THE
RESPONSIVE
EYE

For Fliyeho -
Whose Responsive Eye
Spans many cultures

Emily

THE
RESPONSIVE
EYE

Ralph T. Coe and the Collecting
of American Indian Art

RALPH T. COE

Foreword by Eugene Victor Thaw
with contributions by
J. C. H. King   Judith Ostrowitz

The Metropolitan Museum of Art, New York

Yale University Press, New Haven and London

This publication is issued in conjunction with the exhibition "The Responsive Eye: Ralph T. Coe and the Collecting of American Indian Art," held at The Metropolitan Museum of Art, New York, September 9–December 14, 2003.

The exhibition was organized by The Metropolitan Museum of Art, New York. All works in the exhibition are courtesy of Ralph T. Coe.

This publication was made possible in part by the International Music and Art Foundation (Vaduz).

Additional support has been provided by the Mary C. and James W. Fosburgh Publications Fund.

Published by The Metropolitan Museum of Art, New York

John P. O'Neill, Editor in Chief
Emily Walter, Editor, with the assistance of Elizabeth Powers
Bruce Campbell, Designer
Sally VanDevanter, Production
Robert Weisberg, Desktop Publishing
Jean Wagner, Bibliographic Editor

Photography of objects in the catalogue by Bruce Schwarz, The Photograph Studio, The Metropolitan Museum of Art

Map designed by Anandaroop Roy

Typeset in Adobe Garamond
Color separations by Professional Graphics, Inc., Rockford, Illinois
Printed on 130 gsm R-400
Printing and binding coordinated by Ediciones El Viso, S.A., Madrid

Library of Congress Cataloging-in-Publication Data

Coe, Ralph T.
   Ralph T. Coe and the collecting of American Indian art / Ralph T. Coe; foreword by Eugene V. Thaw ; with contributions by J.C.H. King, Judith Ostrowitz.
        p. cm.
Includes bibliographical references and index.
Catalog of an exhibition at the Metropolitan Museum of Art, New York, Sept. 9–Dec. 14, 2003.
   ISBN 1-58839-085-3 (Hardcover) — ISBN 1-58839-086-1 (Paperback) — ISBN 0-300-10187-2 (Yale University Press)
   1. Indian art—Collectors and collecting—North America—Exhibitions. 2. Indians of North America—Material culture—Exhibitions. 3. Indians of North America—Antiquities—Collectors and collecting—Exhibitions. 4. Coe, Ralph T.—Art collections—Exhibitions. 5. Coe, Ralph T.—Ethnological collections—Exhibitions. 6. Metropolitan Museum of Art (New York, N.Y.)—Exhibitions. I. King, J. C. H. (Jonathan C. H.) II. Ostrowitz, Judith. III. Metropolitan Museum of Art (New York, N.Y.) IV. Title.
   E98.A7C536 2003
   704.03'97'00747471—dc21
                                                2003014817

Jacket illustration: George Walkus, Kwakwaka'wakw, active 1920s–1930s, Yagim mask, 1920–25 (cat. no. 181)

Frontispiece: Lidded basket with handle, ca. 1840. Onondaga peoples (?), New York (cat. no. 16)

Contents

Director's Foreword

It is a personal pleasure for me to introduce Ralph T. Coe and his collection of Native American art to the Metropolitan Museum's public. I have long known Ted Coe, first in his role as museum professional, a role he fulfilled for many years as curator and then as director of the Nelson Gallery of Art (now the Nelson-Atkins Museum of Art) in Kansas City, and subsequently as a devoted follower of the American Indian world and its material manifestations. Two exhibitions have marked Coe's public relationship with Native American art. Both were curated by him, and both were landmarks in the exhibition history of Native American art. The first, "Sacred Circles: Two Thousand Years of American Indian Art," which opened at the Hayward Gallery in London in 1976 and traveled the following year to the Nelson Gallery, included hundreds of objects covering the North American continent and ranging in date from thousands of years B.C. to the early twentieth century. It was a tour de force of organization and connoisseurship, an exhibition that brought to a close the prevalent chronological continent-wide approach to presentations of the topic, an approach initiated by the Museum of Modern Art in 1941, with the exhibition "Indian Art of the United States."

A decade after "Sacred Circles," Coe embarked on a different path. His exhibition "Lost and Found Traditions: Native American Art 1965–1985" was a display of recently made objects. These he himself assembled over a number of years, driving thousands of miles and visiting Native American communities throughout the United States and Canada in search of representative objects that would illustrate the continuity of the artistic traditions of Native America. After an extended museum run encompassing nine venues, the objects from "Lost and Found Traditions" found a permanent home in the Natural History Museum of Los Angeles County, in a city and region with varied American Indian populations.

With this as a background, what Native American art has Coe chosen to collect for himself? His collecting efforts are highly personal, and he lives in close intimacy with all his objects. They are extremely diverse and include, for example, African sculpture, Indonesian textiles, French Impressionist and modern American works on paper, Pop art, and New Mexican furniture. With little imperative to follow the trends of the art world, Coe has taken his own path. His love of baskets is mentioned in the essay in this volume written by his friend and fellow collector of Native American art Eugene V. Thaw, and his study of the extensive range of objects made for trade in response to European tastes and demands during the nineteenth century is a noteworthy departure from current collecting practice. The collection of course includes the types of objects more customarily found in holdings of American Indian art—the dance capes known as button blankets and the imposing masks of the Northwest Coast, the elaborate deerskin shirts and smoking pipes of the Great Plains, and the beautifully formed ceramic jars of the Southwest.

It is fitting that it was Eugene Thaw who came to the Metropolitan with the suggestion that the Museum mount an exhibition of work from the Coe collection. That suggestion was eagerly taken up and is here realized. "The Responsive Eye" presents a selection from the collection, which, in its entirety, is an assemblage of some eight hundred works.

The exhibition catalogue includes essays, written from various perspectives, on the topic of art collecting. Eugene Thaw writes a personal account about Coe as a collector and how his own interest in Native American art was sparked by Coe's knowledge of and passion for the field. Coe himself tells of his journey from his parental home in Cleveland, surrounded by French Impressionist paintings, to the exploration of Native American art and culture and a life in the Southwest. J. C. H. King presents a history of the collecting of Native American art. And Judith Ostrowitz investigates the appreciation of Native American art in the context of theory and text.

During the course of organizing the exhibition and writing this catalogue, Ted has extended his always gracious hospitality toward the Museum staff, and for this I am deeply grateful. I am also indebted to Julie Jones, Curator in Charge of the Department of the Arts of Africa, Oceania, and the Americas, for her indispensable participation in all aspects of this project.

With this exhibition we also celebrate the promised gift of the entire Ralph T. Coe collection of Native American art to the Metropolitan Museum. A group of objects has already been given, and these are included in the exhibition. With such gifts, the Museum will vastly increase its holding of American Indian art. It is with deep appreciation that I thank Ted Coe for his generosity and acknowledge his commitment to the art and cultures of Native America.

The Metropolitan Museum is extremely grateful to the International Music and Art Foundation (Vaduz) for its generous support of the exhibition catalogue. We likewise thank the Mary C. and James W. Fosburgh Publications Fund for its important contribution to the exhibition catalogue.

Philippe de Montebello
Director
The Metropolitan Museum of Art

Collector's Acknowledgments

The task of organizing and producing a project as complex as "The Responsive Eye" has engaged many individuals in the administration and staff of The Metropolitan Museum of Art. To paraphrase the nineteenth-century French painter Eugène Boudin, Perfection is a collective work. Without this particular person or that special person at the appropriate time and place, acting in concert, the desired result would never have been achieved. During the long process of realizing this exhibition, I had countless opportunities to observe the elaborate interaction required of different sectors of the Museum. Deserving of my thanks are surely many whom I may never actually meet.

First of all, I wish to thank the Director, Philippe de Montebello, for his interest in exhibiting this selection from my American Indian art collection, where it can be viewed by one of the most knowledgeable art audiences in the Western world. At this time I want also to express my gratitude to Honorary Trustee of the Metropolitan Museum Eugene V. Thaw for the advisory role he has played in bringing the entire project into being.

Julie Jones, Curator in Charge of the Department of the Arts of Africa, Oceania, and the Americas, deserves my appreciation for seeing this exhibition through all its stages of inception and preparation. Without her perseverance and counsel it simply would not have taken its present form. The staff of her department and that of the Robert Goldwater Library were invaluable in the preparation of both the catalogue and the exhibition, and I thank them all. Museum conservators Ellen Howe and Christine Giuntini analyzed the objects for condition to ensure their continued integrity, and I am grateful for the high level of professional attention they bestowed upon this collection.

I would like to express my appreciation to John P. O'Neill, Editor in Chief, and to his staff in the Editorial Department. Emily Walter, editor of this catalogue, played a judicious role not only as an exemplary wordsmith, but in creating a sense of order in what might well have become a haphazard assembly of disharmonious objects. With a deft hand, she brought precisely that sense of cohesiveness to which I hope visitors to this exhibition and readers of this catalogue will respond, as Indians put it, "with good heart." Ms. Walter was ably assisted in this effort by Elizabeth Powers, who verified a plethora of factual information. Sally VanDevanter spent many long hours at the exacting task of ensuring that the color reproductions would be pristine and true. Jean Wagner worked magic with a mass of details to create a cohesive and accurate bibliography. Mary Gladue had the formidable task of keyboarding the manuscript, accomplishing a feat of organizational wizardry. Vivian Harder, under the supervision of Robert Weisberg, Desktop Publishing Manager, performed the demanding job of typesetting.

Bruce Schwarz, the Museum's Senior Photographer, spent weeks at a time photographing these objects, in both New York and Santa Fe. I am grateful for his acute insight in bringing out the special character that defines the essence of American Indian art. This aesthetic has, in turn, inspired the catalogue's designer, Bruce Campbell, to create a classic design format with which to present the qualities of each object in extenso. Perhaps he was influenced by his early and continuing interest in nature and in American Indian cultures.

Assistant Registrar Lisa Cain and her staff were adept in their handling of the details of transportation between Santa Fe and the Metropolitan Museum, and I appreciate her conscientiousness in performing this behind-the-scenes but nonetheless crucially important task. Bailie and his staff at Untitled, based in Albuquerque, packed and supervised the shipping of all these objects with their usual thoroughness and care, which I appreciate now as I have in the past. Dan Kershaw, Exhibit Designer, Constance Norkin, Graphic Designer, and Clint Coller and Rich Lichte, Lighting Designers, in the Museum's Design Department, have ably and carefully presented these special works of art to the New York public.

I am grateful to Susan Herter of Santa Fe, who graciously agreed to read the catalogue and because she was responsible for putting me in touch once more with Susanna Alde, a former exhibitions officer for The American Federation of Arts, New York, who had worked with me on "Lost and Found Traditions" and is now a resident of New Mexico. I engaged Ms. Alde to inventory my collection, organize it in a properly annotated form on computer, and record it digitally. She became an indispensable liaison on basic matters affecting this exhibition before its final shipment to New York.

Over many years of collecting, I am mindful of art dealers, connoisseurs of the field, specialists, and enthusiasts. I am particularly grateful to the following with regard to this project:

Ann McMullen, Curator, National Museum of the American Indian, Smithsonian Institution, Washington, D.C., for sharing with me her expertise on attributions of eastern North American splint basketry.

John Kania of Kania-Ferrin Gallery, Santa Fe, for the thoughtful discussions we had on both Southwest and California basketry as well as Hopi katsinas.

Joan Lester, of Tufts University and the Children's Museum of Boston; Alexandra O'Donnell, conservation expert in Woodland Indian art; and Stanley Neptune, Penobscot artist and culturalist of Old Town, Maine, for their analysis of the Tomah Joseph birchbark box.

Robert Davidson, Haida, White Rock, British Columbia, eminent Northwest Coast sculptor, for his comments on his Woman Masks in this exhibition.

Professor Peter Furst, of Santa Fe, an authority on shamanism, for his comments on the Tlingit transformation puppet.

William Plitt, conservator, Tesuque, New Mexico, for extended consultation on Native American materials.

Ann Rowland of the Museum of the Aleutians, Unalaska, Alaska, for reaffirming Christine Dushkin as the weaver of the miniature basket.

Bruce Hartman, Director of the Carlsen Center Gallery of Art, Johnson County Community College, Overland Park, Kansas, for information on his father's Thomson River Salish basket.

Andrea Fisher Gallery, Santa Fe, for providing potter Diego Romero's date of birth.

Katherine Red Corn, Osage Tribal Museum, Pawhuska, Oklahoma, for providing the birth and death dates for Georgeann Robinson.

Sarah Novalinga, Canadian Inuit, Belcher Island, Quebec, for a radio-phone conversation about Native culture and kayaks.

Barry Walsh, Holden, Massachusetts, for providing the dates of katsina carver Jimmy Keywaywentewa.

Sarah Peabody Turnbaugh, Curator, the Museum of Primitive Culture, Peace Dale, Rhode Island, for sending me documentation with regard to that museum's Acoma polychrome pot, as it relates to mine.

Additionally, I would like to thank the following for their long-term support of my collecting and for many conversations on American Indian artistic culture:

Taylor A. and Sandra Dale, Santa Fe
James Economos and Gil Hampton, Santa Fe
Donald Ellis, Dundas, Ontario
Jim and Joyce Growing Thunder Fogarty, Polvadera, New Mexico
Leona, David, and Peter Lattimer, Vancouver, British Columbia
John Molloy, New York and Santa Fe
Henry C. Monahan, Santa Fe
Richard A. Pohrt Sr., Ann Arbor, Michigan
Richard A. Pohrt Jr., Ann Arbor, Michigan
George Terasaki, New York, New York
Gaylord Torrence, Curator of American Indian Art, Nelson-Atkins Museum of Art, Kansas City
Ted Trotta Jr. and Anna M. Bono, Shrub Oak, New York
Eleanor Tulman Hancock, New York, New York

Ralph T. Coe
May 2003

Foreword

| Eugene Victor Thaw |

When I started to collect American Indian art after moving to Santa Fe, New Mexico, it was a totally new field for me, although I was an experienced collector in other fields. Coming to my rescue at that time as mentor and guide was Ralph T. Coe, universally known as "Ted," whom I had known in my art-dealing days as the eminent director of the great Nelson Gallery of Art in Kansas City. Ted and I renewed our acquaintance and soon became great friends, since each of us was starved in Santa Fe for conversation and pure gossip about the international art world of New York, London, and Paris, which we both had left behind. We had in common many friendships and episodes in our separate careers, and we now exchanged nostalgic stories about Sir John Pope-Hennessy, James Rorimer, Sherman E. Lee, and other giants in the museum world.

I also shared with Ted a passion for objects and an old-fashioned belief in connoisseurship as an innate talent and a learned discipline for distinguishing quality and authenticity. We commiserated with one another about the intellectual revisionism infecting scholarly pursuits, which was making connoisseurship unfashionable, even irrelevant. Visiting Ted's house in Santa Fe for the first time was an extraordinary experience. Like an Aladdin's cave, it was filled with treasures of many cultures, most of which I could not identify. Taking a potluck chance I pointed to a mask displayed on a stand under a beautiful seascape by Gustave Courbet and asked "Tlingit?" It was a name I somehow remembered from art book perusals and, sure enough, Tlingit was correct. Ted was pleased and said many museum directors visiting his house would not have known that tribal identification.

A little later, in my new Santa Fe life, my wife, Clare, and I began to look around the local galleries and to buy a few minor pieces of Native American art to enliven our adobe house. Trying to learn as we went along, we soon discovered that the dealers would pull out a book to show us comparisons to the pieces we were considering. It was usually the same book each time, the catalogue of the great exhibition "Sacred Circles: Two Thousand Years of North American Indian Art" held in London in 1976, the Bicentennial year. *Sacred Circles* was the bible for American Indian art collectors, and it was written by Ralph T. Coe for the exhibition he had also curated.

Years later, Ted organized a second landmark exhibition, "Lost and Found Traditions: Native American Art 1965–1985." This show, commissioned and circulated by the American Federation of Arts, was conceived by Ted to demonstrate that the traditions of Native American art were alive and well throughout the various tribal regions and that, in fact, a little-noticed renaissance of such cultural activities was under way.

Ted traveled widely to prepare this now-legendary exhibition and met with artists whose talent and craftsmanship often matched or even exceeded that of historic examples in museum collections. Carvers, basket weavers, potters and painters, beadworkers, quillworkers, woolen-blanket and button-blanket makers—in all the fields of traditional Indian artifacts, Ted found contemporary masters. The stunning effect of seeing so much recent Native American art of such high caliber more than verified the thesis of the show and was an overwhelming experience. The exhibition traveled to nine museums and remained on the road for seven years, from 1986 to 1993.

How did Ralph T. Coe, educated as an art historian in Western European painting and sculpture, who worked in major museums and trained with many of the great experts in Impressionism, old master paintings, and Renaissance sculpture, become one of America's leading authorities on the art and culture of Native American tribes? It is an interesting tale, and it illustrates profoundly that the skills which art historians employ to illuminate and put in order the arts of our own Western tradition are the same skills with which we can discern meaning and judge quality in the arts of native peoples. (We no longer refer to "primitive art," the term used throughout the modernist era for such art objects. It was in fact a misleading name since much of this art is highly sophisticated and intentionally made to be beautiful—hardly primitive in any sense.)

While Ted's training as an art historian and museum curator was certainly helpful, it was his experience as a collector that turned him into one of the foremost authorities in the field. In Native American art, he is essentially self-taught. Of course, he tried to interest those museums that he served to collect this material, and he sometimes succeeded. But in Ted's years of museum work, American Indian material culture was not usually considered art but rather ethnology or anthropology, and objects of Native art were always called "artifacts."

Museums of natural history were the places to find significant collections of this material, not art museums, and to a great extent this is still true. But with the 1941 exhibition "Indian Art of the United States" at the Museum of Modern Art in New York, curated by Frederic H. Douglas and René d'Harnoncourt, the tide turned somewhat and the impetus of the 1976 "Sacred Circles" exhibition and Ted Coe's additional drumbeating since then have helped to create an atmosphere in the art-museum world conducive to exhibiting Native American art as art. In Denver, Seattle, Detroit, Kansas City, Milwaukee, Portland, and several other cities, art museums have accumulated significant collections of Indian art, major parts of which are on continuous display. Ted Coe has certainly been one of the principal figures in bringing this about.

I referred to Ted as essentially self-taught in this field. But what a strenuous educational effort he performed! When I first moved to Santa Fe and renewed my acquaintance with him, the automobile he was driving had over 300,000 miles on its odometer. He had worn it out, as he had done several cars before that one—driving from Indian reservation to reservation, to the Arctic circle to live among Eskimos, to British Columbia, and through much of Alaska, becoming intimately acquainted with the Northwest Coast tribal civilizations, participating in potlatches, eating whale muktuk, gut soup from the Plains, and other exotic foods, attending powwows, sleeping on the floors of tipis in a sleeping bag or bedroll, often at real cost to his stomach and his general physical health. Ted combed the trading posts for superior contemporary art objects. After purchasing, he would track down the artists themselves, chat with them to learn their concerns and to monitor the great traditions of such art, the techniques, and how they were passed down.

For "Sacred Circles" he went in search of whatever was best of its kind in collections public and private all across America and Europe. To choose excellent examples in virtually every category type and subtype, Ted had to see everything there was to see. He even persuaded the British Museum to let him browse in its vast collections and to become a lender to the exhibition, since London was the first of the two cities where it was shown. The other was Kansas City. For "Lost and Found Traditions," he literally collected the exhibition himself, making purchases while on the extensive and punishing automobile trips to tribal centers and outposts, to trading posts and out-of-the-way dwellings of fine, but unsung, artists. He also depended on knowledgeable traders for contacts and continuing help, to say nothing of the Indian elders in the United States and Canada, whose role was indispensable to the life of the project.

No academic training or degree program could prepare a scholar to have the expertise that Ted acquired in the long years he has spent looking at and studying probably more Native American tribal art than anyone of his generation. The breadth of his knowledge across the spectrum of the many cultures comprising North America's indigenous peoples is truly remarkable. And, of course, this constitutes a tremendous advantage for Ted Coe the collector.

For the full story of the Coe collection, however, one must go back to the beginning. Ted's father, Ralph M. Coe, was a distinguished collector of Impressionist and early modern paintings, living in Cleveland, Ohio. The family house on Lake Erie, when the collection was intact, was visited regularly by eminent artists, critics, and art historians—Bonnard, Gertrude Stein, John Rewald, and, of course, the major art dealers of paintings. Father Coe often took young Ted to visit the dealers and see their stocks. At home were major paintings by, among others, Gauguin, Cézanne, Renoir, Courbet, and Rouault. Ted, in those easier days, had the run of the Cleveland Museum of Art, with access to the curators all the way up to the great Cleveland directors, William Milliken and, later, Sherman E. Lee. His father, after all, was a benefactor and trustee. One of his sisters, Nancy, married William D. Wixom, curator of medieval art at Cleveland for many years and then head of the same department at The Metropolitan Museum of Art and the Cloisters.

It was, therefore, not exactly accidental that Ted chose art history as his major in college at Oberlin, which also has a distinguished museum and exceptional teachers, and, in those days, art historians like the late Wolfgang Stechow. At Oberlin, before going on to Yale, he spent a summer of intensive study on one of his great interests, ornithology, and expanded his already broad knowledge of architectural history. But in graduate school at Yale, seduced by objects, he opted, after his degree, for an internship in Renaissance bronzes under the legendary John Pope-Hennessy at London's Victoria and Albert Museum. Ted, it seems, always preferred hands-on contact with works of art, which, if one were talented and privileged, could be had in a museum career, but seldom in a college teaching life.

The Great Depression depleted the family fortune. After his father died, Ted chose some paintings remaining in the estate rather than cash or securities for his share. For many years, he lived and collected art on the very limited funds he earned from museum salaries and from occasional writing. Of course, in his younger days, African, American Indian, and tribal art in general was priced at nothing like the levels we see today. Yet the best things were always relatively expensive when they were recognized. This is where Ted's advantage as a collector came into play, for often he was the first to recognize a masterpiece among a group of mediocre pieces and buy for a song what the dealer was not able to spot. Superior knowledge and sheer connoisseurship enabled him to assemble, with very little money, the major private holding of Native American art, only a portion of which has been chosen for this exhibition and this catalogue. A good example of what I am talking about is the Coe collection of New England and Eastern Woodlands splint baskets. Ted has around a hundred examples, mostly historic nineteenth-century pieces, but some beautiful modern ones as well. The prices when he assembled this group (probably the finest in private hands anywhere) ranged from $25 to $100, only occasionally a bit more. Clearly, the baskets were not then generally prized and few buyers were bothering to pick out the best examples available. Ted saw as works of true art and craft what to the rest of the world were merely souvenirs. Similar stories could be told about other major groups in his vast collection of more than a thousand pieces.

In his essay "Collecting American Indian Art" in the catalogue for "Lost and Found Traditions," Ted describes in some detail his immersion in American Indian culture and patterns of life—Indians' sense of humor, their conception of time and their rejection of schedules and deadlines, their great hospitality but utter reserve and reticence about spiritual beliefs. And he became a consummate diplomat in his relations with Indians, particularly Indian artists. A brief quote will give some idea of his experience:

Reading the signals is an acquired art that no one outside the culture can be wholly versed in. This includes unkept appointments. The first time I was stood up I asked about it later. "Well, he didn't turn up with the things I wanted to show you, so I went on," I was informed, with obvious reluctance that the matter should be discussed at all. Since this is normal Indian procedure, I also adopted it. If another matter intervened, I took advantage of it, as they would do in similar circumstances, and turned my car in the other direction. When I would show up later, no questions were ever asked, and I learned not to ask any either—not wishing to offend. In time, it all works out for the best.[1]

In working with American Indian artists and works of art, both new and old, the terms "tradition" and "culture" keep appearing and reappearing, in conversation and in descriptive or theoretical writings. They are so ubiquitous and so often used as a verbal weapon that it is very hard, in discussing Native Americans from outside the parameters of their societies and family circles, to define those terms in any way that a non-Native can apprehend. For the Indian participants in various discussion sessions that Ted attended, "tradition" and "(our) culture," though nearly indefinable, were thought to be understood by those within the culture. As circular as this argument sounds, it seemed, from the many discussants whom Ted sought out for enlightenment, that one could intuit a true sense of tradition only from inside the circle of Indian life—with past and present merging into one, with time existing only as a continuum rather than as a calibrated measure of passing moments, and with collective wisdom continually passed on by tribal elders.

In one of the most moving passages of his essay prefacing *Lost and Found Traditions,* Ted attempts to demonstrate Native American thinking about these crucial ideas, especially among the artists. Many Indian artists are not at all unsophisticated about the modern world, its advantages and its defects. They suffer, in these mechanized days, from a loss of various correct and crucial materials with which to make their art in the proper way. That, in fact, is the only Native meaning close to our word for "traditional": making it the way it should be made. There is no Indian word for our dictionary definition of tradition as something like technique or information handed down from another time. Ted writes, "The Indian view is that tradition, like time, cannot be measured. It exists within everything, a sort of wholeness or allness that man touches, or establishes contact with, at every point, but particularly when he is in a ritualistic state."[2]

For Native Americans, there is an intimate connection between making art objects and serving a spiritual purpose. Even the sometimes disparaged activity of decorating with beading or feathers such items as lighters or cigarette cases, salt and pepper shakers, or soda or wine bottles, has a deeper purpose than just to produce quick-money tourist pieces. Ted quotes the famous Flathead/Cree painter Jaune Quick-To-See Smith about this ubiquitous small-scale work: "We have this urge to decorate everything, to take something ordinary and make it ours, and this is one form it takes today."[3]

Of course, a lot of pretty poor tourist art has been made for a couple of centuries. In the days following the removal of Native Americans to reservations, much of this art and craftsmanship has served to nurture "cottage industries" that have meant the difference between starvation and survival. Within all this activity, the occasional masterpiece was born. The Indians knew right away whether something was a superior object within the "tradition" and who among them were the best artists. This is something that Ted came to know, as accurately as an Indian elder, from his long experience with the many objects he held in his hands and from his many visits and interchanges with the artists themselves. For these artists, respect for the past while making the "new" does not mean that the past is "handed down," as we, in our culture, use the word "traditional." Rather, it means that past and present are one.

To close, I want to give one more example of the depth and radiance of Ted Coe's perception of Indian thought:

> Only one entity is sufficiently vast and permanent to relate to the unstated Native American concept of tradition: nature. This is not nature limited to its physical forms and environmental cycles, but nature viewed as a force that cannot be transgressed if man is to survive. Actions contrary to the laws of nature engender disruption. So in song, dance, and the concomitant arts, Indians sought harmony with the seasons, the sun, the cycles of growth, decay, and renewal of which they are part. They proposed to establish an exquisite harmony between their own existence and nature's round. While the white man seeks to dominate nature, the Indian seeks to live with nature. The Indian mindful of tradition seeks to "center himself" in the balance of nature, which extends outward in ever-widening circles from family, to clan, to surrounding tribes, and to the directional limits, where the sky takes over, and then to the stars beyond. He seeks congruity with these circles of power and sacredness, which are boundless.[4]

The presence of the Coe collection at the Metropolitan Museum fills a long-standing gap in the great tribal arts holdings that the Museum has gathered from major gifts over the years. Accompanied by this catalogue and the reminiscences of Ted Coe, the collection is a treasure that will resonate today and in generations to come.

1. Coe 1986, p. 27.
2. Ibid., p. 46.
3. Ibid., p. 44.
4. Ibid., pp. 48–49.

The Re-Education of an Art Collector: From Aesthetics to Culture

RALPH T. COE

For Nancy Coe Wixom

I. In My Father's House

Born in 1929, I was brought up in Cleveland, Ohio, by a pair of cultivated parents to whom I shall always be grateful (figs. 1–3). In 1882 my father, Ralph M. Coe, was born on a kitchen table in a formidable Victorian stone residence on Euclid Avenue, then the finest residential street in the city. Today, it is a parking lot. His father, Lord M. Coe, born in 1819 near Penn Yan, New York, ran away from his family farm estate and "went to sea," i.e., the city of Buffalo, at the foot of Lake Erie. In time, he became a well-known Great Lakes skipper and eventually owned a tugboat-towing company based in Cleveland. At the pleadings of his wife, Lorinda Benton Coe, whose family had settled at Chardon, Ohio, in 1826, on a Connecticut land grant, he gave up the "sea" and founded, in 1864, the first iron drop-forging company in that part of the country. Years later, my father commissioned, in 1909, the New York Ashcan School painter George Luks to paint my grandfather. The portrait, completed only a few days before his death, resulted in a fierce and stern piece of turn-of-the-century verism that hangs today in my study. Immediately below it are displayed several prehistoric American stone axes, two African sculptures, and an early-nineteenth-century Aleut model canoe with hunter. Alongside the portrait are three framed sketches by Luks—one of our old Irish cook, Essie, hands on hips; another of the family electric car, looking like a baby buggy; and the third depicting the well-known art critic of the New York *Herald,* Frederick J. Gregg, in a futuristic, drunkenly stumbling pose, emerging from Mouquin's in New York City, accompanied by the legend, "A bad mixture Kimmel + Scotch?—Gregg on his way home." At the top of the sheet, Luks inscribed, "P.S. Yes, Huneker [the art critic James Huneker] christened the big canvas, George." Every time I glance at this sketch, I absorb something of the bohemian art world of old New York, when my father and erstwhile pundits would gather at such legendary restaurants or chat at McSorley's bar.

My mother, Dorothy T. Coe, was born in 1891. Her father, James Horace Tracy, after medical training in Berlin and New York, made his way to the Upper Peninsula of Michigan,

Figure 1. Ralph M. and Dorothy T. Coe in front of their Bratenahl home, ca. 1940

Figure 2. View from the front lawn of the Ralph M. Coe residence, 13303 Lake Shore Boulevard, Bratenahl, Cleveland, Ohio, ca. 1945. The architects of the 1923 house were Meade & Hamilton. Photo: Forbes Keith

Figure 3. Partial view of the living room in the Ralph M. Coe residence, 1959, with paintings by (left to right) Redon, Monet, Renoir, Morisot, and Renoir. A totem pole model (cat. no. 89) is on the stand at the right. Photo: Ted Gorka

where he set up a clinic with three nuns to assist him and became a Jack of all medical trades. Perhaps he felt the same call of the wild that I have made part of my experience. When Grandfather Horace died in Michigan, he left an estate insufficient to educate his two surviving children—one of whom was my mother. Mother's aunt had married the son of General Stephen C. Kearney, who had "conquered" New Mexico in 1846. General Kearney's son, Henry, had acquired mining interests in the West and led a life of ease in New Jersey and New York. He accepted my mother as a financial responsibility, sending her to Miss Porter's finishing school in Farmington, Connecticut. Her own mother remained quietly in the background, and Henry Kearney's wife, my mother's Aunt Alice, took over most of her upbringing. Alice Kearney was a domineering, strict, and overbearing Victorian woman, under whose tutelage my mother chafed. When Uncle Henry Kearney died, my mother decided to take herself to Cleveland. To support herself, she became a department store buyer, to the great dismay of Aunt Alice. One of the young set she made friends with was an eligible bachelor, Ralph M. Coe. Another friend said of him, "Oh, he's a charming man, but he collects those awful pictures." Having developed an independent mind, my mother thought those "awful pictures" just fine. My mother and father were married in 1923.

Mother's gentle but spirited humanity and also this sense of feminine independence made her a leader in Cleveland art circles. She had a graciousness that dovetailed perfectly with my father's stubborn wit. When my father made the long train journey to Lakewood, New Jersey, to ask formally for my mother's hand, a starchy Aunt Alice was charmed. She was quite astonished to find that Ralph M. Coe was not a savage from the wilds of Ohio, but a Yale graduate who spoke civilized English just as she did.

As a child, my mother had lived in a Paris apartment on the Rue de Rivoli. She could remember rolling a hoop in the Tuileries Gardens and visiting, at the age of nine, the Paris World's Fair of 1900. She also recalled "a beautiful painting in the Luxembourg Museum full of color which depicted a bench in a park surrounded by flowers with a woman's ribbon hat hanging down from a tree." She could not remember who painted it, but it is easy to identify as a Monet from the Caillebotte bequest—the earliest gift of Impressionist art made to the French people. Over the years, my mother would develop her acute visual sense. When the estate of the pioneer modern art collector John Quinn was being sold in New York, it was she who insisted on buying a 1906 Fauve-period Derain of the London Houses of Parliament, one of the most highly abstracted Fauve paintings. She also chose a large Rouault gouache of 1916, of a wintry palace in far-off Poland.

Mother's upbringing in Paris served her well. Not only did she preserve in her features her Norman-French ancestry, but she could speak a passable French and would later put at ease and charm the many European visitors who came to our house to see the pictures. As the Depression wore on and my father's finances became precarious, my mother continued to entertain—doing much of the cooking herself—with an elegance that smoothed over the realities. Born to the graces, she died in 1966, at the age of seventy-five.

The family art bug was certainly contagious, although it only marginally affected my older sister Eunice, who was for many years assistant headmistress at the Riverdale School in New York. For my sister Nancy, who is eighteen months my senior, art held the same fascination as it did for me. A student of art history, she nevertheless had no art-history program in which to study. Consequently, one was created for her—at Skidmore College in New York, where Nancy became their first art-history major. Nancy later joined the staff of the Cleveland Museum and became an assistant curator in the paintings department. She developed an abiding interest in American architecture and to this day is active in architectural preservation projects in the Hudson River Valley, where she has lived ever since her husband, William D. Wixom, became chairman of the Department of Medieval Art at The Metropolitan Museum of Art in 1979.

How did my father become an art collector? He always attributed it to the influence of one of the great literary lions of America in those days, his best-liked Yale professor, William Lyon Phelps, who not only made English and American letters a source of fascination to his students but also stressed the visual arts. As there was no art history yet taught in America, Phelps's lectures served my father as a worthy substitute.

The travels my father took on the train of art did not gain express speed at once. I use the metaphor of a train advisedly, because that's what would take him from Cleveland to New York. His first purchase was a painting titled *Road near Montmartre,* by the nineteenth-century pleinairist Georges Michel, which he bought from the New York dealer William Schlaus for $600, his take in gambling his last night at Yale. (Today, this painting belongs to my sister Nancy Coe Wixom.) By 1912, he already owned important works by the seminal proto-Impressionists Eugène Boudin, Johann Barthold Jongkind, and, especially, Camille Pissarro. He acquired Pissarro's *A View of Charing Cross Bridge, London,* from the London office of Durand-Ruel. In the 1970s, when I was serving on the IRS Art Advisory Panel in Washington, D.C., the painting came up for evaluation, and because of its history I was asked to pronounce on it. My father had bought it for $1,200 in 1912. We had sold the picture at auction in 1958 for $38,000. And I put its current value at between $180,000 and $220,000, which the panel accepted, not about to quibble at "insider" information. Much of my college education was paid for by the proceeds of paintings that were sold. Each one has its own history, and occasionally I encounter one in unexpected circumstances.

Since his college days, my father had been aware of the prodigious survey on modern art by the German art historian Richard Muther, which Professor Phelps probably signaled to him in its English translation, published in 1895–96. The third volume included essays on such painters as Cézanne, Renoir, Monet, and Pissarro, along with lesser lights. Father spent time learning to understand and to appreciate the quality of the abstracted hillocks in Cézanne's *La Colline des Pauvres* (1888–90), a work purchased in 1913 by the Metropolitan Museum. It would have been a very difficult Cézanne on which to teethe. John Rewald explains why: "*The Hill of the Poor* had nothing of the superb vehemence and furious daring of Cézanne's early paintings . . . anymore than it presaged the often tortured and always energy-charged surfaces of his last years."[1] However much its patchy, soft brushwork and prosaic hill forms exemplify the evolving structuralism of Cézanne's art style, they do not arrest the eye of the beholder. Rather, they engage the onlooker in a deliberate process of close observation. My father chose to experience this slow march toward understanding. During a number of visits to New York from 1913 until the end of the First World War, he would return to the Metropolitan Museum and study this virtuous, if untypical, Cézanne. He would scowl at it, sitting on a portable stool provided by a sympathetic guard, and move his glance from side to side.

All my life I've relied on this measured process of aesthetic absorption, whether the work is a Renaissance plaquette or a Native American wearing blanket. It involves returning over and again to the individual work of art. I revisit and bear constantly in mind the objects in my own collection, however large or small, to gain new insights. They are not trophies but instruments of passion, with the power to unexpectedly reveal mysteries. In Cleveland, we would often suddenly decide to "change the pictures" around, to create new meanings by different juxtapositions. And just as we did then, I continually rearrange the objects in my own home today.

Easier on my father's collector's palate was Claude Monet's brand of Impressionism. Father's first Monet, *A View of the Sea Cliffs at Belle Isle* (today in the collection of the Des Moines Art Center), was purchased in 1913 for $2,600 through the London office of Durand-Ruel. The year before, he had actually written to Monet, in the fractured French of a Yale graduate, inquiring if he had any paintings that could be sold to him directly, thus bypassing Durand-Ruel. Monet forwarded Father's letter to Paul Durand-Ruel, with a notation on the back that, yes, he did have some studies on hand he could sell and that he would wait for advice. Unanswered, Father's request was consigned to the depths of the Durand-Ruel Gallery files. It was rediscovered only years later and published in an annotated record of the gallery's business transactions, edited by the distinguished Italian art historian Lionello Venturi.[2] So much for trying to circumvent an influential gallery. Having learned his lesson, Father went on to purchase three more Monets from various dealers: the well-known and oft-exhibited *Jardin à Giverny* (1900), bought in 1917, which I retained after his death; a painting from the Japanese bridge series Nymphéas, *The Green Bridge* (1899), bought in 1919 and subsequently in the Albert Lasker collection; and *Waterloo Bridge* (1901?), the final Monet purchase, made in 1928.

Immediately after the First World War, my father bid in a Manet marine painting at the Baron Denys Cochin auction in Paris. Then, in 1921, he embarked on his second, and last, trip to Europe (the first was in 1907), chiefly visiting Paris, London, and Spain. By that time, he was more than ready for a Cézanne. Accordingly, he called on the great dealer Ambroise Vollard, whom he remembered as "a reclusive eccentric who showed you only what he wanted to offer from a hidden stock. It was a difficult negotiation because Vollard spoke with a lisp and I had only few words of halting French." Nevertheless, a deal was concluded. My father's purchase, *La Maison Abandonnée,* was the first of three Cézannes. The following year, 1922, he also purchased from Vollard, by correspondence from Cleveland, a vertical study of four trees, *Les Arbres Provençales.* A horizontal painting of the same four trees is in the Tate Gallery in London. The third Cézanne was *The Pigeon Tower at Bellevue,* today a treasure of the Cleveland Museum of Art. In Paris, on foot, my father encountered, at the Galeries Barbazanges, one of two Tahitian Gauguins available in Paris. The other painting is today in the Worcester Art Museum. The Gauguin he bought, *Femmes Assises à l'Ombre des Palmiers,* figured in the New York Armory Show of 1913, which he did not attend, though he subsequently became a good friend of one of its major organizers, Walter Pach.

While still in Paris, at the Galerie Bernheim-Jeune, Father was shown *Le Pont Neuf,* Renoir's most memorable urban scene of Paris and perhaps the most beautiful view of the city from this whole period. At the time, he did not buy the picture, although it lingered large in his mind after his return to the United States. He asked a French friend of his, the Cleveland stockbroker Raoul Charpentier, who was often in Paris, to check periodically on this painting until the price was right. When the time came, he purchased it. After the Second World War, the New York dealer Sam Salz visited Gaston Bernheim. Then in old age, he still remembered "M. Coé, qui était si froid."

Other visitors to our home in Bratenahl, on the Lake Erie shore, which my father had built in 1923, included Baron Elie de Rothschild, Gertrude Stein and Alice B. Toklas, and Pierre Bonnard, whose favorite picture was an 1879 Renoir pastel, *Portrait of Jeanne Samary,* which hangs today in my dining room. One look at the shimmering aureole surrounding the Comédie-Française actress, sensuously *en déshabillée,* will tell you why.

Thus, my two sisters and I were bathed in a special art ambience very much *à la française.* In fact, many Europeans told us that our family should be living in Europe. But we opened our house, with an American informality, not only to professors, fellow collectors, and museum curators and directors but to young students as well. When a group would appear, coming up the driveway unannounced, and ask if they could see "the pictures," they were generally welcomed as much as any visiting firemen.

At the age of fourteen, I finally asked my father to explain to me "about those pictures." Particularly one that had two bronze-complected women sitting under a palm tree. After the family had retired for the night, he took me on a tour of "the pictures" and told me that the two exotic women painted by Paul Gaugin were from Tahiti, in the South Seas, where Gaugin had gone to escape the shackles of European culture. I, too, felt liberated before the picture, as though a whole new world had opened up. It is clear to me now that my interest in the arts of Africa, Oceania, Indonesia, and particularly Indian America stems from this initial, dynamic revelation.

Until then, I had been a mediocre student with a very uncertain future, but now everything began to fall into place. I had been bitten by the art bug, infected by its virus, and have never turned away since. My father had, for those days, an important art library (including a volume that Vollard had asked Renoir to sign for my father), and as my sister Nancy remembers, I really "hit the books." Then there were the resources of the Cleveland Museum. Daylong Saturday visits to the museum, which remains to this day my very ideal of what a broadly assembled and connoisseurship-oriented museum collection ought to be, became one of my favorite pastimes, worth the two-hour trolley ride each way. I began serving as my father's de facto art secretary, carrying on correspondence with museums and arranging details for loans. In addition, Father surreptitiously read to me the minutes of the Cleveland Museum's accession-committee meetings, explaining the difficulties of working with one trustee, whom he called "the grand objector," or, returning from a meeting, saying to my mother, "Well, Dorothy, William cried again, and of course we bought it"—one of the most undeniably effective, if one of the more extreme, tactics I have ever encountered to ensure a museum purchase.[3] But for my family, the charmed circle of our surroundings was closing in, as individual works were sold to pay off the family debt incurred during the Depression, which took my father twenty painful years—from 1932 to 1952—to clear. Little by little, three of the four Monets, three Cézannes, and six of the seven Renoirs disappeared. So did the well-known Matisse *Fête des Fleurs à Nice*, the Degas dance pastel, the Toulouse-Lautrec portrait, and the major Modigliani portrait, among others. Just as wars and looting fragmented major European private holdings, the Depression decimated my father's Impressionist collection. While famous in its day, it has become one of America's "lost" collections; ours was one of the worst hit. Time and again, while casually watching television, I have seen one or another of our old paintings suddenly appear on the screen. It is a strange experience of déjà vu, full of Proustian tugs and pulls that thrust the treasured past into the present.

Father was diagnosed with Parkinson's disease in 1952, and we partitioned off a section of the living room as a downstairs bedroom to accommodate him. No more dinners in our paneled dining room with guests such as George Grosz, who raised his glass to German Romantic painting, or Gertrude Stein, who declared that she had come back to America "to teach but not to learn." One of our last visitors was a boyish young art instructor from Ohio State University who painted small Cubist-style airplane models. A shy presence, he mostly looked at the floor. His name was Roy Lichtenstein, and he was engaged to marry a close family friend. Years later, Ivan Karp at the Leo Castelli Gallery in New York showed me (by then a budding young curator) "things you'll just hate"—slides of paintings by Lichtenstein, Wesselmann, Warhol, Dine, and Rosenquist, which at that time were so innovative that they weren't yet on the market. On the contrary, I found much to savor in these images and later owned works by all of them but Dine, the most famous being the monumental *The Kiss,* by Roy Lichtenstein, now owned by David Geffen.

In 1959, my father died quietly in a nursing home. Sherman E. Lee, then director of the Cleveland Museum of Art, wrote of him, "In 1921, on a trip to Europe, 'he departed from the rational,' according to some, in buying a landscape by Paul Cézanne. . . . His wit and friendly advice, his knowledge and enthusiasm, were an inspiration to a staff with whom he maintained sympathetic relations. . . . His collection was fittingly described [by Theodore Sizer, professor of fine arts at Yale University] as 'an inspiration to a younger generation.'"[4]

My earliest personal acquisition was a Nice-period Matisse lithograph purchased in 1946, soon followed by a Juan Gris lithograph. Then I got into drawings. John Rewald, the great historian of Impressionism, was extremely kind to me during my formative years. Several times, he took me, as a neophyte in my late teens, on authenticating expeditions.

One day, we dropped into the gallery of the eminent dealer in French Impressionism Justin K. Thannhauser, who pulled out a painting that Rewald promptly identified as a Pissarro. At our next visit, the same day, he proclaimed another "Pissarro" a fake. In 1946, at Christmas, Rewald obtained a charming Pissarro drawing of the artist's wife's niece Nini dressed in her Sunday best. It was waiting for me under the tree, a gift from my parents. Actually, I was very spoiled at that time by art dealers as well. "So you want to see Monet," Donald Elfers, manager of the New York branch of Durand-Ruel Gallery, said to me. "Come back after lunch and we'll line some up for you." I was led, alone, up to a fifth-floor storage room with rows of Monets leaning against all four walls, about a dozen paintings in each row. After I'd pulled several toward me to have a look, the load would be so heavy I'd have to let them fall back into place. This was about 1948. By today's standards, I had been privy to several hundred million dollars' worth of Monets!

About the same time, I had written an article on Pissarro's late Paris period. It was scheduled for publication in the *Gazette des Beaux-Arts,* and I felt I had "arrived." It had never occurred to me that real life was not that easy. But scholarly family friends remained encouraging. James Rorimer, a curator in the Department of Medieval Art at the Metropolitan Museum and later director of the Museum, thought I was ready for a beginning position and set up an appointment for me to meet the then director, Francis Henry Taylor. But Taylor refused me point-blank. I ended up instead enrolled in graduate school at Yale, rooming in the attic of a doctor for whom I mowed the lawn and caught mice, ceremonially plopping them into the flames of his backyard incinerator. I had a ball studying with George Heard Hamilton and serving as a section teaching assistant for the undergraduate survey course in art history. A seminar in Roman relief sculpture bored me to tears.

That spring, I strongly felt the need to experience something else besides French culture and Roman reliefs. Expressing my ennui to a fellow graduate student, Richard Brilliant (who went on to teach ancient Roman art at Columbia University), while we were chatting in the library stacks, he reached up to a shelf and suggested that, as an antidote, I take home with me a recently published book by the celebrated Mexican painter and folklorist Miguel Covarrubias, *The Eagle, the Jaguar, and the Serpent.*[5] A beautifully illustrated volume, it was a survey of American Indian art. Covarrubias was part of a New York–Mexico City cultural axis and the *Vanity Fair* crowd that centered around Frank Crowninshield. I remembered both of them having been to our house. Covarrubias took a delightful, sympathetic artist's approach in describing a tribal art that was exotic and new to me but which had, in fact, been created in my own backyard, by then-unknown artists from all parts of the continent. The freshness of all this "material culture," as it was called anthropologically, struck me as belonging to one of the world's great arts, as it had earlier struck pioneers in the field such as René d'Harnoncourt, Frederic H. Douglas, and even the painter John Sloan. The next semester, Yale professor George Kubler, an expert on Precolumbian art and New Mexican architecture, granted me a self-generated reading course on North American art and archaeology and encouraged me to haunt the Carlebach

Gallery in New York, a great cabinet of curiosities if there ever was one. There, my eyes were opened to the agonizing beauty of what was then called "primitive art." From Julius Carlebach, I acquired my first Native American object, a Haida totem pole model today in the Museum of Anthropology at the University of British Columbia, Vancouver (fig. 4). It very soon passed out of my hands in favor of another totem pole model (cat. no. 89) that Carlebach called a finer example. Every time I see this first Indian acquisition at the museum in Vancouver, I still regret not having had sufficient funds to keep them both. The first pole was acquired for $150, the second for $350; it seemed a fortune at the time. Thus began my addiction to the art and culture of the indigenous North American peoples.

II. SACRED CIRCLES

During my last semester at Yale, I was asked to serve as teaching assistant for Visiting Professor Sir John Pope-Hennessy, of the Victoria and Albert Museum, London. I knew him and revere him still as the most eminent authority on Italian Renaissance art who has ever written in English on that subject. I also knew that he had a rather fearsome reputation. In his autobiography, published in 1991, Sir John writes, "In the winter and spring of 1955 I paid my first postwar visit to the United States, where I replaced Charles Seymour at Yale, teaching an undergraduate course in Tuscan Early Renaissance painting and sculpture and a graduate seminar on the Quattrocento in Siena. . . . I had a graduate assistant, Ted Coe, who had been brought up in Cleveland with a major collection of nineteenth-century paintings and who became a close friend." He states further, "I remember . . . an American bicentennial exhibition with the title *Sacred Circles* covering two millennia of North American Indian artifacts, selected with great visual acumen by a specialist I had first known as a graduate student at Yale twenty years before, Ralph T. Coe."[6]

Figure 4. Haida totem pole model, Museum of Anthropology, University of British Columbia, Vancouver. Formerly in the collection of Ralph T. Coe

By that time, after having served as curator of paintings and sculpture and as assistant director at the Nelson Gallery of Art in Kansas City, Missouri, I was director of the museum, soon thereafter called the Nelson-Atkins Museum of Art (fig. 5). The exhibition to which Sir John refers is "Sacred Circles: Two Thousand Years of North American Indian Art," which opened at the Hayward Gallery in London in 1976. One of the chief celebrations of the American Bicentennial in Europe, it included more than 670 objects

Figure 5. Ralph T. Coe, in 1977, shortly after becoming director of the Nelson Gallery of Art, Kansas City. The photo was taken in the nineteenth-century paintings gallery. Photo courtesy of the Nelson-Atkins Museum of Art

Figure 6. Installation view, "Sacred Circles: Two Thousand Years of North American Indian Art." Exhibits included a late-nineteenth-century Northern Plains woman's dress (background) and the famed Powhatan's mantle (foreground). Photo courtesy of the Hayward Gallery, London

on loan from both public and private collections in the United States, Canada, and Europe (figs. 6–8). The visits I made to these institutions and collectors to assemble the exhibition became the foundation of my experience at first hand of the full spectrum of Native American art.

The idea of organizing an exhibition of Indian art and the intriguing notion of showing it in Britain was not initially mine, but the inspiration of a Kansas City socialite, Maggie Phinney. Maggie learned about my interest in Native American art from Laurence Sickman, the preeminent connoisseur of Asian art and director of the Nelson Gallery. Long resident in London, she was married to Robert T. Phinney, the European representative of Braniff International Airways. A committee of American women living in England was formed, and the next time I was abroad I decided to seek the advice of my old mentor

Figure 7. Among the Arctic objects in "Sacred Circles" was (in the left case) a Yup'ik mask (1895–1900) now in the collection of The Metropolitan Museum of Art. Photo courtesy of the Hayward Gallery, London

Figure 8. War bonnets from the Northern Plains Oglala Sioux (left) and Arapaho (right) tribes, in "Sacred Circles." Photo courtesy of the Hayward Gallery, London

John Pope-Hennessy, because I was very much at sea as to how one might proceed. It just so happened that Sir John was the one person in the whole of Great Britain who could make this exhibition a reality. Not only was he about to become director of the British Museum, which had one of the most important collections of North American Indian ethnography in the world, but he had become chairman of the exhibition panel of the Arts Council of Great Britain, the main engine of international art exhibitions for the British Isles. "I think I'll speak to Joanna Drew [the director of the council] about this," he proclaimed. And that was that. About two-thirds of the way through the organization of the exhibition, the Arts Council decided to cut the contents in half. Not only did this diminish the scope of the exhibition, but it threatened to jeopardize the entire project. Sir John again came to the rescue. Phoning up the Arts Council, he spoke to Joanna Drew: "Joanna, I think we'll just do that exhibition as planned." And down went the receiver. Taking a risk concerning a field he knew nothing about, Sir John showed himself the true humanist that he was. Nothing of interest passed his attention. When I was asked to announce the exhibition to a group of British dignitaries at the American Embassy in order to promote its forthcoming venue, first Sir John and then John Walker, former director of the National Gallery in Washington, D.C., where I had once worked, introduced me. Both confessed that they knew next to nothing about "Red Indians," but they convinced the assembled company to give their stamp of approval to the first definitive exhibition of American Indian traditional culture to be held in the British Isles. With the organizational thrust of the Arts Council behind it, "Sacred Circles" went forward at a level that could not have been foreseen.

III. Traditions Lost and Found

A group of three hundred Kansas Citians who had chartered a plane to attend the opening of "Sacred Circles" in London decided then and there to raise sufficient funds to bring the whole exhibition to the United States for a showing at the Nelson Gallery. At the time it seemed, even to me, to be an impossible undertaking. Every lender, whether a private collector or a museum, had to be approached separately to resecure their loans. A great deal of money had to be raised on incredibly short notice to underwrite everything from transportation costs to the hiring of a separate staff to administer the exhibition at its second venue. As a result of the perseverance of an army of fund-raisers—most of all, the prominent collector of ethnic arts Morton I. Sosland of Kansas City—together with significant start-up grants from both the National Endowment for the Arts and the National Endowment for the Humanities, "Sacred Circles" had its American showing in 1977.

Above all, there was much more Native American participation in Kansas City, which lent an authenticity not possible in London. This was a crucial difference between the two showings. At the Nelson Gallery, the exhibition was opened officially by a delegation of Indian dignitaries from British Columbia, all members of the Git'ksan peoples of the Pacific Northwest, noted for their genius as carvers of masks and totem poles. Thirty-seven tribe members gathered around Joan Mondale, wife of the vice president—representing President Jimmy Carter—and myself to enter the nine galleries. The Git'ksan carver Chuck Heit had made a figurative speaker's baton for the occasion, which I carried as a symbol of the authority vested in me by the Indian community to open the exhibition; I guard it still as a talisman.[7] At that time, federal funds for cultural projects were still plentiful. Together, the two National Endowments provided over half a million dollars to bring Native American artists and dancers from all over the United States and Canada to participate in the exhibition. The artists' demonstrations and dance performances, special events not to be seen outside the tribal world, infused the show with the presence of a living culture.

In all this, there was a sense of creative energy that brought home the fact that Native American culture, generally believed by the greater American public to have faded into nonexistence, was very much alive. Even anthropologists had largely given up collecting contemporary material culture, with the exception of the arts of the Southwest, and believed that the only good Indian art was part of the faraway past. But here it was, in the vigorous presence of tribes from all over the continent. Performances were given in an atmosphere of celebration and the unexpected. At one presentation, a group of about twenty Plains Kiowa women in full regalia appeared to perform what had been announced as a routine round dance for their ancestors. Remarkably, it turned out to be a sacred Ghost Dance, held to commemorate their forebears who had been massacred in 1890 at the Battle of Wounded Knee. One time, pausing at a demonstrator's booth, I asked a distinguished Haida elder, Selina Peratrovich, then nearly ninety, if she might make for me a traditional basket of split spruce root, a weaving technique that can be extremely taxing. Her daughter, Dolores Churchill, objected that she was "too old," but several months later, to my surprise, the basket arrived in the mail.[8] This was my first Native American commission, and it initiated a whole new direction in my collecting, one that was to change my life.

I started to follow a new course. It all began in the late summer of 1977 with a telephone call from the United States Information Agency in Washington, D.C. The USIA had received inquiries from several U.S. embassy cultural attachés in Europe about the possibility of an exhibition of Indian art to be circulated by the agency, and what did I think of such a project, based on my experience with "Sacred Circles." I thought back to all the demonstrators and performers at the exhibition and said, Why not do the opposite of "Sacred Circles"? That was a historical survey, with loans from museums and private collectors. Why not organize a show of living Native American art collected fresh from the field? It would mean long visits to Indian country and would demonstrate that quality art is still being produced today. I thought Europeans would find such an exhibition an intriguing challenge. The idea appealed to the USIA. A budget was set, at $85,000, and the American Federation of Arts, then headed by Wilder Green, was consulted to see if there was an interest in having it tour under their auspices, sponsored by the USIA. But the project blew to smithereens. Wilder Green and I met in Washington to sign a contract, he as organizer and myself as curator. We had our pens in hand when a voice came roaring

Figure 9. Ralph T. Coe and Piegan Blackfoot Chief John Yellow Horn, in Brocket, Alberta, Canada, 1982. Photo courtesy of Ralph T. Coe

down the hall: "Stop it! Don't let them sign!" A breathless lawyer exploded into the office: "You can't use taxpayers' money on foreigners. It's illegal." The "foreigners" turned out to be Canadian Indians from whom I had already bought objects, with this exhibition in mind. I said, "Indian peoples know no borders. A Sioux in Manitoba is the same as a Sioux in North Dakota." That argument was summarily dismissed. It seemed that found traditions were going to be lost. Wilder and I slaked our disappointment at a nearby bar.

Badly in need of counsel, I called William Woodside. Then CEO of the American Can Company, Bill had demonstrated his philanthropic bent by contributing a considerable sum to the American venue of "Sacred Circles." We met for lunch in New York, and I described to Bill and his wife, Migs, the plight of what had by now been baptized "Lost and Found Traditions." A week later, a meeting was set up between Bill Woodside and Wilder Green. The eventual result was a $400,000 grant given to the American Federation of Arts by the American Can Company Foundation.

I hopped into my Chrysler LeBaron and set off to find and research objects to include in the show. I already knew that if an object was on the artist's trading table, you bought it then and there, or never. "I can make you another" might be the intention of the maker, but in reality, the harsh exigencies of Indian life demanded that whoever first had the cash was the first to be served. In my travels, I learned to keep ready cash on hand by stashing it unseen in a compartment I made by slitting the ceiling fabric of my car and inserting it within. I learned to keep my car in a generally inconspicuous, unscrubbed state. This proved extremely useful, as when I was staying at a motel in St. Ignatius, Montana, at the edge of the Flathead Reservation. My car, chockablock with newly acquired art, remained untouched, while the gleaming Cadillac just next to it was broken into and robbed in the middle of the night. As an Indian friend at the Hoh River Reservation on the Puget Sound murmured to me after carefully inspecting—and approving—the condition of my car, "Ah, an Indian car. . . ."

In many field transactions, I was powerfully aware that I was not buying commodities in a non-Native sense but that I was stepping back into a very long and honorable tradition of Indian trade and exchange which had nothing to do with dollars and cents. Rather, it was a reenactment of an age-old social contract projected into the contemporary scene, proving that ancient ways were alive and well. In other words, Indian communities had bypassed assimilation by absorbing what they needed from the outside world, rather than the other way around (figs. 9, 10).

Figure 10. Ralph T. Coe, with Eskimo host, on St. Lawrence Island, Alaska, 1988, at a shingle beach not usually open to non-Native visitors. Photo: Sara Wolch

The "Lost and Found Traditions" exhibition opened at the American Museum of Natural History in New York City in 1986. The initiating ceremonial was conceived and executed by the Iroquois Confederacy and began with prayers offered in Iroquois by the Tuscarora artist Rick Hill. From this point on, the exhibition belonged to the Indians. The opening reception was held in the museum's grand Hall of Oceanic Birds. Rick Hill welcomed us to the exhibition and with due solemnity gestured toward the ceiling: "This is the first time in the history of the Haudenosaunee [the collective term for the six Iroquois tribes] that the Tadodaho [chief of the Iroquois Confederacy] has held a convocation under the wrong end of a whale." He was referring, of course, to the gigantic whale suspended above us, giving the assembled—and very dignified—company a dose of Indian humor. Then the more than five hundred guests, Indians and non-Natives together, all joined hands in concentric circles, and in a great round dance moved as with one heartbeat. Thus was called forth the spirit of high purpose and celebration that prevailed throughout the nine showings of "Lost and Found Traditions." The exhibition traveled, from Anchorage, Alaska, to Portland, Oregon, from New York City to Los Angeles, California, from Albuquerque, New Mexico, to Columbus, Georgia, crisscrossing the continent from 1986 to 1994. Its last venue was in Sweden.

From the very beginning, it was felt that "Lost and Found Traditions" should be donated intact to a public institution at the end of its tour. There were 383 objects in the exhibition and approximately fifty additional objects held in reserve. Museum field collecting of American Indian art and material culture in the United States had, except in the case of the Southwest, largely ceased from the Second World War on, with the exception of a little-recognized effort by the Department of the Interior's Indian Arts and Crafts Board. It was hoped that the objects in "Lost and Found Traditions," though only a small sampling of what was available, would be sufficient to remedy, symbolically, the woeful lack of systematic museum field collecting between 1965 and 1985. Because the American Federation of Arts held title to the objects, institutions were invited to apply to them to receive the collection as a gift. Twenty applications were received and carefully reviewed by a committee that met in New York at the AFA office. I was one of six voting members. After due deliberation, the collection was awarded to the Natural History Museum of Los Angeles County. For two reasons. First, while the most varied population of Native Americans in this country resides in southern California, the Indian collections at the museum, though distinguished, were heavily weighted in favor of California. A wider selection was needed to reflect the great variety of tribal representation in the region. Second, the museum was in the process of expanding its hall of American Indian culture, and it expressed the desire to include contemporary work in the new space. Ironically, while "Lost and Found Traditions" was conceived as an exhibition meant for art museums, its mission, to gain respect for contemporary traditional arts *as art,* was accomplished primarily in museums of ethnology and natural history.

The timelessness of American Indian art constitutes a flowing stream of renewal. Certainly one can specialize in a particular category of Indian culture, but to ignore the contemporary aspect breaks that flow. Concentrating only on what has been validated by age obscures the continuity that still underlies Native cultures. Nearly ten percent of the objects seen in the present exhibition are contemporary, and work made after 1950 constitutes a significant presence in my collection.

As my experiences broadened and my inbred romantic notions were superseded by the reality of contemporary Indian life, I developed a few standards of my own to serve as exhibition criteria. In "Lost and Found Traditions," I had included Native American artists with deservedly famous names, but, equally, I had sought new talent that represented the progression of Indian artistry from youth to old age as part of the continuum of culture. The youngest contributor was twelve years old and the oldest nearly ninety. I collected what I encountered, rather than trying to find what I imagined existed. Naturally, I kept in the back of my mind a catalogue of ideal classic objects to fill my tabula rasa, but I worked opportunistically, taking advantage of what I encountered in reality. There was beauty to be found not only in classic costumes, masks, pottery, and weavings but in utilitarian objects. Traditional tools such as fleshers, made of elk horn, sinew, rawhide, and metal for scraping hides, could command not only a functional but an aesthetic validity—and were still being made today, in this era of computer technology.

In the Native world, art is embedded in the doing. It is not, as with us, conceived within the framework of a museum. It resides in design, but not necessarily in abstract aesthetics. Often in the field I would ask tribal elders how they would want to have an exhibition of their art to be organized. Invariably they replied, by geography and then by tribe, for, "We are first of the land. We should be considered as sovereign nations, for there is no word for 'art' with us. We are creativity itself." Certainly, I had come a long way from the world of connoisseurship where I began.

IV. A Circle of Objects

When Indians dance intertribally, they do so in a circle. How many times I have stood or sat around a dance arbor arranged in a circle at Indian Days ceremonies, powwows, conferences, and meetings. That general configuration is at the very heart of Native American culture. Several years ago, at the death of a friend, a well-known Sioux dignitary and leader from the northern Plains, the community in which he lived honored him by slowly driving the pickup truck in which his open casket was placed all the way around the tribal dance arbor where he had officiated on so many occasions over the years. In this way, he could once more say good-bye to his world, and all those who knew him could wish him farewell. The concept of circularity—of encapsulation and interconnectedness—is expressed in countless ways. When Rick Hill introduced me to a fellow tribesman who wondered what I was doing in Rick's company, he said, "It's all right, he's been *around*." What he meant was that I had deviated from the path of materialism and ambition, in the linear sense, and had spent time on the good red road, a path that is as circular as it is continuous.

Initially, I collected American Indian art because it was aesthetically appealing. My father had purchased a couple of African masks in 1927, and he was beginning to look at Precolumbian art as well, his interest having been sparked by the extraordinary excavations being conducted by Alfonso Caso at Monte Alban, the ancient capital city in Oaxaca. My parents looked favorably on exploring other cultures. In the last photographs taken of our old Bratenahl house, one can see that what was then called "primitive" art had begun to creep into our strongly Francophile living room (fig. 11). But the distance between them is not very far. The modern art that my parents collected—in particular, the Modigliani portrait—was greatly influenced by African art. Later, of course, it was my own close contact with the Native American world itself that shifted my concentration toward their culture as a whole. Increasingly, I focused attention on Indian America. It was indigenous. It was right here. It had been here all the time. For other-directed Americans such as myself, it was a revelation. I have also collected in other ethnological areas—Africa, Indonesia, the Philippines, Oceania (fig. 12). And I have a passion for acquiring *objets* of the European arts in which I was initially trained. These would include Renaissance bronzes, boxwood sculptures, drawings, Art Nouveau, Art Deco—what might be called *kleinkunst*. And I am curious, as was my father, to know how works of art from different cultures and of varied styles and periods speak to one another. In my home today, two boxers by the seventeenth-century German sculptor Leonhard Kern, derived from a print by Marcantonio Raimondi, glare at each other while the figure of a California Pomo Indian, by the late folk artist Bun Lucas, stands between them, acting as referee!

Figure 11. Living room of the Ralph M. Coe residence, 1959. A Cézanne landscape hangs above the bookcase between a Nigerian Yoruba mask (left) and a Makah Northwest Coast mask (right). Other non-European objects include an African Bamana Chi'wara (foreground). Photo: Ted Gorka

In the years since "Lost and Found Traditions" ceased to offer a "built-in" reason to frequent Indian America, I have continued to travel, one summer covering as much as 16,000 miles in my car. Several times I have driven from New Mexico through Canada to Alaska and back. I have revisited the Plains, the Far West, the Great Lakes, and the Eastern Woodlands. In particular, I have visited the Eskimo/Inuit world—once hiring myself out as a journalist to the Bethel, Alaska, newspaper, the *Tundra Drum*. The first time I visited St. Lawrence Island, which is culturally really part of Siberia, I was flying in a bush plane in a ferocious storm. We had to turn back because we were literally being rocketed over the Russian Chukchi Peninsula; behind the mountains lurked an unfriendly Russian submarine base (this was at the end of the Cold War). A few days later, we were able to land. To my pleasure, I found that the island was home to the Siberian Yup'ik peoples. It is here that the finest Eskimo ivory carvers live and from whom I have acquired a number of exquisitely carved figures. These convivial people are given dispensation to hunt whale each spring, using traditional umiaks, large wood-frame boats covered with walrus skin. They are re-covered each year, and I walked among the frames stored on posts along the streets. On St. Lawrence Island, I felt I had truly left the white man's world.

Recently, I heard on the radio a Plains Indian discussing how to handle a particularly vexing social problem current in the Native American community. To address the problem, she advised forming what is known as a "talking circle." These spiritual circles continue to play an important part in Indian life. In the past, they served as forums for important

Figure 12. Ralph T. Coe residence, New Mexico, 1999. Architect: Bruce Davis, Albuquerque, New Mexico
Photo: Jack Parsons

councils and treaty meetings. Today, they are used to discuss matters of health, racism, youth issues, and personal conflict. In particular, they are venues for the healing arts and sweat-lodge ceremonies.

Several times on the Olympic Peninsula, I was privileged to attend the Makah tribe's Indian Days celebration at their seaside village of Neah Bay, Washington. I would stay over at the motel on the dock, to enjoy the canoe racing, dancing, storytelling, and fresh baked salmon. On the beach I saw young people loosely grouped in circles around an older member of the tribe, learning the old ways and traditions. I have witnessed, and participated in, such events, and the configuration of the circle has imprinted itself on my mind.

Besides its formal values, there is, I believe, another dimension that informs a collection such as this one. It, too, can be experienced as a talking circle. Traditionally, as noted earlier, there has been no word for art per se. Creative expression is part of a whole—the interweaving of song, ritual, objects, and the materials and technology used for their creation—governed by appropriate times for proper usage. It involves a recognition of the close relationship that exists between the human, animal, and natural worlds, an ethos that is distinct from non-Native culture. Even when Western illusionism is introduced to contemporary Native American painting, it seems grafted on. Underneath is a circular way of looking at an interrelated universe, one that is an Indian imperative alone.

The objects in this collection reflect the beliefs, values, and aspirations of diverse yet connected peoples. They incorporate designs and motifs that express ideas about spirituality and about society and its functions. They were not only made, but they were prayed over.

If we take the time to really look at these objects, they draw us into the circle. They invoke the Sioux concept of the *inipi*—a purifying ceremony held in the round. In the Lakota language, the prefix *in* means "to live"—as in living arts, living spirits, living visions. Such a ceremony usually ends with the words *mitakuye oyas in,* meaning "all my relatives," or, inductively, we are all related through the mind's responsive eye.

1. Rewald 1989, p. 204.
2. Venturi 1939.
3. "William" was William Mathewson Milliken, the eminent and dynamic director of the Cleveland Museum of Art from 1930 to 1958. Milliken found the museum in marble and left it in platinum, with the second most important collection of medieval art in the United States. A discriminating connoisseur and one of the few American art museum directors well respected in Europe for his wide exercise of connoisseurship, "Uncle" William, as we called him, was a distinct influence not only on me but also my sister Nancy in our vision of what an art museum ought to be.
4. [Lee] 1960.
5. Covarrubias 1954.
6. Pope-Hennessy 1991, pp. 121, 196.
7. See Coe 1986, p. 270, no. 379.
8. Ibid., fig. 367.

Marginality and Intelligence in the Collecting of Native American Art

J. C. H. KING

Two different phenomena characterize the contemporary private and public collecting of Native American art. One is the collaboration of Native Americans, Native nations, and established museums in the organization of exhibitions, the building of new museums, and the interpretation of Native art and history. At the center of this development is a renewed leadership that vigorously expresses a Native American approach to curating. W. Richard West Jr., director of the Smithsonian Institution's National Museum of the American Indian, in Washington, D.C., leads this movement. The other is the private collecting of contemporary and early Native art, which also flourishes, often only marginally involved with the Native community. This essay looks at private collecting outside the great anthropological and natural history museums of Washington, D.C., Philadelphia, New York, and Chicago, among others, which date from the period 1865 to 1930. These histories of outsider museums and collectors related to the development of Native museums are placed in the context of American taste for Native art and aesthetics. Also briefly discussed are how collectors and museums may or may not collect "intelligently"—in the sense of being systematic—and how Native art is exhibited. The evolution of this history is in many ways indebted to the pioneering work of Ralph T. Coe, who initiated many of these changes in the last part of the twentieth century and whose own collection is celebrated in these pages.

In the creation of the exhibition "Sacred Circles: Two Thousand Years of North American Indian Art," in 1976–77, for the United States Bicentennial,[1] Coe influenced a generation of collectors and museum professionals (fig. 1). The main precursor to his curatorial approach, in which Native American art is presented not in an ethnographic context but as art in and of itself, was the Museum of Modern Art's 1941 exhibition "Indian Art of the United States." This concept was refined in the 1970s, in Norman Feder's book *American Indian Art* and in the exhibition "Two Hundred Years of North American Indian Art," held at the Whitney Museum of American Art, in New York City,[2] and it was greatly expanded by Coe. By opening his exhibition in London and by resourcefully gathering exhibits from overseas collections, he gave this exhibition

Figure 1. Ralph T. Coe in 1977, pictured before the Sioux horse effigy at the exhibition "Sacred Circles: Two Thousand Years of North American Indian Art." Photo courtesy of the Nelson-Atkins Museum of Art, Kansas City

type international exposure, arguing for the centrality of Native aesthetics to American art and to the cultural and historical identity of the United States. He did so from a position marginal to Native culture. Coe was one of a number of individuals and institutions on the periphery of Native society, academic anthropology, and Native studies who changed the outsider's view of American Indian art and the Native world. The organizers of the 1941 MoMA show, Frederic H. Douglas and René d'Harnoncourt, from the Denver Art Museum and the Museum of Modern Art, respectively, were also outsiders, in relatively new institutions that were marginal to the great anthropology collections. Among the first to adopt and develop the idea of Indian art as art, they created a new paradigm for the presentation of Native society past and present (fig. 2). Coe, also from a great but, in terms of a Native collection, marginal institution, the Nelson Gallery of Art, Kansas City, Missouri (now the Nelson-Atkins Museum of Art), framed a similar re-evaluation. Its influence continues to be felt to this day.

THE FIRST COLLECTORS

In "Sacred Circles," Coe presented to the world the great votive Huron wampum belts that were deposited at Chartres Cathedral in the seventeenth century.[3] Their context is that of one of the earliest surviving forms of European collecting, the medieval treasury, an exhibition format that juxtaposed disparate objects, similar to the way it was done in the early modern cabinets of gentlemen and nobles in Oxford and Copenhagen.[4] The Tradescant family at Oxford, noted seventeenth-century British collectors, in acquiring and organizing curiosities into natural and artificial categories, could be said to be among the first intelligent collectors. In the work that they assembled, trophyism was replaced by an organizational principle.[5] In contrast, the first collections in what was to become the United States combined features of the trophy display, the armory, and the business room. This display was exemplified in the home of Sir William Johnson (1715–1774), superintendent of Indian Affairs during the third quarter of the eighteenth century. At his house in upper New York State, he set aside one of the front rooms to conduct business with Native American leaders in the region. Here he displayed the items he had acquired in transactions with Native nations, in the business of war and alliance, and in transferring land to Americans and Europeans.[6]

The collection of Thomas Jefferson, at Monticello, twenty or thirty years later, was, though perhaps without any overarching principle, similar in outline to Johnson's. Jefferson owned relics obtained from what he termed "barrows"—later to be renamed "mounds"—as well as the objects collected by Lewis and Clark during their travels to the West in 1804–6. William Clark (1770–1838), superintendent of Indian Affairs for the Louisiana Territory and governor of the Missouri Territory, continued to acquire Native American art, and in 1816 he formed a collection at St. Louis, from which he selected pieces to present as gifts to visiting luminaries.[7] Like Johnson before him, Clark probably used his collection also as a resource in transactions with Indians. No doubt, both men pointed out to visiting chiefs objects that had been presented to them on earlier occasions by other leaders or members of their tribes. Affairs of state, whether presidential or associated with the War Office, were also a major source for objects, particularly with the founding in 1846 of the Smithsonian Institution, which acquired the great accumulation of the U.S. Exploring Expedition of 1838–42, led by Lt. Charles Wilkes.[8]

Figure 2. The Eskimo Hunters of the Arctic, one of the exhibits at "Indian Art of the United States," The Museum of Modern Art, New York, 1941. Photo courtesy of the Museum of Modern Art

Among the more scholarly, but also commercial, museums founded at the same time were those of the Peale family in Philadelphia and Baltimore. In 1784, Charles Willson Peale (1741–1827) established Peale's Museum, also known as the Philadelphia Museum, a repository of natural history and art. And Rubens Peale (1808–1891), Charles Willson's son, founded his own art and science museum in Baltimore.[9] These were followed, in the 1840s, by the commercial American museums of P. T. Barnum in New York. These ephemeral institutions, many destroyed by fire, are unfortunately poorly documented. Barnum probably regarded the supply of Indian relics as an infinite, replaceable resource, and no doubt he regularly acquired new Indian dresses, as earlier displays became dirty, soiled, and unattractive, or when he decided to sell off objects from his collection. Barnum, who was more interested in Native performances than Native objects, had been in temporary partnership with the artist George Catlin (1796–1872) and Catlin's Gallery when he was in London in the 1840s. Catlin is an important figure in this history because of his involvement with Native culture—as both a painter and a collector, showing his own work alongside that of Native American artists. The great museums that followed, particularly the Peabody Museum of Harvard University, founded in 1866,[10] and the Smithsonian Institution, worked with

Figure 3. Illustration of a European in the dress of a Delaware Indian, from *French and Indian Cruelty: The Life and Curious Adventures of Peter Williamson,* 1758

the scientific paradigm model first espoused by Jefferson. It was their aim to record the art and material culture of aboriginal and non-industrial peoples. Eventually, their collections would be the most extensive in the world.

Taste and Collecting

Rather separate from the history of major museums in the collecting of Native American art is the perception of taste. One of the peculiarities of these early collections is how little the work of Native artists was appreciated in the context of taste in household design. The Plimoth Plantation Museum, in Plymouth, Massachusetts, for example, which presents Euro-American life in the seventeenth century, while it duly notes Native contributions, such as the growing of Indian corn, includes little in the way of Native manufactures or ideas of Native taste. The great Native contributions to colonial life related to the world outside the home: horticulture, hunting, clothing, and transportation. Perhaps the major vernacular use of Native objects in the home during the colonial period and into the nineteenth century was that of basketry: ash splint basketry in the Northeast, birchbark basketry and canoes, coiled splint imbricated basketry in the Coast Salish waterways of the Northwest Coast, and coiled and twined basketry in California. However, very few domestic items—baskets, bags, and carved wood bowls—survive in New England collections from this early period.[11] On the other hand, from at least the eighteenth century soldiers, explorers, and people on the frontiers acquired Native costume and accoutrements for use (fig. 3). After the Seven Years' War (1756–63), when Native American fighting techniques were used by the British in Martinique against the French and in Cuba against the Spanish,[12] Native costumes ended up in European cabinets or in men's studies and women's cozy corners (fig. 4). One collection of exceptional quality was that of Jasper Grant, who was stationed in Ontario at the beginning of the nineteenth century.[13]

Yet these were marginal aspects of taste. Indeed, what the rarity of these collections highlights is that Native American design was not the exotic art of choice. North

Figure 4. "Bachelor's Parlour in Winnipeg, Canada," from a stereocard, 1890. Private collection

Americans—and Europeans—have preferred, and often still do prefer, Asian art. Early museums such as the Peabody Essex Museum, in Salem, Massachusetts, founded in 1799, have until recently exhibited Asian art rather than Native American art and privileged Chinese export wares over those from Native America. In the nineteenth century, the Arts and Crafts movement emerged from the ideas of the English social critic and theoretician John Ruskin (1819–1900) and of linked American artists such as James Abbott McNeill Whistler (1834–1903). Transported from England to America, this movement was recast with an ever stronger Japanese emphasis.

This Asian preference pertains especially to the work of the American architect Frank Lloyd Wright (1867–1959). Wright used the term "Usonian" to refer implicitly to a broad concept of American architecture that complements and melds with the landscape of the Midwest prairies and Arizona desert. Usonianism was related to the idea of wilderness and to the shadow concept, the frontier, more than to a populated Indian landscape or to a Puebloan architecture. Primary source materials for Wright's domestic architecture were often Japanese, and Wright spent much of his career supporting his lifework by dealing in Japanese prints. There are few Native American references in his buildings or in his interiors. One of Wright's great American architectural creations, in Los Angeles, takes the form of a series of interlocking Maya temples, yet it bears the name Hollyhock House (1916–21), after a flower of cottage simplicity. Only rarely— a Zuni water jar at Fallingwater, in the 1960s, for example—is anything Native American seen in Wright's buildings.[14] This separation of local culture and landscape is further underscored by the use of glass, canvas, and water at Wright's Scottsdale studio, Taliesin West (1937), which dramatically dissociates the building from Native vernacular architecture (fig. 5).

Interestingly, much of the early appreciation for Native North America was contextualized with Japanese design. For instance, the beginnings of tourist advertising for the American West and Southwest by railroad companies in the 1880s often employed the Japanese design principle of positive and negative space. Brochures distributed by these companies showed lithographic reproductions of totem poles by the naturalist John Muir (1838–1914) set in Japanese cartouches.[15] These companies, as primary agents of change in the American West, were instrumental in introducing Native taste to the American public (fig. 6). From the 1880s, with the proliferation of hotels and tourist advertising, which emphasized place and the regional exotic, American taste shifted and for the first time turned to a Native aesthetic. The preeminent practitioners were the railway and hotel restaurateur Fred Harvey (1835–1901), in his association with the revived Santa Fe Railroad of the 1890s,[16] and, in the early twentieth century, the railroad magnate Louis Warren Hill Sr. (1872–1948), of the Great Northern Railway.[17] Harvey is known not only as an entrepreneur and for his Pueblo-style hotels and promotion of tourism but also because he was a collector and a dealer in Native American art. This interest marked a change from the initial American response to the Native aesthetic exemplified in, say, the architecture of Santa Fe, which concentrated on the stripping out of Hispanic, Mexican, and Puebloan elements and their replacement with the nineteenth-century American vernacular.

Figure 5. Frank Lloyd Wright (1867–1959), Taliesin West (1937), Scottsdale, Arizona. Photo: J. C. H. King

Figure 6. Photograph of a Navajo rug in a California interior, ca. 1930. Private collection

The Influence of Native Design in the American West and Southwest

The Hispanicized and Indian taste of Fred Harvey was institutionalized in Santa Fe by archaeologists and other professionals, such as Edgar Lee Hewett (1865–1946), the founder of the Museum of New Mexico. It was they who provided a formal approach to the design of such institutions, which have done so much to collect and preserve Native American art.[18] Concurrently, in Los Angeles, Charles Fletcher Lummis (1859–1928) took the Southwest aesthetic west to California, where he launched a crusade to restore the Spanish missions. The photographer Grace Nicholson (1877–1948), at the same time and in the same city, as a collector and dealer, was a—if not the—great patron of Native American basket makers. Her passion for Native art was maintained and baskets were sold in the context of her more commercial interest in Asian art and architecture. The important point here is that it was largely through tourism and marketing that the Western taste for a Native aesthetic developed and led to the creation of Native collections. This taste for Native aesthetics, specifically for geometric forms, was only slightly later reflected in American decorative arts and architecture. In the decorative arts, the influence is expressed especially in the strong abstract geometric forms seen on manufactured textiles—those made by the Beacon Manufacturing Company, in New Bedford, Massachusetts, or by Pendleton, in Oregon, for example (fig. 7).[19] And in architecture, Art Deco design also shows a Native inflection

Figure 7. Brochure from the 1920s advertising Beacon Camp Blankets. Private collection

Figure 8. Northwest Coast Indian mask motif atop an Art Deco cinema, Fairbanks, Alaska. Photo: J. C. H. King

(fig. 8). These influences are ultimately related to Navajo/Saltillo textile design, Western basketry, ceramics of the Southwest, and Mexican architecture, as, for example, at Mitla.

Numerous important exhibitions have been mounted to show the influence of Japanese design on Western art, but only one significant exhibition has described the influence of Native American art. This was the 1984 Museum of Modern Art show "'Primitivism' in 20th Century Art," curated by William Rubin.[20] Remarkably, architectural basketry and textile design were largely omitted, perhaps because they were considered outside the parameters of fine art. But without the sense of place and appreciation of architecture that emerged through tourism, marketing, and travel west, which resulted in changes in taste, none of the intelligent collecting of the mid- and late twentieth century could have occurred. Related to this phenomenon is the disappearance, during the mid-twentieth century, of such concepts as "savage" and "primitive art" in collecting.[21]

George Heye (1874–1957) and Collecting

How then do we suggest which twentieth-century collectors collected intelligently? One way is through the relationships between collectors and suppliers of art, whether Native or non-Native. Artists, dealers, collectors, and institutions and their sponsors are today all part of elaborate networks. Ideas associated with these networks are very much center stage in academic studies, yet they often remain marginal for active collectors. In contrast, the great collector George Heye may be said to have worked with his associates through a command system of relationships. As the preeminent, even monopsonist, collector, he created and dominated the market for Native materials with a combination of wealth and force of character. There was very little in the way of partnership of equals between Heye and his second wife, Thea, and those people who assisted in the formation of the Museum of the American Indian. Yet, Heye managed to build the largest and most important collection of Native American art to date. Indeed, it could be said that his museum was a greater monument than all other private collections put together. None was organized with such single-minded dedication, skill, and avarice.[22] In this, he was perhaps like Henry James's collector, Mrs. Gereth, in *The Spoils of Poynton*. She was said to have been possessed of "a patience, an almost infernal cunning, that had enabled her to do it all with a limited command of money." One can be sure that, like Mrs. Gereth, Heye "waited for [his treasures], worked for them, picked them over, made them worthy of each other . . . watched them, loved them, lived with them."[23] Because of chance—the death of patrons and the Great Depression of the 1930s—Heye left his lifework, nearly one million items from indigenous peoples throughout the Western hemisphere, in a perilous condition in the 1950s. As is well known, there was little endowment and no prospect of financial growth and security. The museum was salvaged in the 1990s through the dedicated work of Native Americans and lawyers, legislators, and anthropologists. Heye, from his grave, was the beneficiary of the ultimate coup, the permanent federal funding for his museum—ironically, at the cost of losing part of his name to the institution, the National Museum of the American Indian. The museum, which is to open in Washington, D.C., in 2004, will no doubt be the focus for collecting on a national scale, an effort postponed since the onset of the Depression. In this, it may become an umbrella organization for institutional and private collections, whether Native or otherwise. In 1998, the museum was appointed by Congress to house 6,500 pieces from the Indian Arts and Crafts Board of the U.S. Department of the Interior, founded in 1935 to foster Indian art.[24] This development is particularly notable at a time of prolonged crisis for other institutions, such as the Southwest Museum in Los Angeles[25] and the Robert S. Peabody Museum of Archaeology at Phillips Academy, Andover, Massachusetts.

MID-TWENTIETH CENTURY COLLECTORS

Other collectors, lesser than Heye, developed personal relationships with Native Americans in acquiring Native art. One of the best documented is Milford Chandler (1889–1981), who collected most actively during the years 1915 to 1926.[26] His acquisitions were made through personal dealings with Native peoples in and around the Great Lakes and the Plains. Chandler was a man of limited wealth, and his transactions and those by his later colleague Richard Pohrt (b. 1911) were made in a climate of supplication and friendship. With little institutional base and slender resources, inequality between the sellers and the buyers was minimal. In a sense, Chandler and Pohrt collected in a very modern way. Other collectors (including Heye and Lummis) employed different collecting approaches and had varied motives. These are described in great detail in a collection of innovative essays published in 1999 and edited by Shepard Krech III and Barbara A. Hail. Much collecting was the result of scientific interest, and some derived from the romantic notions of the "vanishing" Indian. Several institutions had an educational mission. These included the Indian Museum at Fruitlands, founded in 1929 by Clara Endicott Sears in Harvard, Massachusetts, and the museum planned in the 1950s in the Florida Keys by Francis and Mary Crane. (The Cranes' collection eventually went to the Denver Museum of Natural History.) One notable lacuna in Krech and Hail's volume is any discussion about the quality of the collections, in particular whether the objects were well documented and whether they were acquired intelligently. In collecting for educational purposes, some might say it is unnecessary to include the best of type—whatever that value-laden concept may mean. In this, the educator-collectors would have agreed with Picasso, who, when the quality of his collection of primitive art was criticized, responded that it was not necessary to use master-pieces to gain an understanding of stylistic principles.[27] But in a relativistic age, absolutes are a must and quality does matter.

This distinction can be seen very simply in a comparison between nineteenth- and twentieth-century Plains warrior shirts in two exhibitions. One, curated by Joseph and George Horse Capture, was held at the National Museum of the American Indian in 2001.[28] This included superb early shirts with painted pictographs representing exploits, medicine, and trophy tallies. Because of the meanings behind the motifs, these shirts may be considered more important than the later examples exhibited in 1981 at the Haffenreffer Museum of Anthropology, in Bristol, Rhode Island. These, in contrast, are painted only modestly with symbolic designs.[29] Private collectors have, in recent years, been eager to acquire fully painted early shirts, as they communicate, aesthetically, core Native values more effectively than those of a later date. While later shirts reflect, by the absence of full pictographic decoration, the condition of the Plains peoples when they were transferred to reservations, the earlier examples signify the brief moment of warrior life. One judgment is largely cultural, the other is largely aesthetic.

SURVEY EXHIBITIONS AND SURVEY COLLECTING

Teaching with masterpieces, as at the Barnes Foundation in Merion, Pennsylvania, may be a good practice, but it is not a prerequisite for successful education.[30] This idea was taken up, in the mid-nineteenth century, at the South Kensington Museum in London by Ruskin and other educators, who believed that in teaching, reproductions could serve as well as originals. This was something that Chandler and Pohrt particularly appreciated. It later came to be associated with hobbyists and the hobbyist movement, but it did not blur the boundaries between what may or may not be considered authentic. Conversely, as mentioned above, with the MoMA exhibition of 1941, a sense of the quality of the work itself begins to emerge. Norman Feder's refinement of these ideas, focusing on accuracy of attribution and the exhibiting of the "very best," derived not simply from an art-historical perspective. These ideas were reinforced by his perspective as a practical person and as a maker of art-works.[31] Publisher in the 1950s of the magazine *The Indian Hobbyist,* Feder by the 1970s had achieved national prominence.[32] Using the collections assembled at the Denver Art Museum by Frederic Douglas, he reworked the format of both survey exhibitions and collections, as did Coe with "Sacred Circles," and, a year later, Evan Maurer at the Art Institute of Chicago.[33] Feder was also a collector and understood that great curators work within a dialectic of collecting, exhibiting, and scholarship and that these activities reinforce and influence one another. While anthropologists are often rather leery of historians of Native American art, the introduction of concepts about art to the field of anthropology resulted in raising the status and prestige of the study of Native material culture. Regional institutions of national and international prominence, such as the Denver Art Museum and the Nelson-Atkins Museum of Art, whose Native collections pale beside those of, say, the

National Museum of Natural History, have changed the way the American public perceives American Indian art, thus altering the non-Native perspective on Native culture as a whole.

DEALERS

The Chandler-Pohrt collection was first given a published airing in the 1973 exhibition at the Flint Institute of Arts, before being redeveloped for "Art of the American Indian Frontier," which traveled from the Detroit Institute of Arts to the National Gallery of Art, in Washington, D.C.[34] At the same time another collection, that of the Hamburg collector Arthur Speyer, first published in Germany in 1968, emphasized quality and age. This collection was acquired by the National Museum of Man, in Ottawa, where it was curated, contextualized, and presented, by Ted Brasser, to a wider, Canadian audience.[35] From the 1970s on, a dozen or more private collectors, largely in the United States, built continent-wide survey collections, drawing on the insights and experience of Coe, Maurer, Feder, Speyer, and Chandler-Pohrt. With most Native American art of excellence already in public institutions, these individuals relied on the connoisseurship of major museums and on a few prominent dealers as providers and teachers. Their work is shown in the great series of general survey catalogues that have been published over the last twenty years,[36] the most distinguished of which is that of the Eugene V. Thaw collection at the Fenimore Art Museum, in Cooperstown, New York.[37] One way of viewing these highly motivated individuals is as catalysts. In the Native American context, they may function much like Raven or Coyote, endlessly creating and giving but also acting unpredictably, in a manner often uncontrollable by mere mortals. In this sense, dealers exhibit the same characteristic of marginality seen in those twentieth-century institutions and individuals who have effected change in both collecting and in the perception of collecting. Other collectors, such as Adelaide and Dominique de Menil and Edmund Carpenter, worked with museum professionals and Native American artists, as seen for instance in the discussion of Northwest Coast art in the book *Form and Freedom,* by Bill Holm and William (Bill) Reid, published in 1975.

Coe, in his collecting, also exhibits this characteristic, of coming from the outside. He has been able to acquire important objects that are not typical, such as the Pacific Eskimo tea box (cat. no. 198). He is also often interested in objects considered too "ethnographic" by the trade. Similarly, Coe has exploited the market by acquiring objects that are "burned" (or unsalable) through too much public exposure. Indeed, his ability to act "opportunistically" is an important feature of his collecting.

NATIVE MUSEUMS OF NATIVE AMERICAN ART

Museums of Native American art provide a contrasting paradigm for collecting. Long before Europeans arrived in the Americas, Native peoples accumulated regalia and paraphernalia for ceremonial and religious purposes. The burial of pipes by the Indians of the Hopewell culture at Mound City, Ohio, more than fifteen hundred years ago represents one type of collecting. The production and preservation of crest regalia on the Northwest Coast could also be said to be a form of collecting, as could, perhaps, the accumulation of sacred objects in medicine bundles. These can be seen by outsiders as a kind of portable shrine. Indeed, Plains peoples may see museums as vastly enlarged medicine bundles. The creation of Native-run museums is often seen, erroneously, as a recent phenomenon. In 1826, for example, Cherokee leaders attempted to found a museum at New Echota, Georgia, although they were prevented from doing so by the destruction of the incipient Cherokee state and by the forced movement westward of the tribe.[38] Direct Native involvement in museums in fact extends back at least one hundred fifty years. The New York State Museum (then Cabinet) in Albany, founded in 1836, was the repository for two collections built in the mid-nineteenth century by Lewis Henry Morgan (1818–1881) and by the Seneca sachem General Ely S. Parker (1828–1895). Parker's nephew Arthur C. Parker (1881–1955) headed the influential Rochester Museum of Arts and Sciences in the early twentieth century and, at the suggestion of the New-York Historical Association, published *A Manual for History Museums*. The book includes a pithy section on collecting material for historical displays, such as period rooms, and emphasizes the importance of documentation.

Today, Native museums and cultural centers are a focus for the expansion of collecting. The principles involved are rather different from those invoked by private collectors. Museums are important as symbols of nationhood, particularly as expressed by those tribes enriched by the gaming industry. They promote preservation, recovery, and the development of tribal identity, and they assume moral practice as a central tenet. This is combined with an emphasis on cultural specificity. In contrast, in the globalized world, urban museums emphasize shared, universal values. Most important, Native museums contribute to the education of the public in cultural values—the cyclical and non-linear nature of time, for example, and the importance of land and family.

Krinsky's 1996 monograph on contemporary Native American architecture, subtitled *Cultural Regeneration and Creativity,* focuses on the building of museums and cultural centers. Many of these institutions have their own web sites, which articulate their collecting philosophies. The Alutiiq Museum and Archaeological Repository, in Kodiak, Alaska, is a good example. Although not one of the larger new museums, it has grown rapidly. Opened in 1995 with a grant from the Exxon Valdez Oil Spill Trustee Council, in 2002 it already had a collection of 50,000 items. The ethnographic section includes objects made within the recent past, contemporary art, and replicas of prehistoric artifacts and historically significant specimens. The Makah Cultural Resource Center, in Neah Bay, Washington, has a collection of similar size, largely from the Makah archaeological site at Ozette, excavated in the 1960s and 1970s. Their displays include exceptional replicas as well as archaeological finds.

Another significant feature of Native museum collections is the contributions made by local leaders. One such collection is that of Nipo Tach Num Strongheart (1891–1966), in the Yakama Nation Museum, Toppenish, Washington. A performer with Buffalo Bill's

Wild West Show from the age of ten who later had a career in Hollywood, he left 10,000 artifacts and books to the museum. Another collection, of Pomo baskets made by her family and friends, was assembled by Elsie Comanche Allen (1899–1990) and exhibited in the Grace Hudson Museum, Ukiah, California.[39] This collection, interesting for its documenting of Native-owned basketry through the lean years of the mid-twentieth century, acts as a link between the contemporary world and the heroic years of art basketmaking in the early twentieth century. It is particularly remarkable for the number of baskets identified as to maker.

The process of repatriation, or "de-collecting"—a process that is more radical than simply deaccessioning—in some Native museums, is also an important element of collecting. While the moral imperatives behind repatriation have a global reach, only in Canada has museum practice, and in the United States has the law, provided an effective framework for achieving resolution and, perhaps, closure of this issue. Repatriation may be seen as an aspect of relations between tribal and nontribal museums, but it is part of a larger picture, namely, the proper use and interpretation of Native materials in museum collections and the realization of

Figure 9. Brochure from the Ah-Tha-Ti-Ki Museum, Big Cypress, Florida, 1999

appropriate cultural relations with originating peoples. On the other hand, while repatriation is a significant development in the whole concept of collecting, curiosity about other cultures and the impulse to collect are very much a part of American and European culture. In a sense, what matters most is not what people or institutions own but whether they make the best use of what they own.

One of the primary Native museums in Florida, the Ah-Tha-Ti-Ki Museum at Big Cypress (fig. 9), has chosen to acquire major historical works, including paintings and costume. At the time of opening in 1997, it was stated museum policy that the Seminoles would "regain" the artifacts then in the Smithsonian Institution, Washington, D.C., and in the George Gustav Heye Center of the National Museum of the American Indian in New York City.[40] Museums in Florida are important because it was Florida Natives who led the way in the development of high-stakes gaming, so controversial today, identifying a radically new way of providing resources for Indian nations. Another, rather different approach to the repatriation of collections is that adopted by the Agua Caliente Museum, in Palm Springs, California, which owns the registered trademark "The Spirit Lives." Representing the Agua Caliente band of Cahuilla Indians and other Cahuilla peoples, the Cahuilla Intertribal Repatriation Committee was formed to establish a collaborative project to repatriate objects that meet the criteria of the federal Native American Graves Protection and Repatriation Act of 1990.

LIMITS ON COLLECTING

Perhaps it is also worth considering the seldom-addressed question of how individuals validate their collecting and how they ensure the survival and thus the memorialization of their collections. Many of the greatest collectors, such as J. P. Morgan and Sir Richard Wallace, while leaving institutions in their names, did not save the entirety of their collections for posterity.[41] Numerous collectors more or less failed to preserve their collections at all. Charles I lost his head, and William Beckford and William Randolph Hearst lost their money. Yet liberal, though perhaps unfocused collectors have left important accumulations—Hearst himself, with his gift of the great group of Navajo textiles to the Natural History Museum of Los Angeles County.[42] Others who did likewise include Eric L. Harvie of Calgary, whose heterogeneous interests extended to the superb group of Haida argillite carvings now in the Glenbow Museum, Calgary,[43] and Sir Henry Wellcome. Wellcome's collection in the British Museum, and elsewhere, includes besides important Tsimshian objects and manuscripts, hundreds of archaeological specimens, in chert and ivory, still more or less undocumented. These were acquired incidentally during the 1920s and 1930s. Some came from early accumulations of a typological series of arrowheads and stone points—"relics"—a collecting model that generally ceased to be of interest to archaeologists in the first half the twentieth century. Intelligent collectors know limits and boundaries. They know when to stop and when permanence is more important than rank growth. Few people want their collection to end up in a Hearst-style giveaway at Gimbels,[44] or to be dispersed at Sotheby's. Many people give their art to institutions that demonstrate respect for art. But not all collectors want permanent housing for their collections. Those who sell may say, for instance, that they want others to experience the same excitement that they experienced in the chase and frenzy of acquisition.

RELIC COLLECTORS

Relics constitute perhaps the one category of Native collecting that can quite easily be caricatured and stereotyped. As long ago as 1935, Arthur Parker was emphatic about the subject: "Getting Indian relics is not the object of archeology. To hunt relics is like having an unlettered person dig into the ruins of some vast library of priceless knowledge."[45] While amateur archaeology today is often illegal, as, for instance, on federal lands, collectors still maintain large accumulations of flaked and ground tools, such as points and adzes. These are often of a certain minimalist aesthetic and attractive to handle and to look at, but without proper documentation they may be of little value. In the mid-1970s, when I first started working at the British Museum, I received a phone call from an American collector who wished to sell his lithic materials, or relics. The collection was described in terms of tonnage—seven tons, to be exact. In no other field would a collection be sold by tonnage—birds' eggs, drawings, medical equipment, airplanes. In the sense of being an active collecting institution, of course, the British Museum is a marginal museum with very limited budgets. No dealer or auction house with typical objects—a raven rattle or a Plains pipe bag—need bring them to the Department of Ethnography for an opinion or a possible sale. So it is usually people outside the market who offer such material. Relic collecting, in the sense of being a nineteenth-century activity, is today considered to lie outside the realms of good taste and good practice. It was once much favored. William Blackmore, for example, the English speculator in Hispanic land grants, collected relics for his museum in Salisbury in the 1860s, and the Blackmore Museum housed a great array of flaked points, typologically arranged, undocumented and uncatalogued except to states. A century and a half later, the phenomenon of relic collecting is situated rather differently.

In his novel *Utz,* Bruce Chatwin talks of the eighteenth-century lust of the Saxon monarch August the Strong for porcelain from his Meissen manufactory as "porcelain sickness" (*Porzellankrankheit*).[46] There is not, of course, anything equivalent in North America. Collectors of Native art are not really possessed by "Indian Sickness." Yet there is a fairly indefinable—but undeniable—syndrome in which non-Natives identify with Native Americans in a complex nexus of interest, much of which is associated with Indian hobbyists and relic collectors. It is an interest that goes back to medieval times, to the Wildman, the Woodsman, the Savage, and the search for anti-heros, who, in their simplicity, represent the antithesis of urban civilization. And it encompasses, in its European peculiarities, both the wilderness activities of the Boy Scout movement and the novels of Karl May, as wellsprings of authenticity. Relic collecting is another aspect of this complex whole. It possesses separate forms of refined typological organization, market structures, and guarantees of authenticity (with certificates, of course). In psychological imperatives, it seems to connect both to illegal activities, such as collecting birds' eggs and other wildlife specimens, and to an obsession with militaria. One unfortunate result of relic collecting is the destruction of sites and scientific data, such as the General Electric Hopewell site in the Midwest,[47] or the scouring of the Mimbres Canyon for ceramics. An extreme manifestation of this business is the organization of flaked tools in pretty, framed pictures, a validation of collecting that could be considered, at best, tasteless. Taste itself has been described by Sally Price as related, perhaps symbiotically, to connoisseurship.[48] Joseph Alsop had earlier linked these subjective relativities to money. In his book *The Rare Art Traditions,* Alsop maintains that "current prices always tell the current story of taste."[49] Yet with Indian relics, this is not quite the case. Indian points may indeed fetch high prices, but the collecting of points may be considered, at the very least, morally ambiguous. Alsop, of course, was not interested in Native American art. A similar disinterest is reflected in the near exclusion of Native North America from accounts of looting—in the historical study *Art Plunder* (1960),[50] for example, or in *The Plundered Past* (1977), a book about modern trade in antiquities.[51] The nearest equivalent of these studies, one describing the lust for Native art from the Northwest Coast, is Douglas Cole's *Captured Heritage* (1985), perhaps the single most influential monograph about institutional collecting. It is written largely from an ethno-historical rather than an antiquarian perspective.

THE COLLECTING OF CONTEMPORARY NATIVE AMERICAN ART

Ralph T. Coe's "Sacred Circles" was an exhibition that more or less excluded contemporary art. Ten years later, his "Lost and Found Traditions: Native American Art, 1965–1985," redressed this balance by surveying contemporary art across the continent.[52] No one else had attempted this, and no one is likely to attempt it again—at least not in the same way. What was particularly impressive about this effort was that Coe collected most of the material himself, that is, field collecting took place in circumstances of relative equality between the maker and the collector of the object, much like the collecting transactions of Chandler and Pohrt fifty years earlier. Again, the important point is Coe's capacity to effect change in the perception of Native American history, art, and anthropology despite his position of marginality. More recent surveys of contemporary art, such as those associated with Canadian national institutions—"Indigena," "Land Spirit Power," and "In the Shadow of the Sun"—have been focused rather differently, often on conceptual and two-dimensional art.[53] As one would expect, the best contemporary collections of Native art are held by regional museums, which have easy access to artists and to regional suppliers. Beginning in the middle of the twentieth century, institutions such as the Heard Museum in Phoenix and the Philbrook Museum in Tulsa have regularly mounted competitive regional exhibitions of Native American art. From the 1970s, museums in the Northwest—the Museum of Anthropology in Vancouver, for example—have promoted contemporary artists, such as Bill Reid and Robert Davidson (see cat. nos. 183, 184); and the Provincial Museum of British Columbia (now the Royal British Columbia Museum), in its exhibition "The Legacy," presented internationally an early integrated view of historical and contemporary Northwest Coast art.[54] Regional museums have developed excellent shops and galleries—for commercial purposes, of course, but which incidentally ensure that public collections can filter shop stock and acquire the best available contemporary objects. This world, however, remains little known. There are few publications about contemporary dealers in Native American art, and even someone as prominent as was Grace Nicholson has neither a Pierre Matisse–style full-length biography nor the general fame of a Leo Castelli. Even given the modesty and marginality of Native art collecting in the wider art market, collectors, galleries, and museums act very creatively, as seen, for instance, in two recent exhibitions at the Wheelwright Museum of the American Indian in Santa Fe, "Clay People"[55] and "Painted

Perfection."[56] What these seemingly modest shows do is, apparently, reduce the authorial role of the curator, enabling the artist to communicate more directly with the viewer.

Finally, Coe and "Sacred Circles" played a significant role in my own education. When I began work at the British Museum in 1975, I had no experience with the Native American collections. Nor had anyone ever worked with the collections. Coe's involvement with the museum as one of the primary lenders meant that numerous authorities, including Edmund Carpenter, Norman Feder, Bill Holm, George MacDonald, Peter Macnair, and Ben Stone, visited London and the British Museum to see Coe's exhibition, or perhaps simply because they had learned, because of the show, that the museum had a collection of Native American materials. Bill Reid, who visited the British Museum at this time, seems likely to have been the first Indian recorded as having visited the British Museum. All these individuals helped to identify objects, and they provided detailed information about the collections in London. Coe himself was particularly helpful in this respect, as he had been exceptionally generous, with his extensive knowledge and his advice, to many collectors, including Morton and Estelle Sosland in Kansas City[57] and Eugene and Clare Thaw in Santa Fe (see pp. 1–6). More generally, of course, it is Coe's publications and his articulation of many elements of Native American art in his own collection that will stand as a monument to his life's work.[58]

1. Coe 1976a.
2. Douglas and d'Harnoncourt 1941; Feder 1971a and 1971b.
3. Coe 1976a, p. 79.
4. Dam-Mikkelsen and Lundbæk 1980.
5. MacGregor 1983.
6. Burch 1990.
7. Ewers 1967.
8. Viola and Margolis 1985.
9. Sellers 1996.
10. Browman 2002.
11. Willoughby 1935.
12. Brumwell 2002, p. 225.
13. Phillips 1984.
14. Zevi and Kaufmann 1965, p. 77.
15. Muir 1978, p. 72.
16. Howard and Pardue 1996.
17. Walton, Ewers, and Hassrick 1985.
18. Wilson 1997.
19. Kapoun and Lohrmann 1997.
20. Takashina et al. 1988; Rubin 1984.
21. Sally Price touches only marginally on Native American art; see Price 1989.
22. Force 1999.
23. James (1897) 1987, pp. 42–43.
24. Montiel 2002.
25. Reynolds 2002.
26. Pohrt 1992.
27. Halle 1993, p. 144.
28. Horse Capture and Horse Capture 2001.

29. Hail 1980, pp. 68–78.

30. Greenfeld 1987.

31. Herold 2001.

32. Feest 2001.

33. Maurer 1977.

34. Penney 1992.

35. Benndorf and Speyer 1968; Brasser 1976.

36. Ewing 1982, for example, and Wardwell 1998.

37. Vincent, Brydon, and Coe 2000.

38. Archambault and Sturtevant 1996, pp. 407–8.

39. Abel-Vidor, Brovarney, and Billy 1996.

40. See the Web site http://abfla.com/1tocf/seminole/semus.html

41. Mallett 1979, pp. 180–202.

42. Blomberg 1988.

43. Sheehan 1981.

44. Swanberg 1962, pp. 499–500.

45. Parker 1935, p. 176.

46. Chatwin 1988, p. 50.

47. *ACPAC Newsletter* 1994.

48. Price 1989, pp. 15–18.

49. Alsop 1982, p. 395.

50. Treue 1960.

51. Meyer 1977.

52. Coe 1986.

53. McMaster and Martin 1992; Nemiroff, Houle, and Townsend-Gault 1992; Canadian Museum of Civilization 1993.

54. Macnair, Hoover, and Neary 1980.

55. Batkin 1999.

56. Struever 2001.

57. Walker Art Center 1972.

58. Many people have helped with this paper, making suggestions, corrections, and improvements. I would like particularly to thank Barbara A. Hail, Morton I. Sosland, Eugene V. Thaw, and also Christian Feest, Leslie Sklair, Colin Taylor, and Gaylord Torrence.

The Collecting of Native American Art

"Full of Blood, Thunder and Springy Abandon"

History, Text, and the Appreciation of Native American Art

JUDITH OSTROWITZ

The history of response to Native North American art since the great acceleration of its entrance into non-Native life in the mid-nineteenth century was mediated at first by the projects of influential scholars.[1] That the appreciation of indigenous art by outsiders was, and is, a cross-cultural endeavor suggests that these projects were acts of interpretation specific to the histories of those who generated them. For the most part, early scholarship identified Native American works as artifacts, the props and traces left behind by Native practice. They were not yet thought of as autonomous works of art, objects that could be considered for their beauty alone. Consequently, authorities linked these pieces with explanatory texts. Volumes were written by anthropologists, collectors, and others who sought to know the nature and meaning of objects that originated in Native cultures, in what they considered a systematic and scientific way, and ultimately to share that knowledge with larger audiences, particularly in museum environments. Non-Native standards for the evaluation of beauty, as an issue separate from didactic purpose, were eventually developed, initially as an adjunct to this quest for information about cultures of origin. This information was recorded by non-Native authors who observed native practices and participated in consultations with those who were termed Native "informants," the local authorities and community representatives whom they interviewed. Only very infrequently did Native thinkers make direct contributions that affected the written record or strategies for museum collection.[2]

Public appreciation of Native American art as works of great visual interest was later developed in tandem with the extrication of its forms from these scholarly texts. Not surprisingly, this aestheticization process took place in the modern period in relation to the practices of Western art museums and commercial art galleries where non-Native works of art were then also displayed and understood primarily through perceptual means, in association with contemporary ideas. Art theorists of the mid-twentieth century, some of whom were deeply appreciative of abstract art, were most active in this process. Their sympathetic regard for Native American form on this basis was intended, at least in part, to raise the profile of these arts and cultures in the estimation of Western audiences. By doing so, they established certain ideas among art viewers about universality and the potential accessibility of Native art forms to a broader audience through acts of observation, not erudition. The meanings of these artworks were thought to be available through the commonality of human experience, and therefore new non-Native audiences became increasingly empowered, no longer dependent upon scientific and scholarly mediators, or collectors of text, for insight. In spite of the high ideals and humanistic motivations of these modernists, their influence also resulted in some change in the status of Native American peoples, inadvertently obviating their participation as consultants, and in some cases as experts and gatekeepers, for information about traditional arts.

It is interesting to observe that today, at the turn of the twenty-first century, several young, influential Native American artists have returned to the practice of referencing texts, broadly defined, in their creation of postmodern works of art. The proper comprehension of these pieces depends, once again, on the relative degree of access to specific local knowledge. They are understood differentially by their various audiences, according to their knowledge base and group memberships. In this manner, many artists now "take back" the universal access once understood by modernists and admirers of Native American art, who were informed by mid-twentieth-century art theories. These changes in theoretical approach over time are deeply related to matters of agency and ownership of Native American art on those occasions when it is presented in public places.

WRITING THE MEANING OF NATIVE AMERICAN ART

One may look to the anthropological texts about the art of any region of Native North America in this regard, but I will begin here with Franz Boas and the enormously influential legacy of explanatory material that he created in relation to Northwest Coast art and culture. I choose Boas because he proposed an important dichotomy in the appreciation of aboriginal art, identifying the potential for pleasurable visual experience as distinct from the comprehension of meanings and ideas.[3] In the introduction to his book *Primitive Art,* first published in 1927, he discussed the accessibility that general criteria for the appreciation of beauty allowed. "In one way or another esthetic pleasure is felt by all members of mankind. No matter how diverse the ideals of beauty may be, the general character of the enjoyment of beauty is of the same order everywhere."[4] Boas also specified that characteristic or "fixed forms," which reflect standards of excellence, particularly of technical perfection, qualify objects as true works of art and elicit widespread appreciation. And he ascribed a universal appeal to such evidence of expert technique that might result in recognizable qualities of symmetry and rhythm which were appreciated the world over.[5]

However, Boas was explicit on the culture-specific nature of the meaning of these artistic forms. He postulated a "twofold source of artistic effect, the one based on form alone, the other on ideas associated with form."[6] Only those highly conversant with the specific philosophies, beliefs, and practices that engendered these forms might gain access to their larger significance and come to appreciate the ideals that they embodied. Here, no universal or intuitive approach would be helpful in gaining access. The acquisition of contextualizing information would be indispensable. Boas commissioned the acquisition of an enormous amount of written material that he amassed and published with relatively little attempt at interpretation. It was his belief that precise and supposedly unadulterated accounts of specific cultural practices were designed to avoid the pitfalls of generalization and ultimately to provide insight about historical and environmental influences.

Boas and other anthropologists of the early twentieth century, Alfred Kroeber and Bronislaw Malinowski, for instance, have been discussed by scholars as avid collectors of information or as "salvage anthropologists." They stockpiled texts and artifacts on behalf of future audiences against the day that, as they supposed, Native cultures would disappear from the face of the earth.[7] Every display, every object in storage, and each page in the archives of museums that was collected during this period were documents that referenced and aided in the conceptualization and preservation of a larger Indian reality, of an imagined high point in the history of "Indian life."[8]

A Triangle Must Be a Mountain or a Tipi

Boas also produced important studies based on his own direct observations and analyses of artistic forms.[9] His motivations included the desire to discover the logic behind complex design phenomena, for instance, the application of conventionalized forms to irregularly shaped design fields. He also wished to study changes in artistic form over time to disprove the persuasive theories of cultural evolutionists that were prevalent during this period.[10] These experiments in design analysis were not meant to uncover culture-specific meanings. These, he believed, were accessed only through dialogue with Native peoples and through the close study of their practices. To understand the larger significance of forms, Boas relied on the reports of cultural "insiders" and those of other firsthand observers.[11]

Other anthropologists, Boas's students in particular, wished to build on their mentor's interest in form. But here the parameters of Boas's proposed dichotomy between the appreciation of beautiful form, an understanding of abstract design principles, and technical expertise as opposed to the more privileged understanding of specific, culturally generated meanings began to lose its clarity. Interestingly, the anthropologists Clark Wissler and Alfred Kroeber, both of whom had been Boas's students at Columbia University in New York and ultimately became his colleagues as scholars of Plains Indian art and cultures, seem to have conflated the particulars of design analysis with the accessibility of meaning. Kroeber, for instance, proposed that Arapaho art consisted of "the intimate fusion of symbolism and decoration."[12]

Like Boas, these anthropologists wished to gather data from the study of artworks that would help to resolve the debate among their contemporaries about artistic evolution. Some of them had proposed that nonrepresentational works were conventionalizations that had deteriorated over time from more naturalistic representations.[13] Wissler, for instance, set out to discover if there were "successive steps by which realistic design is reduced to a mere decoration."[14] To this end, both Wissler and Kroeber recorded and studied

Figure 1. Pipe bag, Sioux/Oglala Lakota, 19th century. Hide, glass and metal beads, quill, pigment, and sinew. American Museum of Natural History, New York
Photo: Jackie Beckett

geometric design elements that had been invented by women and carried out in quillwork or beads on moccasins, leggings, pouches, and other items and treated them as if they were pictographs. Kroeber, for instance, had observed that an equilateral triangle pointing downward was referred to among the Arapaho as a heart; a long stripe crossed by two short ones was called a dragonfly; crosses and diamonds could be stars. He believed that several of these forms might be put together to approximate a picture that was related to a specific narrative.[15] Similarly, Wissler observed that a triangle pointing upward was sometimes called a tipi pattern or tent design by Sioux artists. At times it included a little rectangular "door or entrance." A small rectangle was occasionally referred to as a bag or a box in the context of a larger composition. Again, more complex patterns were given names by their female makers that implied that they were "little scenes." For instance, a forked element between two triangles created a pattern that he observed on a pipe bag (fig. 1). Some artists called this "the shooting of arrows from between the hills."[16]

Ironically, most of the Native artists that these two anthropologists consulted resisted any consistent iconographic interpretation of their work. Sioux artists told Wissler that they had nothing in mind when they did most of this work except the beauty of the moccasin or other object that they adorned.[17] The Arapaho artists whom Kroeber consulted provided inconsistent meanings. One maker might indicate that a series of lines on a bag represented rivers or roads, but another might suggest that the same lines referred to a traditional way of fastening such bags by passing a rope across it several times.[18]

The hypotheses that Kroeber and Wissler tested were not without some basis in Plains art traditions. Although most of the Sioux works that Wissler studied were meant simply to please the eye, women did occasionally discuss conventional decorations with consistent symbolic or representational associations. A pattern commonly used to adorn the blue beaded yokes of dresses, for example, was meant to evoke "reflections in water."[19] Geometric configurations often had spiritual significance, such as those forms called "medicine hoops" and "spider webs."[20] In addition, artworks used as mnemonic devices meant to preserve history were known to exist elsewhere in Plains art. Men painted naturalistic works to facilitate the narration of their honorable deeds in military and spiritual contexts, and pictographs were employed to record history in calendrical art. However, these images were quite idiosyncratic and best interpreted by their makers. They alone held the keys to autobiographical and other historical information and the very broad range of visual devices they used to represent important events. Their art might be fully appreciated only when accompanied by related oratory or other cultural practices.

Neither Kroeber nor Wissler was ever able to contribute irrefutable data to the debate about artistic evolution in Plains art. Kroeber concluded that "realistic-symbolic" and "decorative-technical" approaches coexisted.[21] Perhaps, if they had not been preoccupied by this particular research question, they might have pursued different, text-based explanations for the significance of these arts.

Relatively little information survives about the prestigious women's societies in the Plains region that honored members for extraordinary artistic achievement. Accounts of the projects of Cheyenne women indicate that certain acts of decoration were carried out in a ceremonial context and regulated so that quillwork was considered equivalent to the acts of bravery that brought men honor in warfare. Few written reports of such practices survive. One, by George Bird Grinnell in his famous volumes on the Cheyenne, was first written in 1923, and another account was published by Alice Marriott in 1956. They describe associations of Cheyenne women who pledged to complete decorative art projects, according to prescribed procedures, that would bring good fortune to designated members of their families. The geometric ornamentation of robes, tipi liners, moccasins, backrests, bags, and pillows under ritual supervision was believed to improve the fortunes of a brother or husband going to war, to heal a sick member of the family, or to help in childbirth. As Grinnell remarked, "Although the tendency among observers is to see a meaning in every Indian design, many of these designs are not always symbolic."[22] Apparently, meaning is not limited to the signification of symbols. On some occasions, it is meant only to be understood by the context of its creation and display.

It is interesting to note here that Boas also remarked upon the existence of pattern names used by Tlingit artists in the Northwest Coast region as components of Chilkat blanket designs. Names of design elements refer to features like the eyes, ears, or claws of animals. Cannily, Boas published some conflicting interpretations of specific blanket designs by the anthropologists John Swanton and George Emmons side by side, as captions for illustrations.[23] In fact, correct interpretations of the designs on these robes were probably known only by their makers and their original owners. Boas's publication of ambiguous interpretations of Native symbols may frustrate the scientifically minded reader, but his methods were consistent with his belief that cultural meanings were not conveyed by visual means alone. They could not be easily read by an interested outsider unless he understood the "code."

Several of Boas's students maintained a keen interest in the study of the formal characteristics of Native American art. Herman K. Haeberlin, for instance, in the course of his brief career, hypothesized a "science of esthetics" the application of which would yield greater knowledge of culture type. The prevalence of an artistic approach in any culture area would constitute its "style." As if looking ahead to the universalist notions of modernists, he indicated that there might be an equality of all human acts of perception, noting, "A hasty survey reveals devices of composition that are in principle the same as some employed in our own art."[24] Styles might vary, but, according to Haeberlin, residents of all culture areas possess similar faculties and, by extension, similar abilities. As the anthropologist Ira Jacknis has noted, Haeberlin's efforts to establish connections between so-called primitive art and Western art rely on formal relationships, discovered, at least in part, through the use of intuition.[25]

Also following Boas, Haeberlin proposed that scholars of Native art seek out the unique responses of individual artists to conventionalized form and other restrictions imposed by artistic tradition. This approach followed methods already practiced among historians of Western art who were accustomed to the study of individual artists. Similarly, Boas's student Ruth Bunzel produced an influential study of Pueblo pottery in 1929 that associated design principles with the artistic practices of specific Pueblo groups. Her most significant contribution, however, is related to the expression of creative artistic approach by the individual as it operated within the confines of those principles. These scholars and others helped to position the study and appreciation of Native American art as the appropriate concern of twentieth-century modernists.

The Modern Period and the Aesthetization of Native American Art

At the turn of the twentieth century, most non-Natives, living through a period of rapid transformation as a result of increasing urbanization and industrialization, held to the belief that Native peoples possessed an enduring relationship with nature that they themselves lacked (these ideas survive in some ways today). Many looked to Native Americans to provide them with a glimpse of their own past, as if their indigenous contemporaries still lived in a manner common to the early history of the entire human race. As Marvin Cohodas wrote in 1992, this nostalgia contributed to the development of new opportunities for the marketing of Native American art to outsiders. Connoisseurs maintained a high regard for what they considered historical or past forms. They also valued handmade works, as a reaction against mass production. Ideally, collectors hoped to locate artists whom they considered authentic because of their relative lack of interest in commerce.

These consumers soon discovered decorative works of Native art (often the textiles, pots, and baskets produced by women) that met non-Native criteria for supposed historical accuracy, as well as an accompanying preference for forms and materials that originated from nature. As this new market took shape, it is not coincidental that some Native artists of the period were identified as masters and began to be known by name. Their products were especially coveted because they had been imbued with special value by those who had exclusive access to these individual artists and therefore had a hand in selling their work.

In the 1930s and 1940s, the desirability of such artworks for outsiders and the development of criteria for their evaluation increased and was encouraged by certain groundbreaking exhibitions and other related developments. Important landmarks of this process have already been the subject of much scholarly consideration. One key exhibition, influential in this process, was "Indian Art of the United States," held at the Museum of Modern Art, New York, and organized by Frederic H. Douglas and René d'Harnoncourt for the Indian Arts and Crafts Board of the U.S. Department of the Interior. According to W. Jackson Rushing's 1992 study, the curators wished to present works in the exhibition, particularly those that had been recovered from prehistoric civilizations of North America, as distinguished for their visual qualities alone.

As a strategy, d'Harnoncourt encouraged an aesthetic response through the design and layout of the exhibition. A display of Mimbres pottery, for example, was presented in an environment of "neutrality, austerity, and a lack of textual information that encouraged a purely aesthetic encounter with the ceremonial bowls."[26] D'Harnoncourt understood the useful relationship between text-free exhibition design and the facilitation of cross-cultural dialogue. What must be noted here is that once these objects were freed from historical and cultural specificity, made "neutral," they were no longer the privileged business of the Native people who created them. Although it was understood that they had once been used in a traditional manner, they were now made available for comprehension and appreciation by outsiders. By extension, these things could be considered appropriate for collection and for display in the non-Native home. For instance, in the "Indian Art for Modern Living" section of the MoMA exhibition, a study gallery was set aside to highlight the facility of contemporary Native peoples with abstraction. This facility, which was well illustrated by so-called decorative works of art such as textiles and pots, exemplified a style already understood and in vogue in the non-Native art world.[27] If these works were to be considered compatible with the sensibilities that engendered modern environments, it was necessary that they be accessible and known directly by their non-Native admirers. Stylized and geometric forms lent themselves to the intellectual musings of aficionados who were free to ignore the original ceremonial and functional aspects of these works. Some objects, such as the Mimbres pots, had even been associated with burial practices. This was a matter of lesser concern in an art-world environment. But the illusion that funerary arts could be effectively neutralized and used for aesthetic purposes was to have significant repercussions later in the century.[28]

In projects like the MoMA exhibition, designed to provide a larger public with greater access to Native art objects and, consequently, to stimulate a market for them, a new definition or complicated "place" for them was proposed. The art had to retain compelling qualities that denoted cultural difference. This was a part of its charm and mystery.

But perhaps more important, these specific differences, expressed as characteristic forms, permitted the development of criteria for connoisseurship. Works were identified as the products of distant cultures, such as the long gone Mimbres people, or of the nineteenth-century ancestors of the geographically distant Nootka (now called Nuu-chah-nulth) from the west coast of Vancouver Island. Distinct local styles and substyles were characterized, as if produced by "artistic schools," as they are known in the Western tradition. Ironically, because these differences were catalogued, viewers the world over were informed that they were capable of understanding these works. Visual acuity was all that was required, not the specialized knowledge and group memberships of Native peoples or any familiarity with the voluminous texts that had been produced by turn-of-the-century anthropologists. These works of art were considered exciting because they were made by those with specialized knowledge, handed down from generation to generation. On the other hand, art lovers were meant to understand that "good design" exceeded the limits imposed by such exclusive status. Visual images were to be considered the lingua franca of the entire human race, permitting any number of outsiders to gain authority as explicators of these forms.

Interestingly, just a few years earlier, in 1932, the art teacher Dorothy Dunn had launched the influential Studio School at the Santa Fe Indian School, a location where Native watercolor painters had been active for at least a decade. Dunn had proposed to her new students that they would do well to develop distinctive tribal styles, identifying themselves with specific cultural and geographic origins. However, according to the art historian J. J. Brody, they chose to engage instead with the development of a more general "pan-Indian" approach.[29] Dunn had thought that here, too, the implication of Native "schools of artistic practice" might suggest legitimacy. In addition, although it may seem contradictory, Dunn encouraged her students to balance ideal microidentities with ambitions for participation in cross-cultural art worlds. Again she was disappointed in her efforts, and she lamented that they did not think that their own practices qualified them to participate in a "universal fine art."[30]

The die was cast in the 1930s and early 1940s. The idea was to establish an ideal measure of "difference" as central and identifiable in the public presentation of Native American art, but at the same time to allow clear modes of access for outsiders—to have non-Natives become connoisseurs of Indian difference in order to address and invite their gaze.

Projects with similar intent followed in other regions of North America for decades. In 1967, the anthropologist Wilson Duff and the artist and art historian Bill Holm, both non-Natives, together with the Haida artist Bill Reid, organized the very influential exhibition "Arts of the Raven: Masterworks by the Northwest Coast Indian" for the Vancouver Art Gallery. All three men were, each in his own way, well versed in traditional Northwest Coast culture and practices. Yet, according to Doris Shadbolt, acting director of the museum, the exhibition was about "art, high art, not ethnology." This principle was illustrated by a selection of works that the curators represented as "masterworks," by virtue of their excellence as examples of complex graphic arts in the northern style, as well as sculptural pieces that were meant to exemplify the intellectual and expressive accomplishments of artists in the region. Consistent with the requirements and interests of museum curators and collectors of modern art, individual masters were identified and lauded, especially the Haida artist Charles Edenshaw.[31] Stylistic criteria as well as the superior vision and virtuosity said to be evident in the work of certain individuals were accessible through acts of keen observation, without knowledge of traditional practice. This reliance upon perceived cues for the appreciation of Native American art was meant to suggest the grandeur of these traditions, comparable to the arts of the non-Native world.

Modernism in the Non-Native Art World

In the non-Native art world at mid-twentieth century, similar ideas about the universal appeal of high art paralleled and exceeded the themes described above. Abstract Expressionists and, later, Op artists and Color Field painters, among others, insisted that their visual works could stand alone and were accessible solely by perceptual means, without reference to objects, phenomena, and discourses that existed beyond the perimeters of their canvases. Clement Greenberg's work was influential in establishing the idea that the experience of form was all that was essential for the appreciation of art. Modernists, Greenberg claimed, "must try, in principle, to avoid dependence upon any experience not given in the most essentially construed nature of its medium."[32] Greenberg and others, like their counterparts among historians of Native art, argued that visual phenomena were independent and defended the possibility of complete knowledge through perception alone, made possible by standing before a canvas without reference to other resources or texts.

As described above, by the 1960s, some non-Native art historians of Native American art had internalized such concepts, ideas about the completely self-referential nature of works of high art. Soon they began to apply these notions in a manner that affected the production of new work. On the Northwest Coast in particular, important scholarship engendered the development of increasingly complex criteria for aesthetic excellence based on deductions made through the visual analysis of works known from museum collections. As has been noted many times, Bill Holm's influential study of the design principles that directed the creation of works in the northern Northwest Coast graphic tradition, *Northwest Coast Indian Art: An Analysis of Form* (1965), resulted from his remarkably astute observations about these compositions. Although extremely knowledgeable about traditional cultures of the Northwest Coast region, Holm at this point in time worked with his eyes and with his own hands to produce a manual of style rather than an ethnographic study.

The art historian Rosalind Krauss has written with skepticism about these concepts, which originated in the modernist period, in her study of non-Native art-historical practices, but similar questions might be raised about interpretations of Native art projects. She has challenged claims to the "autonomy [of art]," the "thinking that [artists] can bracket it off from the world, from its context, from the real."[33] On the Northwest Coast, for instance, even those art historians and anthropologists who were intimately involved with cultural practice were able, in the same way, to "bracket it off," to put Native traditions aside, as a result of their extreme preoccupation with visual cues alone.

In 1971, the first version of the influential exhibition of Northwest Coast art "The Legacy: Continuing Traditions of Canadian Northwest Coast Indian Art," was displayed at the British Columbia Provincial Museum, now the Royal British Columbia Museum (RBCM). Its curators, led by Peter Macnair, then curator of ethnology, developed distinct criteria for the inclusion of living Native artists in the exhibition and these were recorded in the exhibition catalogue. Lineage and some contribution to "surviving traditional culture" were cited. However, following the descriptions of each of the local styles now considered standard for the region, it was stated that among the participants, "all are artists who reached maturity by clearly demonstrating that they understand and can execute the old forms of sculpture or two-dimensional design."[34] By 1971, design rules developed from the formal analysis of early works of art were being applied to the Northwest Coast as key to the evaluation of even the newest work. There was no requirement for the pieces to have been created for use as a part of traditional practice. It was sufficient that the artists were well versed in traditional Northwest Coast styles, as these had been delineated through processes of visual study by art historians and museum curators of the modern period.

Although less abstract and complex, stylistic criteria for artistic excellence and historical continuity had been delineated for other regions of North America for some time as well. Cues had been enumerated to identify formal relationships between traditional arts of the nineteenth century and contemporary works, inadvertently creating convenient methods of establishing legitimacy for pieces destined for museum status as well as for more popular markets.

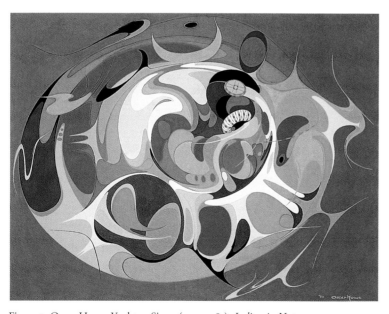

Figure 2. Oscar Howe, Yankton Sioux (1915–1983), *Indian in Nature*, 1970. Watercolor. Fine Art Collection, Heard Museum, Phoenix, Arizona

As cited earlier, artists from the pueblos of the American Southwest had also been engaged in an artistic dialogue with outsiders, making pots for anthropologists as well as paintings on paper for sale to appreciative non-Native artists and others, since the turn of the twentieth century. From the beginning, painters created a visual record of traditional practices. By the 1930s, they were inclined to produce relatively flat and decorative paintings peopled with figures dressed in minutely detailed costumes, largely in the manner that artists of the Studio School in Santa Fe had established. A couple of decades later, however, some young Indian artists were chafing at the restrictions that such clearly

Figure 3. Fritz Scholder, Luiseño (b. 1937), *Indian Wrapped in Flag,* 1976. Acrylic on canvas. Private collection. Photo courtesy of the Heard Museum, Phoenix, Arizona

Figure 4. T. C. Cannon, Caddo/Kiowa/Choctaw (1946–1978), woodcut after the painting *Osage with van Gogh,* or *Collector #5,* ca. 1980. Fine Art Collection, Heard Museum, Phoenix, Arizona

delineated visual criteria for the identification and patronage of their work required. In the Plains and Southwest regions, painters who produced works in the "traditional style" were the ones awarded prizes and were most successful in the marketplace. In 1946, for example, the Philbrook Museum of Art presented its first "Annual National Exhibition of American Indian Painting," which was established to perpetuate stylistic references to existing traditions. The work of some artists, however, was excluded from the exhibition because of the canon established by the museum. Yankton Sioux artist Oscar Howe, in particular, preferred to treat themes that derived from legendary history in a more subjective and abstract way, experimenting with color and form in the modern manner (fig. 2). Howe accused the Philbrook of holding Indian artists back and not permitting them the opportunity to express individuality. He composed an influential letter in 1958 that ultimately resulted in the creation of a new "non-traditional painting" category for Philbrook Annual entries.

Native artists of the 1950s and 1960s wondered if their identities depended on providing visual references to past forms or if, instead, they should provide evidence of legitimacy by adopting the powerful non-Native preoccupation with innovation. Either way, their work would be defined by how it looked on paper or canvas, not by its relationship with cultural phenomena or social life.

By the late 1970s and early 1980s, painters like Fritz Scholder (Luiseño) forcefully addressed the world by painting *Indian Wrapped in Flag* (fig. 3) and T. C. Cannon

(Caddo/Kiowa/Choktaw) challenged the excessive influence of the market for Indian art by painting *Osage with van Gogh,* or *Collector #5* (fig. 4). Ironically he placed the Indian in the armchair of a collector, thus advertising the prizes that in this case a Native person had gained through wealth and connoisseurship.[35] Works by these artists spilled over the edges of the design field to address larger issues.

The Problem of Commonality

More recently, ideas about the universal appeal of delineated forms and the consequent accessibility of their meanings have been problematized. As art historian Keith Moxey has suggested, aesthetic values do not exist in works of art themselves but are produced within historical and social contexts that constantly shift over time. Moxey's argument follows upon his critique of Kant's conception of aesthetic value as unchanging, as available through "correct" processes of evaluation in all times and at all places.[36]

Instead, the extrapolation of meaning and the development of standards of value and beauty by historically positioned observers must be understood as interpretation. An examination of the ahistorical methodologies and cross-cultural comparisons that were adapted by non-Native art historians in the twentieth century indicates a privileging of "text-free" interpretations meant to extend to the arts of every period and place. They sought to dignify the arts of Native American peoples as highly skilled and appealing, specifically according to the criteria set by Western modernists. At the same time, the appropriation of these "leveling" methodologies may have accomplished greater parity for the work of these art historians themselves in their attempt to establish the field of Native American art scholarship as comparable with the projects of historians of Western art.

In 1976, Ralph T. Coe, whose collection is the subject of this exhibition and catalogue, curated "Sacred Circles: Two Thousand Years of North American Indian Art." One of the theses of his presentation was the advantages that might be obtained through cross-cultural comparisons of masterfully conceived works of art.[37] Coe was well aware of the "texts," or ethnographic contexts, derived from the study of Native cultures and social histories and applied them to the understanding of the works in the exhibition. Yet he also suggested, as a method for appreciation, the extrication of Native

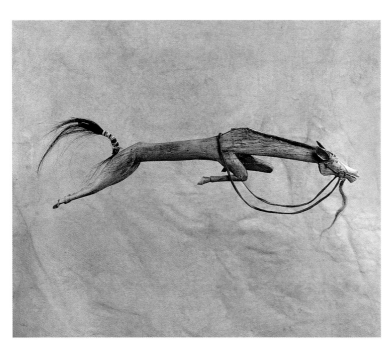

Figure 5. Horse effigy, Sioux, 19th century. Wood, hide, horsehair, paint. Museum of the South Dakota Historical Society, Pierre, South Dakota

"Full of Blood . . . and Springy Abandon"

art from its anthropological context for purposes of formal comparison with the "high arts" of other great world cultures. In his introduction to the exhibition catalogue, he explained: "It is one thing to accept Indian culture as anthropology and quite another to apply to it the standards of aesthetic appreciation reserved, let us say, for a Renaissance bronze or a Han tomb sculpture. Yet does not the unique Sioux wooden horse effigy . . . , full of blood, thunder and springy abandon, bear comparison with the Kansu horse?" (fig. 5).[38]

In sharing his perception of the "springy abandon" of the horse effigy, Coe provided a foothold for the interpretation of the sculpture by appreciative museumgoers of the 1970s. But what had become of the object's "difference," of the painstakingly recorded meanings as they were understood by the museum anthropologists of the late nineteenth and early twentieth centuries? With this egalitarian perspective, might not difference "lose ground" when the pleasures of beautiful form are extolled as available to all discerning viewers, so that the skill and imagination of Indian artists may be justly honored? This perspective necessitated some repositioning of privileged information concerning traditional practice as preserved in Native communities or in the form of scholarly text. Such a shift provided a perceived means of access to an art formerly meant only for Native audiences, scholars who were deeply committed to a study of Native life, and the readers whom they chose to inform.

NOW, THE INTERTEXTUAL

At the turn of the twenty-first century, such methodologies for the understanding of Native American works of art are no longer justifiable. Definitions for Indian art based solely on formal criteria or, alternatively, on the comprehension of privileged texts, for that matter, are clearly inadequate. Today, non-Natives consume staged representations of indigenous life as a routine part of their travels, museum forays, and television viewing. Indians interview their own elders, but they also read Boas, Kroeber, or whomever when they wish to find out more about the historical documentation of their cultures in order to claim it, alter it, or refuse it as they see fit. Consequently, some contemporary Native American artists embrace multiple audiences and perspectives, selectively exploring many possibilities.

A case in point is Lawrence Paul Yuxweluptun, a Canadian First Nations

Figure 6. Lawrence Paul Yuxweluptun, Coast Salish (b. 1957), *Smash, Crash, Bang the Legend,* 2000. Acrylic on canvas. Courtesy Lawrence Paul Yuxweluptun

Figure 7. Jolene Rickard, Tuscarora (b. 1956), *Corn Blue Room,* 1998. Mixed media, installation view. Canadian Museum of Civilization, Quebec. Photo: Harry Foster (s2002–2860)

artist of Cowichan Salish descent, who, while a participant in traditional life, has also made forays into the non-Native artistic strategies of Surrealism, virtual reality, and, recently, an invented art form that he calls Ovoidism.[39] This appears, at least superficially, to be related to the "post-painterly" abstract works of the 1960s by such artists as Ellsworth Kelly, Jules Olitski, and Kenneth Noland. The ovoid form that Yuxweluptun uses in his compositions, for instance, in his painting *Smash, Crash, Bang the Legend* (fig. 6) is, in fact, one of the design elements named by Bill Holm in his 1965 study, a form that Northwest Coast artists have painted and carved for centuries. It has become a signature of the tradition, but it is now unclear who assigned it such status. Was it Bill Holm, Peter Macnair, or pre-contact Native artists themselves? In addition, Yuxweluptun's heritage, the Coast Salish artistic tradition, has been described as less complex than the design strategies of groups farther north, those renowned for their elaborate manipulation of ovoids, trigons, and other graphic elements. Consequently, Coast Salish art has received less scholarly attention and admiration by those trained as modernists. No wonder this artist has been motivated to consider the nature of the emblematic ovoid.

The vast majority of viewers will most likely access Yuxweluptun's work with ovoids as visually appealing, abstract compositions, but they will remain completely unaware of his allusions to historical Native works and even less informed about his oblique references to the mid-twentieth-century scholars who "bracketed off" such forms for description and analysis by perceptual means. The intellectualization of Northwest Coast design by some art historians of the modernist period seemed to establish them as gatekeepers of the tradition. But, in his paintings, Yuxweluptun "takes the ovoid back" and outdoes these scholars by owning the design element in three worlds—with traditional, modern, and postmodern strategies.

Other contemporary Native artists create works that incorporate "texts" and permit differential access by their viewers, based on their knowledge, personal histories, and group affiliations. Who can know all the implications of the work by Tuscarora artist Jolene Rickard titled *Corn Blue Room* (fig. 7), made for the 1998 exhibition "Reservation X: The Power of Place in Aboriginal Contemporary Art"? Intertextual references to Rickard's family history, traditional Iroquois practice, photographic technologies, and the history of non-Native installation art render this sophisticated work nearly opaque to all but a few viewers. In the same exhibition, Marianne Nicholson, a Kwakwaka'wakw artist, referred to traditional-style architecture and all the social history that such houses embody by creating an installation called "House of Origin," made up of two-dimensional works suspended in sheets of glass to approximate the shape of such a structure. The "invisible" walls enclosed images related to traditional textiles as well as written passages in Kwakwala, Nicholson's native language, from the legendary history of her family and small community, Kingcome Inlet, on the west coast of British Columbia. A viewer would have to be positioned much as Nicholson is herself in order to participate completely in this piece.

Until now, the ongoing battle for the public recognition of non-Western art and culture, the desire to "level the playing field," has alternated, strategically, between ideas about "difference" and concepts related to universality. In periods when difference has been highlighted, there has been a corresponding drive to collect and produce explanatory texts. In other periods, the elevation of Native American art in the estimation of outsiders has been related to ideas about its universal visual appeal and the common approaches that are perceived to exist in the production of value and standards of excellence for all art. These ideas have been explicated through intensive studies of artistic form, temporarily subordinating contextual narrative.

Coe himself spelled it out when he spoke of the "springy abandon" that anyone might perceive and appreciate, if they would only evaluate the Sioux horse effigy without limiting themselves to anthropological documents about traditional context or place of origin. This historical alternation of paradigms for the appreciation of Native American art suggests the incompatibility of ideas about general accessibility with theories of historical particularism and cultural relativity. Modernists in the twentieth century pursued the identification of grand phenomena, developing encompassing theories about human nature itself. Now that several young, twenty-first-century postmodern Native artists have regained some measure of agency over the public display of the traditional, private business of their tribes, perhaps related to recent triumphs in land claims and the successful repatriation of artworks from museums, they have, simultaneously, restored the centrality of text. Ideas about difference are now embedded in their public presentations. They tackle a herculean task. For they must appeal to viewers according to current aesthetic criteria, yet they must refer as well to selected texts to accommodate the multiple points of reference of their new, far-ranging audiences.

1. Several writers about the history of museums, anthropology, and the representation of cultures have characterized the period that began roughly in the middle of the nineteenth century and continued through the first decade of the twentieth century as "The Museum Period." Many of the great museum collections of Native American art were assembled at this time by anthropologists who wished to represent Native life in a "complete and systematic" way. They attempted to do so by amassing comprehensive texts about traditional practices as well as large collections of a great range of artworks and artifacts. As a result, many readers and museum visitors regard this period as a point of reference for authentic Native American art. See Sturtevant 1969; Cole 1985; and Stocking 1985.

2. Among those rare examples of Native people who made such direct contributions to this cross-cultural dialogue were, first and foremost, George Hunt, who coauthored with Franz Boas "Kwakiutl Texts" (1902–5) and "Kwakiutl Texts, Second Series" (1906). Louis Shotridge, a Tlingit man, was trained in phonetics by Franz Boas at Columbia University and went on to collect for the University of Pennsylvania Museum and develop its display of Northwest Coast art, creating a model of his traditional home village of Klukwan, Alaska (Cole 1985, pp. 255–67). In the decades that followed, some Native participation in anthropological projects gradually increased indigenous agency, but this did not become influential or an important part of the public record until the last decade of the twentieth century.

3. Aldona Jonaitis indicates this dichotomy in her "Summary of Boas's Art History," in Jonaitis 1995, p. 37.

4. Boas 1955, p. 9.

5. Ibid., pp. 9–17.

6. Ibid., p. 13.

7. For ideas about the "'Salvage' Paradigm" of the early twentieth century, see Clifford 1987.

8. See my earlier suggestion that objects and images in museum collections are the salient features of larger, unseen territories in "The Map and the Territory in the Grand Hall at the Canadian Museum of Civilization" in Ostrowitz 1999, pp. 47–82.

9. See, for instance, Boas 1908. Many aspects of design analysis are also addressed in Boas 1955.

10. Jonaitis 1995.

11. Using terms that are now perhaps "out of style," Marvin Harris provided the most direct characterization of Boas's position in this regard. He calls Boas an "emicist"—an ethnographer preoccupied with the importance of the "native point of view." See Harris 1968, p. 316.

12. Kroeber 1901, p. 309.

13. Jonaitis 1995, pp. 16–20.

14. Wissler 1904, p. 231. Wissler cited the influence of studies by Alfred Haddon as seminal to his hypotheses. See Haddon's *Evolution in Art* (1895), as described in Jonaitis 1995.

15. Kroeber 1901, p. 309.

16. Wissler 1904, p. 238.

17. Ibid., p. 234.

18. Kroeber 1901, p. 318.

19. Wissler 1904, p. 240.

20 Ibid., pp. 248–49.

21. Kroeber 1901, p. 310.

22. Grinnell 1923, vol. 1, p. 168.

23. Boas 1907.

24. Haeberlin 1918, p. 260.

25. Jacknis 1992, p. 145.

26. Rushing 1992, p. 208.

27. Ibid., p. 214.

28. See, for instance, repatriation policies and legislation, in particular the Native American Grave Protection and Repatriation Act (NAGPRA) of 1990.

29. Brody 1997, p. 182.

30. Dunn 1968, p. 254.

31. Shadbolt 1967, n.p.

32. "The New Sculpture," in Greenberg 1961, p. 139.

33. Krauss 1996, p. 12.

34. Macnair, Hoover, and Neary 1984, p. 85.

35. For some insight into the conflicts experienced by Native American artists of the Plains and Southwest regions grappling with the requirements of the market and with the ideals of modernism, see the essays in Archuleta and Strickland 1991.

36. See Moxey 1994, p. 37, for a more complete explanation of the work of Jan Mukarovsky and others who discuss Kant's work.

37. The exhibition was organized by Ralph T. Coe in 1976, in cooperation with the Arts Council of Great Britain and with the support of the British-American Associates. It was on view in North America in 1977 at the Nelson Gallery of Art, Kansas City.

38. Coe 1976a, p. 13.

39. See *The Art of Yuxweluptun* at http://www3.bc.sympatico.ca/artist/index.htm.

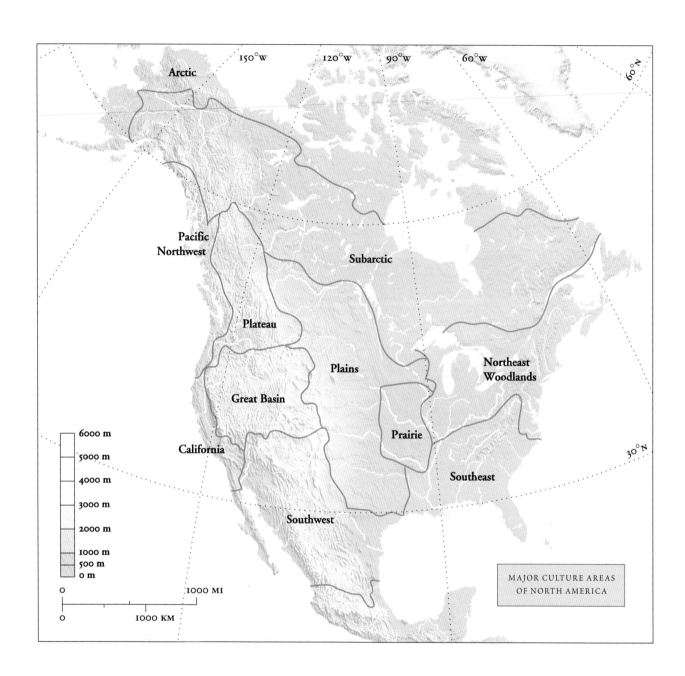

Arctic

Pacific
Northwest

Subarctic

Plateau

Plains

Northeast
Woodlands

Great Basin

California

Prairie

Southeast

Southwest

6000 m
5000 m
4000 m
3000 m
2000 m
1000 m
500 m
0 m

0   1000 MI

0   1000 KM

150°W   120°W   90°W   60°W

60°N

30°N

MAJOR CULTURE AREAS
OF NORTH AMERICA

I

PREHISTORIC NORTH AMERICA

The Unseen Past

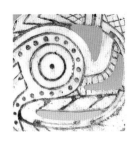

1. Bottle

ca. 1400–1600

Caddoan peoples, Perry County, Arkansas (?)

Ceramic

Height 8 in. (20.3 cm); diameter 7 ¼ in. (18.4 cm)

RTCNA 580

The Mississippian culture occupied most of the southeast of the region now the United States from A.D. 1000 until the arrival of the Europeans in the sixteenth century. Its architecture, sculpture, astronomy, and social structure were well developed and display features that may indicate influences from both the prehispanic Caribbean and Mexico. Platform mounds constructed along the lines of those in Mexico occur at Mississippian sites such as Moundville, in Alabama; Spiro, in Oklahoma; and Etowah, in Georgia. By the sixteenth century, mounds were no longer being built. Had not the Europeans been so exploitative, the tribes of the southeast—Cherokee, Choctaw, Muskogee, Seminole, Creek, and the Indians of Florida—might have continued to develop and to increase the power of their already outstanding cultures.

In the late Mississippian period (1400–1600), which corresponds chronologically to the late Middle Ages and the Renaissance in Western Europe, potters in southern Missouri and northern Arkansas developed, over a relatively short period of time, one of the great ceramic traditions of the ancient Americas. Because Anasazi pottery from the Southwest has been so thoroughly studied and had such wide public attention, Caddoan pottery has been largely overlooked and has remained the private province of archaeologists and, until recently, amateur collectors.

This Arkansas bottle exemplifies the high level of execution and refinement these ceramics can attain. The curvilinear design of spirals and circles provides a shallow but vital surface energy that beautifully coalesces with the formal shape. There are many variations of the curvilinear design motif. Here, covering the the entire surface, it belongs to the interlocking phase of the category called Rhodes Incised, most commonly excavated in Arkansas.[1] The spiral retained its importance in southeastern art in historic times and remained a major feature of late-eighteenth- and early-nineteenth-century Cherokee sashes. It is still seen today on bandolier sashes made for stickball players and is one of the rare Precolumbian motifs that has survived intact.

1. A vessel of similar profile, with the same type of neck and underlaid, incised curves, although somewhat stubbier in proportion, is illustrated in Maurer 1977, p. 66, no. 12. It was found in Garland County, near Hot Springs, Arkansas.

2. Seed jar

ca. 1300–1550
Mississippian peoples, Clark County, Arkansas (?)
Ceramic
Height 11 in. (27.9 cm); diameter 5 ½ in. (14 cm)
RTCNA 582

The tall form of this seed jar is unique to Mississippian Arkansas. It was likely excavated in Clark County. Here, shape dominates, and while important, the incised decoration distinguishes only the upper portion, as opposed to the overall design on the bottle made by the Caddoan peoples (cat. no. 1). Notable here is the subtlety by which the seeming contraction of the round aperture at the top contrasts with the expanding nature of the linear decoration, which both frames and calls attention to the opening while it directs the eye downward to follow the entire form of the pot. An accidental aesthetic refinement is the way the soft shading and mottling of fireclouds, incurred by changes in temperature during firing, enrich the pot's dark buff body.[1]

1. This jar and the preceding bottle (cat. no. 1) were included in the "Sacred Circles" exhibition in London in 1976, which was probably the first time such pottery was shown as art in Europe; see Coe 1976a, pp. 66–67, nos. 32, 34.

3. "Crouching man" pipe

ca. 1200–1400
Mississippian peoples, Natchez, Mississippi (?)
Limestone
4 ¾ x 6 in. (12.1 x 15.2 cm)
RTCNA 583

The "crouching man" constitutes a recurrent sculptural theme at late Mississippian southeastern sites.[1] Important examples have been found as far west as Spiro Mounds, Oklahoma, and as far east as Moundville, Alabama. Precisely what this type of figural representation means iconographically has never been determined, though it may derive indirectly from the same matrix that produced effigy sculptures among the Precolumbian Taino from the Caribbean islands, such as the Dominican Republic, Cuba, Jamaica, and Puerto Rico.[2] It is possible that stylistic features traveled not only north through southern Florida but also, more directly,

through the west coast of Florida along the Gulf of Mexico. This would account for diffusion to the southwestern area of what is today the state of Mississippi. Another route was the Natchez Trace, today a national parkway but in ancient times a well-used Indian trail between Lake Pontchartrain northward through the Mississippi River valley.

There is a quite similar crouching man pipe known to be from the Emerald Mound site, Natchez, in the Brooklyn Museum of Art. It is long known, for it was illustrated in Henry Rowe Schoolcraft's *History of the Indian Tribes of the United States,* published in 1857.[3] Untangling paths of

influence is always complex. The Brooklyn Museum pipe also generally resembles, particularly in the face and hairstyle, those of the Precolumbian Huaxtec area on the Gulf Coast of Mexico, not far south of the present U.S. border. This pipe was published, incorrectly, in 1959, as coming from Ohio.[4] Such a confusion of attributions reflects the quandary that has only recently begun to be resolved with regard to this aspect of late Precolumbian cultures.

1. Brain and Phillips 1996, pp. 384–85.
2. Bercht 1997. This is particularly true in Taino three-pointed stones, as illustrated in ibid., pp. 9 no. 9, 83 no. 60, 93 no. 68, and 103 no. 77.
3. Schoolcraft 1857, pl. 8 (between pp. 610 and 611). Both the present example and the Brooklyn Museum pipe are illustrated in Coe 1976a, figs. 39, 40.
4. Burland 1959, pl. 22, bottom left.

| 4. Gorget |

ca. 1200–1400
Mississippian peoples, Bartow County, Georgia (?)
Shell, pigment
3 ¾ x 4 ¼ in. (9.5 x 10.8 cm)
RTCNA 590

Gorgets like this one, with the snake's head and body clearly depicted, are generally placed toward the end of the Mississippian period. Two holes in the upper border are for suspension around the neck. Shell gorgets of this type usually display coiled rattlesnakes; others are engraved with representations of spiders. Snakes are depicted in a more abstract scheme, with the snake's body solidly wrapped around a centered head. A variant of this gorget was excavated from Mound C at Etowah, Bartow County, Georgia, and is owned by the National Museum of Natural History, Smithsonian Institution, Washington, D.C.[1] These two pieces are part of a substantial oeuvre, many examples of which have been found in Tennessee. This may suggest the presence of a workshop or workshops, although the Smithsonian example has a striated diagonal border and is not as carefully executed. This ancient ornament was owned by the Illinois collector Ralph Olsen and then by the dealer George Terasaki of New York City. In the year 2000, I purchased it from Ted Trotta of Shrub Oak, New York.

1. Maurer 1977, p. 70, no. 20.

5. Pipe

100 B.C.–A.D. 300
Hopewellian peoples, Pike County, Illinois (?)
Ceramic
2 ¼ x 5 ⅝ x 2 in. (5.7 x 14.3 x 5.1 cm)
RTCNA 575

This Hopewell pipe of the Middle Woodland period (300 B.C.–A.D. 300) is called a monitor pipe, a reference to the rounded pipe bowl that recalls the Union's ironclad U.S.S. *Monitor,* which had a single, round turret. But while often underestimated by collectors because its form is simple in comparison with Hopewell animal-effigy pipes made during the same period, the best have a formal element of pure artistic concentration.

The surface patina of this excavated pipe shows clearly that it was charred in an ancient fire. It was perhaps cremated with a corpse or set on fire with other objects during a commemorative ceremony. Hopewell tombs were often constructed of logs covered with earth, and when more than one building campaign took place, mounds grew as successive burials were added.[1]

1. See Illinois Archaeological Survey 1968, "Appendix: The Gibson Mound Group," 86 fig. 39 (the Pete Klunk Mound monitor pipe), pp. 119, 121 fig. 51.

| 6. Pipe |

100 B.C.–A.D. 400
Hopewellian peoples, Darke County, Ohio (?)
Kaolinitic pipestone
4 ½ x 6 ¼ x 2 in. (11.4 x 15.9 x 5.1 cm)
RTCNA 576

The Copena complex is associated with the Hopewellian trading network, which flourished between 100 B.C. and A.D. 400 in the Scioto River valley of central Ohio and the lower Illinois River valley in Illinois. Its name derives from the first three letters of the word "copper" and the last three letters of "galena," a lead ore used for making artifacts. When ground, galena could take on a silvery appearance. Copena objects have also been found in southern Illinois, in Kentucky, and as far south as northern Alabama. This extraordinary phalliform pipe was excavated in Darke County, west-central

Ohio, close to the Indiana border. It was among many offerings typically found in Copena burials—copper ornaments and celts, nodules made of galena weighing up to forty pounds, marine shell cups, elbow pipes, and so forth. It is of polished stone, and the bottom shows damage, presumably inflicted by a farmer's plowshare. The rim is chipped, which perhaps occurred when it was excavated. The ridge on the platform from which the pipe bowl extends is marked along its entire length by closely spaced notches. The pipe was once in the Long collection.

7. Plummet

ca. 300 B.C.–A.D. 300

Deptford peoples, Florida

Basalt

⅞ x 4 ¼ in. (2.2 x 10.8 cm)

RTCNA 588

The environment and the passage of time have been very hard on objects made in pre-contact Florida. What archaeologists have exhumed gives us a somewhat ghostly apparition of the artifactual past. For example, sculptures of wood have come out of their ancient burial sites with such extensive surface erosion that a vestigial object is all that remains and we can only imagine what the pristine original really looked like. Other relics have been excavated from watery, seaside shell heaps without attention to scientific methods of preservation, so that they are damaged simply by subsequent exposure to dry air and have survived in a lamentably shrunken and eroded condition.[1] What has survived in better state are small objects of stone—bannerstones, elbow pipes, and engraved discoidals. Often these objects, such as this small plummet from the Deptford culture in Florida, convey, with some clarity, the skill of their maker. Here, one can discern how the sculptor has understood and beautifully delineated the features of a roseate spoonbill, even to the casque at the end of the long bill.

These bird-headed stone effigy plummets, probably a Hopewellian ramification of approximately 300 B.C. to A.D. 300, are in an excellent state of preservation. Just how these delicately fashioned plummets were used is not clear. They could have been fishing weights, or they could have been worn as symbolic jewelry.

I encountered this plummet in 1960, at Willis Tilton's Indian Relics shop in Topeka, Kansas. At that time, the collecting of Native American art was still a kind of free-for-all, and one never knew what might be discovered next, let alone where it might surface.[2] Three close variants are in the collection of the Brooklyn Museum of Art.[3] They exhibit not only very similar profiles but also the same subtle line engraving around the eyes and the bill that joins these features in a surprisingly acute feat of observation.

1. Purdy 1996, p. xvi.
2. The present plummet was included in the exhibition "The Imagination of Primitive Man" (Nelson Gallery of Art, Kansas City, 1962); see Coe 1962.
3. The variants were included in the exhibition "Ancient Art of the American Woodland Indians" (Detroit Institute of Arts, 1985); see Brose, Brown, and Penney 1985, p. 86, pl. 66. A further example, from offshore Cedar Key, Levy County, Florida, is published in Purdy 1996, pl. 55.

8. Birdstone

1500–500 B.C.
Archaic peoples, north-central United States
Limestone
2 x 4 ⅜ in. (5.1 x 11.1 cm)
RTCNA 571

9. Birdstone

1500–500 B.C.
Archaic peoples, Macomb County, Michigan
Ferruginous limestone
2 ½ x 3 in. (6.4 x 7.6 cm)
RTCNA 572

Birdstones found in the northeastern quadrant of the United States and southern Ontario are among the earliest self-contained animal images that have come down to us in Native American art. They are generally thought to be weights that, like bannerstones, were attached to the end of a throwing stick to steady the hunter's aim, but none have been preserved in their original context. The two examples pictured here are of two distinct types. The birdstone at right is a stylized, entire bird form with a tail indicated at the back and a pair of protruding eyes, adding character to the head. The whole image coalesces into a consecutively swelling and diminishing form that has long attracted the interest of collectors. At left is a birdstone known to be from Macomb County, Michigan. It was passed on to Robert Dunham, of Cowgill, Missouri, by the Illinois archaeologist Ken Farnsworth. Shorter and more compact than the other example, it has a vertically oriented structure.

10. Bannerstone

3000–2000 B.C.
Archaic peoples, Branch County, Michigan (?)
Banded slate
6 x 5 in. (15.2 x 12.7 cm)
RTCNA 565

Bannerstones, excavated at archaic sites in the Midwest and eastern United States, were apparently used as weights attached to throwing sticks. Doubtless, they also had some ceremonial significance. This bannerstone is said to have been found in Branch County, Michigan, the heart area from which the notched, ovate group of banded slate bannerstones originates.[1] The eccentric shape of this group has a close parallel in designs found on textiles excavated in the kurgans of the Altai region of southeastern Siberia, where present-day Russia, China, and Mongolia meet.[2] It is interesting to compare the dates assigned by American archaeologists to notched, ovate bannerstones—about 3000 to 2000 B.C.—with those assigned by the eminent Russian archaeologist Sergei I. Rudenko to the Altai designs, which he attributes to the fourth century B.C. In other words, this distinct form appears earlier in the New World than in the Old, calling into question the usual assumptions.

1. See also Knoblock 1939, pp. 380–81, pl. 176.
2. Rudenko 1970, p. 186, fig. 98.

11. Bannerstone

3000–2000 B.C.
Archaic peoples, Fulton County, Illinois (?)
Ferruginous quartz
5 ¼ x 3 in. (13.3 x 7.6 cm)
RTCNA 567

In his classic book on ancient bannerstones, Byron W. Knoblock cites an example in hourglass form as probably the largest extant of the type.[1] The present example, of the same form, is half an inch higher and of equally beautiful translucency. It is also of nearly exact coloration, with shades of white and deep red. Both these objects are from the middle Mississippi valley and represent what Knoblock considers a classic example. The hourglass form, as described by Knoblock, has a deep triangular profile; later examples are flatter and slightly wider; and the final, classic type is thinner still in its construction.[2] The present bannerstone is classified as type no. 6, class C, the most subtle, abstract, and developed of the hourglass form. Knoblock experimented with drilling through a modern sample of ferruginous quartz using a hollow reed and a sand matrix and notes that "the perforation through this bannerstone, which is four and three-fourths inches in length, required 32,769,528 grinding revolutions, 285 hours of actual drilling time, and 128 ¼ inches of cane was worn away."[3] The reader is left to figure out how much more time it would take to drill a bannerstone of the same type, color, and material, but half an inch higher, as here, and to marvel at the superb workmanship required to execute such a perfect object. Something of the determination and stamina demanded of the maker is expressed in the lithic strength of the finished product.

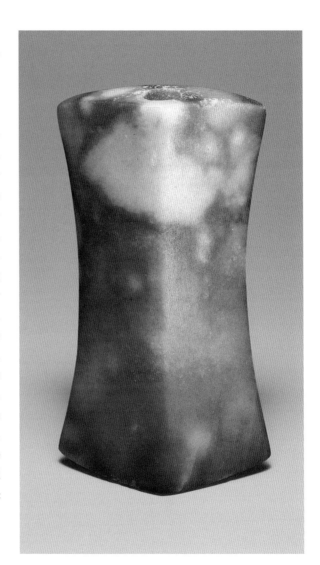

1. Knoblock 1939, pp. 286–87, colorpl. 136.
2. Ibid., p. 288.
3. Ibid.

12. Bannerstone

5000–4000 B.C.
Archaic peoples, Kankakee County, Illinois (?)
Shale
3 x 4 ¾ in. (7.6 x 12.1 cm)
RTCNA 564

This bannerstone in the shape of a double-bitted axe is fashioned from shale although Knoblock published it as "black slate with very thin wings" and identifies it in his system of classification as a class SC (see cat. no. 11).[1] Found in Kankakee County, Illinois, and formerly in the Phillip C. Schupp collection, Chicago, it was acquired by John J. Klejman, New York, from Byron W. Knoblock, and thence to this collector.

1. Knoblock 1939, p. 332, pl. 156, no. 6.

13. Two pelicans and a canoe

16th–17th century
Chumash peoples, southern California
Stone, shell inlay
a. 3 ¾ x 1 ½ in. (9.5 x 3.8 cm)
b. 3 ¾ x 2 in. (9.5 x 5.1 cm)
c. 1 ⅞ x 5 in. (4.8 x 12.7 cm)
RTCNA 557a–c

The Chumash peoples lived in late pre-contact times, near what is now Santa Barbara and the offshore Channel Islands, and their culture continued inland as far as present-day Bakersfield, California. Among the works they produced were beautifully abstracted, large, carved stone bowls, some several feet high. But of particular interest to us are the small black and gray images of hematite-rich stone representing whales, pelicans, and, with this group, not only two pelicans but also a canoe. These objects first came to light in the late 1920s, when sites on the Channel Islands off the Santa Barbara coast were excavated by the then director of the Museum of the American Indian (Heye Foundation), E. K. Burnett.[1] The whales and pelicans were often, but not always, embellished with drilled, circular shell inlays set in a tar matrix, much of which probably came from the La Brea tar pits adjacent to what is today the Los Angeles County Museum of Art. Evidently, such small effigies were used as auspicious charms to propitiate hunting and could also have served as plummets. An acceptable date for their manufacture would be around the sixteenth to the seventeenth century. These three Chumash effigies were for many years on loan to the Israel Museum, Jerusalem, from the American collector Samuel Dubiner. He purchased them at the Stendahl Galleries, Los Angeles, about 1961.

1. Burnett 1944.

II

BASKETS

Hand-Woven Architecture

14. Hinged storage basket

ca. 1840
Passamaquoddy peoples (?), eastern Maine
Painted brown ash splint
Height 22 in. (55.9 cm); diameter 28 ½ in. (72.4 cm)
RTCNA 14

As the eastern shores of North America and the adjacent interior became denuded of game, the trapping of which provided Native Americans with badly needed income, the Passamaquoddy peoples turned to making baskets for their livelihood. In time, "basket families" could be seen taking their wares to sell in town, walking with them strung over the shoulder and down the back. As late as the 1960s, I found a few such baskets being sold by their makers in the Saint John, New Brunswick, weekend market. They were quite plain compared with the more complex and elegantly decorated examples of earlier times, but very pleasing in their simplicity. The next time I visited this market, they had gone.

I found this large hinged storage basket in an antiques shop, Patchwork Samplers, in Clayton, Missouri. A one-time owner of this giant container was Harvey Geason of Marietta, Pennsylvania, in 1976. It was subsequently purchased by John and Valerie Arieta, two American, London-based dealers in ethnology with numerous sources in the British Isles and the United States.

The basket, with a circular shape on a square base, is archetypal of its class, generally supposed to be Penobscot, from northeastern Maine. When the Arietas owned it, a newspaper fragment, now gone, was pasted on the interior, bearing a date imprint of 1850.[1] Originally, there had been a knob—probably turned or carved hickory—at the top center of the lid and also a European-type latch, indicated by the holes for attachment. As to place of origin and tribal authorship, Ann McMullen, curator at the National Museum of the American Indian, Washington, D.C., agrees that it was made in Maine, but she favors a Passamaquoddy over a Penobscot attribution because of the use of yellow and green paint. (The Penobscot used more dark blue during this period.)[2] She calls attention to the "peak" form of the lid, which also seems uncharacteristic of Penobscot work, and notes that the narrow splints are slightly uneven in execution, suggesting that they were done with a knife rather than cut across a basket gauge, which would have provided uniformity of the desired width. This would support a date of about 1840, as suggested here.[3]

1. Personal communication from John Arieta, about 1997.
2. Personal communication from Ann McMullen, June 2, 2002.
3. For earlier domed baskets, see McMullen and Handsman 1987, pp. 132 no. 93, 137 no. 101.

15. Lidded trunk

ca. 1860
Oneida peoples (?), New York
Stamped and painted brown ash splint
14 ½ x 24 x 15 in. (36.8 x 61 x 38.1 cm)
RTCNA I

For years, the greatly varied brown ash splint baskets from the Eastern Woodlands—New England, New York, the Canadian Maritimes, and the Great Lakes—were sold far and wide simply as Americana. Now recognized as Native American, the baskets are being studied and appreciated for what they are. Both the horizontal and the vertical splints were swabbed with different colors, creating a checkered design. Often they were further patterned with potato and wood stamps in buttermilk paint. The sturdy natural-colored farm and pack baskets were made by the men, while the more elaborate baskets were usually the province of the women. Large to miniature lidded trunks were well-known specialties. Late in the Victorian period, fancy trinket and sewing baskets were made, some of them in the shape of fruit and, rarely, imitative of high Victorian hats (see cat. no. 67).

This brown ash splint basket appears to be Oneida, with influence from southern New England tribes.[1] After the conclusion of the Revolutionary War, many Christian Indians from southern New England moved to eastern New York, settling a community called Brothertown. The Stockbridge moved nearby. Some of the Stockbridge then moved to Wisconsin, and some of the Brothertowns moved back to Connecticut, where they intermarried with the Oneida. Subsequently, Oneida basket makers began to include in their designs four-part motifs in medallion shape, like those of the Brothertowns, as seen here.

Another factor that argues for an Oneida attribution is the preference for more variegated and brighter colors, especially the liberally applied orange and mint green. The medallic designs of the Oneida were first outlined with stamps and then vibrantly colored in, the procedure followed here. The basket's surface is covered with decorative motifs. The Oneida settled in both New York and eastern Massachusetts. New York baskets are similar to this one, while those made by the Massachusetts basket makers are usually painted rather than stamped and have swabbed splints.[2] As this trunk is stamped and painted and without swabbed splints, the attribution would seem to lean toward the Oneida of New York rather than those of eastern Massachusetts.

1. Personal communication from Ann McMullen, 2002.
2. Ibid.

16. Lidded basket with handle

ca. 1840
Onondaga peoples (?), New York
Stamped and painted brown ash splint
14 ¼ x 13 x 8 ⅜ in. (36.2 x 33 x 21.3 cm)
RTCNA 6

While Oneida and Onondaga baskets from about 1840 to 1850 are very similar, the use of reddish, swabbed wefts on this purse-shaped basket would indicate an Iroquois Onondaga origin.[1] The basket was purchased from Hastings House Antiques, in Essex, Connecticut, one of the best sources for quality splint baskets until it closed several years ago.

The designs applied to splint basketry, particularly in southern New England, were, in part, suggested by the decorative elements found in wallpapers and appliqué stencils of the early colonial settlers, adding a kind of nostalgia and charm born of the closeness of Native Americans and settlers living side by side. The lidded basket with handle seen here perfectly exemplifies this charm, with stamped outlines of pink foliate elements offset by green leaves that are dabbed on freehand. The pattern also reflects the gradual absorption of design concepts over time rather than the deliberate adoption of a specific motif, which created a whole new vernacular of artistic expression.[2]

1. Personal communication from Ann McMullen, June 2, 2002.
2. For earlier baskets of this type, see McMullen and Handsman 1987, p. 134 no. 96.

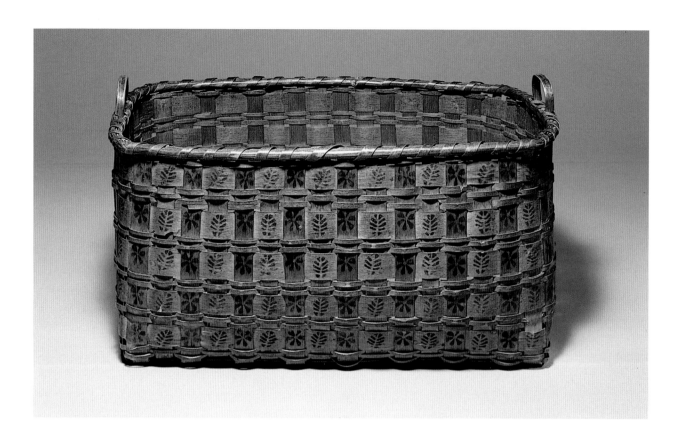

17. Work basket

ca. 1850
Quinnipiac or related peoples, southwestern Connecticut
Stamped and painted brown ash splint
8 x 17 ¼ x 12 ¼ in. (20.3 x 43.8 x 31.1 cm)
RTCNA 24

Baskets in this form were originally made in central Massachusetts. They usually have one wide weft alternating with one narrow weft and two different decorative stamps, sometimes quite complex and based on open circles. According to Ann McMullen, such baskets were made by wandering descendants of disbanded Praying Indian towns, Christianized Indian communities, and can be tribally identified as Natick, Ponkapoag, and related Massachusetts groups.[1] The present basket is stylistically even closer to baskets that show up and probably originated in the southwestern corner of Connecticut. Basket makers seem to have been active there from about 1840 to 1880 because, as coherent groups, they had lost their lands and survived as best they could by their craft, only as scattered, isolated families. Baskets similar to this one have also appeared in the coastal area between New Haven, Stamford, and Greenwich, Connecticut. Note that this example has the requisite two narrow wefts, a strict repetition in stamping, and a highly rhythmical progression from bands of narrow to wider splints. The two dark brown leaf designs, evidently specific to this area, are highly uniform in their application, creating an overall design. The regularity of the stamping would argue for a wood rather than a potato stamp, which would have deteriorated with repeated use. Traditionally, there was a division of labor in the fashioning of such baskets, the men being responsible for the handles, the women for the baskets. On this example, the joining of the hickory handles to the rim adds a note of elegant refinement.

1. Personal communication from Ann McMullen, 2002.

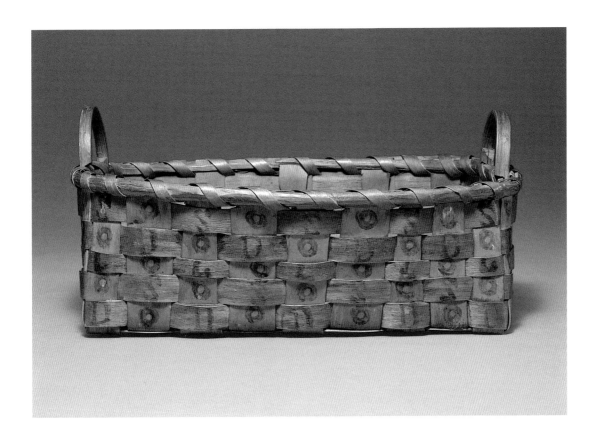

18. Berry basket

1840–60
Pequot peoples (?), southeastern Massachusetts
Stamped and stained brown ash splint
3 ¾ x 11 ½ in. (9.5 x 29.2 cm)
RTCNA 71

With this berry basket, the Eastern Woodlands Native American sense of humor is expressed as a pun on the concept of trading and selling between two disparate peoples—them (the makers) and us (the buyers). The evenly spaced splints are stamped with letters applied in a sly confusion, but when decoded they spell out the word "sold." During the many years I have spent with Native Americans, I have had much experience with deadpan Indian humor, but this was one of the most subtle and also the most ingratiating. Because the basket itself is a commodity, the question arises,

Who gains and who loses? The producer/seller is getting paid by the dominant culture, but the buyer is getting his money's worth.

I acquired this basket from Joel and Kate Kopp, the proprietors of the well-known and now defunct folk art gallery America Hurrah, in New York City. Before the Kopps relocated their store to Madison Avenue, they owned a more modest emporium on East Seventieth Street. Joel was kind enough to let me browse in his second-floor storage area, where this basket popped into view.

19. Lidded storage basket

ca. 1940
Winnebago peoples, Wisconsin
Stained brown ash splint
Height 15 in. (38.1 cm); diameter 13 ¼ in. (33.7 cm)
RTCNA 132

While brown ash splint basketry was a phenomenon of the Eastern Woodlands, after 1820 some of the Brothertown, Stockbridge, and Oneida tribe members who had lived there moved west to central Wisconsin, where they introduced this art to the Winnebago peoples long in residence there. Splint basketry also spread in Canada and from New York State westward; hence, excellent enclaves of Ojibwa splint basketry occurred in Michigan and western Ontario. Of these Great Lakes manifestations, the baskets of the Winnebago are most easily recognized. They were not made on reservations but on Winnebago farmlands associated with Wisconsin towns such as Tomah, Wittenberg, Neilsville, and Baraboo, to say nothing of the picturesque tourist center Wisconsin Dells. In comparison with the baskets of other tribes, Winnebago work is notable for its architectural strength. This is exemplified in the extra support placed around the shoulder of nearly all Winnebago baskets unless there is already a rim to provide this added stability. The lidded storage basket seen here shows a variant on the shoulder reinforcement that encourages the weaver to slope the shoulder element inward, which in turn gives rise to a very prominent woven lid. Also notable is the sturdy handle and its heavily articulated attachments, carved from oak rather than the hickory preferred among the eastern tribes. Another characteristic of the Winnebago approach is to prominently define the decorative ribbonwork accents. To an eastern basket maker once active in Connecticut or Massachusetts, this emphasis might appear overdone, but to a Winnebago master, it serves to enhance the architectonics of her craft.[1]

1. For additional commentary, by a Winnebago basket maker, see Coe 1986, p. 100, nos. 96, 97.

Attributed to Ernestine Walls

Chitimacha, 1917–1988

| *20. Pair of baskets* |

1970s or later
Chitimacha Indian Reservation, Charenton, Louisiana
Dyed river cane
a. 8 x 13 ½ in. (20.3 x 34.3 cm)
b. 7 ⅛ x 13 ½ in. (18.1 x 34.3 cm)
RTCNA 367a, b

This pair of southeastern baskets and the following lidded trunk (cat. no. 21) are Chitimacha in origin and were made in the late twentieth century by two of the most distinguished weavers active at the Chitimacha Indian Reservation, Charenton, Louisiana.

The visual effect of these basket bowls derives from their volumetric character. Another interesting feature is the continued use of natural walnut and butternut dyes rather than the synthetic dyes in common use since the 1960s. Many other baskets with this type of design—bull's-eye medallions—were made from the turn of the twentieth century until midcentury, but this pair seems to have been made in the 1970s. Ernestine Walls was a member of a very small tribe.[1] In such a society, a strong identification with tribal history is a necessity for survival. It is this strength that seems to be echoed in the powerfully architectonic character of Ernestine Walls's basketry. Another similar basket of equal size and shape by the same artist is now in the Whitecloud collection, New Orleans.

1. I wish to thank John Darden, basket maker and curator of the Chitimacha Museum, Charenton, Louisiana, for providing me with information on this artist.

Ada Vilcan Thomas

Chitimacha, 1924–1992

21. Square lidded trunk

April 17, 1987

Chitimacha Indian Reservation, Charenton, Louisiana

Dyed river cane

15 x 13 in. (38.1 x 33 cm)

RTCNA 347

The Chitimacha tradition was continued after the death of Ernestine Walls by the masterful Ada Vilcan Thomas. At that time the sole remaining full-blood Chitimacha basket artist, she wove this large lidded trunk in 1987. In contrast to the Native dyes still used by Ernestine Walls, Ada Thomas used chemical dyes because local riverine lands and bayous had been sprayed with chemicals, heavily damaging the vegetal source of Chitimacha dyes. The design on the lid and body of this commodious square trunk is continuous, and the technique is a double weave, creating an air cushion between the two layers that is noticeably pleasant to the touch. The double-weave technique was also used with mastery by Cherokee weavers in the Qualla Boundary area of North Carolina. The interior is plain, while the exterior features the traditional Muscadine Rind motif and the lid displays the "worm tracks" design. Perhaps Ada Thomas was recalling a *coussin,* a square ottoman or bolster, once quite common in southern Louisiana homes.

22. Basketry bowl

1915–20
Panamint peoples, southeastern California
Plant fiber
Height 3 in. (7.6 cm); diameter 6 ¼ in. (15.9 cm)
RTCNA 544

This small, flared basketry bowl represents the ultimate in California weaving from the southern desert region. Technically, it is the finest basketry on view here, and only the bowl made by Lena Dick (cat. no. 23) is comparable, although they are quite different in form and approach. With approximately sixty stitches to each inch, it has the smoothness of silk. The extraordinary refinement of this piece is attributable to the fact that the weaver used a three-rod coil but peeled the willow to produce the exquisite horizontal lines of vertical stitching. The plant motifs call to mind the cacti of the desert, and the forms seem to evaporate into space like seeds into dry air. While the maker has not been identified, there is another Panamint basket, of the bottleneck type, that is in all probability by the same hand.[1] Only a weaver sensitively in touch with her environment could have created such a concentrated mirror of the desert world—not barren, but teeming with organic life.

1. Butterfield and Butterfield, San Francisco, sale, April 25, 1991, lot 4188.

Lena Frank Dick

Antelope Valley Washoe, 1889–1965

23. Basketry bowl (degikup)

ca. 1925–30

Coleville, California

Plant fiber

Height 4 ¾ in. (12.1 cm); diameter 7 ⅝ in. (19.4 cm)

RTCNA 530

Degikup, a term for basketry bowls, was invented for the sophisticated buyer's market by Abe Cohn, the Carson City, Nevada, dealer and proprietor of the Emporium Company. He is best known as the patron of Dat-So-La-Lee (Louisa Kayser, d. 1925), the greatest of all western basket makers and perhaps the most renowned basketry artist of North America. Dat-So-La-Lee was a Washoe Indian who lived near Lake Tahoe. Her great fame has tended to overshadow a school of Washoe basket makers who lived south of the primary community of Washoe. Because the Washoe territory south of Lake Tahoe drops over the state line from California into Nevada, the Antelope Valley Washoe have been artificially associated with Nevada rather than with the greater Lake Tahoe cultural area. Lena Dick was the most skilled weaver of the Antelope Valley Washoe. This basket, which she made when she was in her thirties, is woven with a stitch count of thirty-five to thirty-seven stitches per linear inch,[1] and it displays the artist's great control of the globular *degikup* shape. The flamelike motif on two sides seems almost to burst from the confines of the bowl. As the flame-stitch design points upward, the frondlike designs on the opposite sides point downward, creating a dimension of perfect balance.

There are essentially four stages in the evolution of Lena Dick's work. The first is an adaptive period, when she uses designs and forms generally accepted as having been developed by Dat-So-La-Lee. During the second stage, her stitchery becomes more refined and the designs more animated. The third period lasts approximately five years, from 1925 to 1930—when this basket was made—and is when she developed her greatest technical skills. Lena Dick's eyesight began to fail after 1930. From then on until she died in 1965, she made baskets mainly by touch that are without designs and far less controlled, husks of her former genius.

1. Personal communication from John Kania, 2001, accompanied by a certificate from Professor Marvin Cohodas, University of British Columbia, Canada.

24. Feathered basket

Early 20th century
Clear Lake Pomo peoples, California
Plant fiber, feathers, shell
Diameter 12 in. (30.5 cm)
RTCNA 531

Baskets such as this one are a tour de force of Pomo basketry art. In addition to their aesthetic appeal, they were of deep symbolic import. Their function as emblems of wealth and largesse is embodied in the shell money that embellishes the surface. It took untold virtuosity to interweave these myriad feathers—of the western meadowlark (yellow), the flicker (orange red), and the mallard duck (deep blue green).

The basket was purchased in 1962 from the New York dealer Julius Carlebach. Carlebach bought it as a "sewing basket," and originally it had a label indicating a Clear Lake, California, provenance.

25. Feathered basket

Early 20th century
Pomo peoples, California
Plant fiber, quail feathers
Height 3 ⅜ in. (8.6 cm); diameter 7 ¼ in.,
with quail feathers (18.4 cm)
RTCNA 532

Pomo basket makers raised their art to what is often acknowledged to be the finest basketry made by any indigenous people. The more elaborate forms reach their zenith when feather imbrication is added to the weaving process. The Pomo have been credited as the only Native Americans to have elevated a craft to an independent art; in other words, it is art for art's sake. Many of their baskets were made as gifts—at the time of a birth, for example, or to one's mother-in-law—or they were placed on a pyre and burned with the mortal remains in funeral ceremonies.

Pomo feathered baskets such as this one from the early 1900s rely on the maker's dexterity and the tightness of the weave—in this case, a T-weave—for their aesthetic appeal. The topknot motifs in the bottom register echo the real feathers on the surface, creating a give-and-take between tensile strength and ethereality.

After 1870, there was an increasing market for Pomo baskets, and the resulting rivalry among collectors helped to sustain the art during very difficult times, as Native cultures became increasingly deprived. Since the end of the Second World War there has been a welcome stabilization of the culture, and superb Pomo baskets are still being made today.

26. Trinket basket

1890–1900
Pomo peoples, California
Plant fiber, glass beads
Height 2 ¾ in. (7 cm); diameter 5 ⅞ in. (14.9 cm)
RTCNA 533

27. Basketry bowl

ca. 1920
Pomo peoples, California
Plant fiber
Height 7 in. (17.8 cm); diameter 12 in. (30.5 cm)
RTCNA 534

Beaded bowls tended to be made for the trade, though such a refined example as this one could have been intended as a gift basket exchanged between relatives and friends as a token of honor and respect. The pinwheel dynamic of the design is apparent only when the basket is viewed bottom-side-up. Viewed from the side, the joined diamonds can also be considered X motifs, providing an interesting visual double entrendre. In either case, the beaded rectangle that mediates between each motif provides a fulcrum and is therefore crucial to the balance of the design.

The graduated zigzag, discoidal design of this otherwise rather typical Pomo basketry bowl seems to make it whirl in space or, when held, levitate out of one's hands. The technical virtuosity of this basket is evident in the contradiction between the vertical rows of stitching and the horizontal progression of the ascending zigzag lines. The zigzag motif has been identified as "deerbacks" and the rim decoration of small rectangles as ant motifs.[1]

1. See Bedford 1980, p. 20, no. 36.

28. Large Utility basket

ca. 1900
Pomo peoples, coastal California
Plant fiber
Height 18 in. (45.7 cm); diameter 32 in. (81.3 cm)
RTCNA 620

This and the following Pomo basket were made for utilitarian purposes and are not in the gift basket category. The present example is an outsize container executed in openwork weave and probably used for the storage of fishing nets by the coastal Pomo peoples. The functional nature of the basket did not distract the weaver from creating an aesthetically pleasing architectural masterwork. The lattice twining lends a pneumatic, billowy character, quietly accented by the redbud rings that provide an overall sense of control. The sling by which the basket is suspended for hanging (not visible here), while it is of Pomo manufacture, is made of commercial twine and did not originally accompany the piece. It is also later in date. The basket was collected by the Reverend Leo Brown (see cat. no. 30).

| 29. Burden basket |

Mid- to late 19th century
Pomo peoples (?), California
Plant fiber
Height 14 in. (35.6 cm); diameter 15 ⅜ in. (39.1 cm)
RTCNA 546

Equally utilitarian to the preceding basket (cat. no. 28) is this one of typically conical shape, though it is somewhat smaller than average. By means of a sling, it rested on the back of a Pomo woman when on berry- and acorn-gathering expeditions. Six horizontal bands with various motifs alternate with plain bands to endow this basket with a severe geometric strength. The design bands are of split redbud, and the foundation is willow warp rods and sedge root. The basket is of Pomo origin, although to which group it is ascribed has not been ascertained.

30. Basket tray

ca. 1900
Yurok peoples, northern California
Plant fiber
Diameter 15 ¼ in. (38.7 cm)
RTCNA 547

The technique used for this Yurok basket tray is plain twining, and three colors are used. The neutral color is bear grass; the black is maidenhair fern; and the red is giant chain fern dyed with the inner bark of white alder. Parallel zigzag lines, referred to as "long worms," are enclosed within three tripartite motifs.[1] The basket's relatively small size probably identifies it as a receptacle to catch ground acorn meal, a staple of California Native cuisine. The sense of the grinding motion is echoed in the bold circular design treatment.

The basket was formerly in the collection of Leo Brown, a Methodist missionary who had a small private museum in Eureka, California. He is known to have collected directly from reservation Indians, especially in the 1950s.

1. For typical northern California designs, see Fields 1985, pp. 78 fig. 95, 88 figs. 124–31, 70 figs. 66–68.

31. Basket tray

ca. 1910
Akimel O'odham (Pima) peoples, Arizona
Plant fiber
Diameter 18 ½ in. (47 cm)
RTCNA 548

The Akimel O'odham peoples live in south-central Arizona along the Gila and Salt Rivers. This name, which they prefer to the one by which they have become known, Pima, translates as "river people." They are generally accepted as descendants of the ancient Hohokam peoples, who thrived from A.D. 200 to 1450 in what is today Phoenix, down to the northern part of the Sonoran Desert in Mexico. To this day, the tribe adheres to its agricultural roots and basketry has continued to be an economic staple for them, despite the fact that its production has diminished over the last half century.

This tray is a fine example of the Akimel O'odham figurated style from about 1910, when non-Native customers still appreciated the classic forms and designs of southwestern basketry. It displays sixteen animal and human figures united into a dynamic pinwheel pattern that maintains a sensitive balance between open intervals and design motifs. The male and female figures holding hands as they dance in a circle and the four anthropomorphic horned toads represent the universe. Syncopation is provided by the rhythmic design of the figuration, and the joined hands create a sense of both contained energy and energy radiating beyond the confines of the basket itself. The cross motifs between the figures, which are often seen on Akimel O'odham and Papago basketry, are called *pan ika kita* and represent the tracks of the coyote. These convey an element of humor, as the coyote is a trickster figure.

Coiling of this tray is to the left, using a bundle of cattail leaf that is then sewn with split and peeled willow for the tan areas and devil's claw for the dark relief designs. It would be very difficult for any but the finest basket maker to achieve, using only two tones, a composition of such remarkable rhythmic clarity.

Collected in 1896
White Mountain Apache peoples, Arizona
Plant fiber, Navajo silver button
Diameter 19 ⅜ in. (49.2 cm)
RTCNA 636

This White Mountain Apache basket is accompanied by a most unusual document that takes it back to the day in 1896 when it was finished. One of the many tourist explorers who ventured to the Southwest at the end of the nineteenth century was a Chicagoan named Hugo Kugenhaumer, who was also an amateur photographer. According to Kugenhaumer's granddaughter, he came upon a basket maker at work, and she agreed to sell him the basket she was working on for twelve or thirteen dollars. Because it was unfinished, Kugenhaumer went off hiking. When he returned a week later, the basket was finished and the weaver allowed him to take this glass-negative photograph of her protectively holding the basket and smiling shyly, as if hesitant to part with it.[1] Unfortunately, her name is not known, but the photograph is a rare historical record. Apache women were often extremely sensitive about being photographed, and outsider interest during this period focused on Apache men, famously known as warriors and therefore given more attention by journalists and photographers. Very few close-up photographs of Apache women from the end of the nineteenth century have survived, and for this reason the photograph is, in some ways, as important as the basket.

The sexpartite design is united at the center and plugged with an old Navajo button. Each of the sections includes a varied design composed of arrangements of deer, arrows, and human figures with hands upraised, perhaps celebrating a hunt. The charm of the basket resides in no small way in its slightly uneven pictorialization, an effect exactly the opposite of that achieved in the Akimel O'odham figural basket (cat. no. 31), which features perfect symmetry rather than occult balance.

1. Information supplied by Hugo Kugenhaumer's granddaughter in the late 1990s to the Santa Fe dealer Robert Ashton, from whom I bought the basket.

33. Basket

Late 19th century
Tlingit peoples, southeastern Alaska
Plant fiber
Height 8 ¾ in. (22.2 cm); diameter 10 ¾ in. (27.3 cm)
RTCNA 625

Sitka, Alaska, was a center for the sale of baskets fashioned entirely in the Tlingit tradition but made for sale to visitors. This basket features two circumferential designs known as "waves," with a narrow intervening band called "half the head of a salmon berry."[1] The rim is delicately accented by a narrow checkerboard pattern. A label inside, reading "Mrs. H. M. Cross Collection, 1911," is of special interest. Edie Cross, to whom the label refers, was an old-time dealer-collector who lived in Sidney, British Columbia,

outside Victoria. Active from the early twentieth century until the 1960s, she is best remembered as the owner of a pair of celebrated Tsimshian stone masks, unique in all Northwest Coast art. One is preserved at the Canadian Museum of Civilization, Gatineau, Quebec, and the other at the Musée de l'Homme, Paris.[2]

1. These designs are illustrated in Turnbaugh and Turnbaugh 1986, pp. 29–32.
2. Illustrated in Bancroft-Hunt 1979, p. 63.

Isabella Edenshaw, Haida, ca. 1858–1926

Charles Edenshaw, Haida, 1839–1920

| 34. *Lidded basket* |

Late 19th–early 20th century

Tlingit peoples,

southeastern Alaska

Plant fiber

Height 3 in. (7.6 cm); diameter 4 in. (10.2 cm)

RTCNA 624

| 35. *Lidded basket* |

1885–90

Old Masset, Haida Gwaii (Queen Charlotte Islands),

British Columbia

Plant fiber, paint

Height 3 ¾ in. (9.5 cm); diameter 4 ¾ in. (12.1 cm)

RTCNA 172

Baskets such as this one, which had pebbles inserted into a raised center portion of the lid—adding the unexpected element of sound when the basket was opened or shaken—were customarily made for tourist appeal. But in no way was quality sacrificed, as is evident here in the exceptionally restrained and succinct rendering of a standard design known as "shaman's hat." This is a tightly twined tour de force of basket weaving, with twenty-four stitches per inch on the lid and only slightly fewer on the cylindrical body. The lid motif is a variant of the "tail of the raven" design.

Charles Edenshaw was as excellent a painter as he was a carver and jeweler. His wife, Isabella, was a superlative basketry artist in her own right, and their collaboration produced a number of baskets of uncommon refinement, a group of traditional hats, and woven table mats painted with Northwest Coast imagery. This small lidded basket is one of several very similar baskets that can be attributed to this couple. One practically identical basket, with a rattle lid, now in the Haffenreffer Museum of Anthropology, Bristol, Rhode Island, was collected between 1884 and 1889 by Emma Shaw Colcleugh, a Rhode Island journalist who traveled in the Arctic and sub-Arctic in the late nineteenth century. The painting on that basket accords exactly with Charles

Edenshaw's style during the 1880s.[1] A shallow tray that was collected at Massett, in 1898, by Charles F. Newcomb and is today in the Canadian Museum of Civilization, Gatineau, Quebec, displays a painted beaver crest that is slightly looser in drawing, which supports a date in the late 1890s.[2] Another cylindrical basket on which is painted a killer whale is owned by the Seattle Art Museum.[3] It is the most subtly balanced of the baskets described here and probably the latest, dating perhaps into the 1900s. The present, earlier example is tighter in design and less fluid in drawing. Baskets such as these were commensurate with traditional practices, but they were also sold as objets d'art suitable for a Victorian setting. Because of the refined sensibilities of these two artists, the integrity of their work was not compromised in the transition. (See also cat. nos. 91, 92.)

1. Krech 1994, p. 120, fig. 11-37.
2. MacDonald 1996, p. 28, pl. 16.
3. Brown 1998, p. 117, fig. 5.16a, b.

April Churchill, Haida, b. 1951
Robert Davidson, Haida, b. 1946

36. Basket with killer-whale images

1983
Old Masset, Haida Gwaii (Queen Charlotte Islands),
British Columbia
Plant fiber, paint
Height 8 ¾ (22.2 cm); diameter 10 ½ in. (26.7 cm)
RTCNA 154

Traditional basketry on the Northwest Coast waned during the second third of the twentieth century, largely as a result of a dearth of tourists interested in acquiring fine work. However, a few traditional basket makers survived. These included the Tsimshian basket maker Flora Mather and a matriarch of Haida basketmaking, Selina Peratrovich, whose daughter, Dolores Churchill, inherited her mother's mantle and remains today an active basketry artist. Dolores's daughter, April, wove this large, classic basket, in collaboration with the eminent contemporary Haida artist Robert Davidson, who painted the dramatic killer-whale designs. It was very ambitious for its time, when the revival of basket weaving was just beginning to gain recognition. The painting, consisting of three continuous killer-whale designs, is based on a silkscreen by Davidson titled *T-Silii-AA-lis* (Raven-Finned Killer Whale), which was issued in 1983.[1] Before I acquired the basket the following year, Davidson expanded the design threefold to form a frieze around the circumference. To accommodate the extra space, the killer-whales' heads are foreshortened and the raven fin is tucked closely underneath. To underscore the rhythm of the composition, a modified whale's-tail motif was inserted between each of the three images, increasing the visual impact by a serial presentation, almost like a filmstrip. The blue-and-red star painted on the bottom of the basket is Davidson's personal mark.

Years later, sitting behind Dolores Churchill on a bus, as part of a group going from London to Oxford, I mentioned to her that since I had last seen her, I had acquired a basket by her daughter. On hearing my description she responded, with characteristic understatement, "Oh, we always wondered where that one went."

1. Thom 1993, p. 103.

37. Hamper

Late 19th century
Thompson River Salish peoples, British Columbia
Plant fiber
16 ½ x 19 in. (41.9 x 48.3 cm)
RTCNA 634

This husky, broad-shouldered hamper, notable for its strong, bulbous form effectively brought to completion by the firm placement of the lid, is both a typical and exceptional example of southern Northwest Coast basketry art. Its unique aesthetic is restricted to the Olympic Peninsula and interior of Washington State and the interior of British Columbia. The beautifully imbricated designs are said to represent faces, and indeed, the traditional Thompson Indian name for this motif is "masks" or "half faces." The design is executed in a geometric style that perhaps reveals some indirect and remote connection to the ancient Chinese mask form *tao tie,* which is here highly simplified but nonetheless still recognizable. Around the time I bought this basket, my curiosity had been piqued by the concept of cultural diffusionism, the spread of ancient motifs between the Orient and the Western world.[1] It was this interest and the presence of the idiosyncratic design that led to the purchase.

The hamper was once owned by the Frohman Trading Company in Portland, Oregon, a well-known early source for baskets from California and the Northwest. I acquired it from Edward Hartman of Lee Summit, Missouri, who had an excellent eye for Native American art and who owned a machine shop for the repair of tractors, an apiary for gathering honey, and a quality Indian trading establishment.

1. Coe 1972 and Coe 1976b.

38. Lidded basket

Late 19th–early 20th century
Aleut peoples, Aleutian Islands, Alaska
Beach grass, silk thread
Height 5 in. (12.7 cm); diameter 3 ½ in. (8.9 cm)
RTCNA 617

Christine Dushkin, Aleut, b. 1923

39. Lidded basket

Late 1980s–early 1990s
Sand Point, Aleutian Islands, Alaska
Beach grass, silk thread
Height 1 ¾ in. (4.5 cm); diameter 1 in. (2.5 cm)
RTCNA 618

Aleutian Islands baskets are so compactly woven that they appear to be related as much to the most refined textiles as to any known form of basketry. This is true of the Attu Island basket (left) and even more so of the miniature lidded basket (right), which I spied in a corner of the Native Alaskan Craft Cooperative, in Anchorage, Alaska. The latter has the fineness of silk and is woven with a remarkable thirty-two stitches to the inch, which explains why Aleutian basketry is admittedly some of the finest in the world. The weaver, Christine Dushkin, originally from Sand Point in the Aleutian Islands, now lives in Anchorage.

The conical lidded Attu basket is one of a number that have survived, all displaying similar schematic designs. They are decorated in the middle register with eight-pointed floral stars, usually two, dramatically opposed and elegantly spaced between narrow bands, so that the beauty of the plain twill is accentuated.[1] Such containers appear to be a uniquely nineteenth-century type. Aleutian basket weaving is believed to have originated at Attu, at the western extreme of the island chain, and spread through two intervening weaving regions, Atka and Unalaska, the latter closest to the Alaskan mainland. The art historian Lydia Black has written of this art form: "Since the earliest contact time the excellence of Aleut basketry was recognized and valued. Sailors, merchants and travelers carried Aleut baskets to their distant homelands. After 1867 [the year Alaska was sold to the United States by Russia] the Aleut baskets, especially the famed Attu baskets, became a major item of commerce. The last church built on Attu, destroyed in World War II, was built with the proceeds of the sale, or exchange for building materials, of baskets made by seven Attuan basket weavers. It took the women an entire year just to prepare the grass for the project."[2]

1. A similar rye grass basket with a slightly less prominent Attu-type knob, which in the present example almost resembles an Aleut cap, is illustrated in Fitzhugh and Crowell 1988, p. 56, fig. 57. For early Aleut gut caps, see Varjola 1990, p. 184, nos. 267–70.
2. L. Black 1982, p. 164. Facing p. 164, fig. 113, shows an Attu basket probably by the same maker as the present example or from the same family workshop.

III

NORTHERN WOODLANDS
UTILITARIAN OBJECTS

The Inner Character of Wood

40. Paddle

1850–75
Iroquois peoples, Quebec or Ontario
Wood
42 ½ x 4 ½ in. (108 x 11.4 cm)
RTCNA 594

This monumental and exceptionally elaborate wood paddle for the preparation of cornmeal mush or soup turns utility into meaningful sculpture. Like the chip-carved decorations sometimes applied to crooked knives, it exhibits both a quasi-Victorian sense of nineteenth-century artistic elaboration and a Native American pastoral simplicity of form. The paddle is distinguished by a formal grandeur of conception. The ceremonial overtones, underscored by the freestanding figurine of an Iroquois orator at the top, indicate that it was customarily used only at major communal or sacramental events. The orator holds a miniature version of the large paddle on which he stands, thus creating a kind of pun—the paddle is presented as both functional and symbolic.

The paddle probably dates to between 1850 and 1875. A Quebec or Ontario provenance is suggested by the fact that it surfaced in England, having been taken from Canada as a souvenir by a British visitor. It subsequently belonged to a New York City connoisseur-collector. Mush paddles of wood are still carved by the Iroquois today, but as smaller mementos of their culture rather than as full-scale implements.[1]

1. For a contemporary paddle, see Coe 1986, p. 78, no. 45.

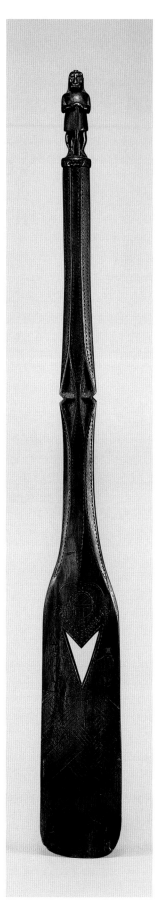

41. Cradleboard

ca. 1860
Mohawk peoples, Quebec and New York
Painted wood, rawhide ties
26 x 10 ½ x 10 ½ in. (66 x 26.7 x 26.7 cm)
RTCNA 226

Perhaps the most spectacular of all Woodlands Indian wood cradles is this type, made by the Mohawk (Iroquois), whose largest reservation is on the divide of the U.S.–Canadian border. These consist of a sturdy board, often, as here, with a gray background color and a bentwood protector attached to shield the baby's head. At the back of the cradle, as seen at right, is the main feature: a relief-carved and gaily painted floriated panel divided near the top with a turned, wood brace into which the bentwood head shield is pegged.

There is a tangible European influence here, more specifically, French Canadian. It is visible in the spindle-like profile of the back brace, but it appears most notably in the relief-carved designs. These are composed mainly of two open sunflowers, one above the other, and a subsidiary leaf-and-floral pattern that recalls motifs found in the French Canadian folk art of Quebec, such as woven bed and table covers. Because the Mohawk peoples lived in one of the most populous areas of Quebec Province, cultural exchange was to be expected. Iroquois clan symbols—bear, wolf, deer, and turtle—were typically carved at the corners of such cradles, although they are absent here. The green and rusty red pigments convey a sense of the verdant woodland environment in which the Iroquois lived. Specifically, the sunflower motifs conjure up a sense of birth and renewal in their sensuous display. A resurgence of Mohawk culture in our own times has favored the continuation of this traditional cradle type, often with somewhat modernized designs.[1]

1. For a cradleboard made in 1981–82, see Coe 1986, pp. 75 no. 39, 116.

| 42. Belt cup |

Before 1850
Penobscot or Passamaquoddy peoples, collected in Maine
Wood
2 x 3 x 4 in. (5.1 x 7.6 x 10.2 cm)
RTCNA 284

| 43. Bible marker |

Mid-19th century
Maliseet peoples, New Brunswick
Wood, metal, silk ribbon
1 ½ x 3 ⅝ in. (3.8 x 9.2 cm)
RTCNA 282

The idea of the belt cup is integral to woodland lore. Used as a portable drinking vessel, it enabled trappers, campers, paddlers, lumberjacks, and other travelers through the forests to obtain a drink of water en route, just as I used a tin cup attached to my belt as a youth in arboreal Canada. This particular example—paper-thin and whittled with great finesse—recently came to light in Maine and is attributable to the Penobscot or Passamaquoddy peoples. Like crooked knives, it is embellished with a personalized metaphor on the woodland habitat—a handle composed of two engaging beavers face-to-face. To hold the cup to a belt, a thong was passed through the handle.

The early adoption, in the seventeenth century, of Catholicism by Canadian Algonkian Indians was nowhere more significant to Native American life than with Maritime tribes, such as the Maliseet of New Brunswick Province. In church, a ribbon was customarily used to hold the Bible open to the lesson being read. It is not known exactly when Indian-made Bible markers such as this one became a part of Maritime Indian church furniture. This elegantly carved pointer has an old silk ribbon attached—through a handmade pot-metal socket—to a carved miniature heart, a motif common to Indian trade silver. The back of the wood face is fitted with a clip to hold the pages in place. The front, seen above, is engraved with still smaller hearts, each one speared by crossed arrows, along with two medallion circles like those found in Micmac/Maliseet quillwork (cat. no. 53). Small-scale chip carvings along the edge of the pointer lend an additional aspect of delicate charm to this tiny object of faith.

| *44. Crooked knife* |

Before 1870
New England or eastern Canada
Wood, metal
9 ¼ x 6 in. (23.5 x 15.2 cm)
RTCNA 330l

Crooked knives, an Indian-American folk art, were carved by northeastern tribes from New England and the Canadian Maritimes. This form of utilitarian knife spread across northern Canada and New York State, into the Great Lakes area. While there are undoubtedly non-Native influences that affected the varied repertory of forms and motifs, the genre remains an Indian manifestation. The handle on this knife, for example, swells to a delicately configured fiddlehead, a fern that is steamed and eaten as a delicacy in the northern woods.

Crooked knives were grasped by the carver with his thumb typically fitted into an indentation on the back of the handle. When the knife was thus secured, it was pulled toward the carver's chest. In dexterous hands, a crooked knife could be wielded with amazing agility and speed. The blades were fashioned from files, altered knife blades, and straight razor blades—or the local blacksmith could make one for you. The classic way to secure the carving blade to the knife handle was by tightly wrapping them into one unit with piano wire. All that remains on this knife of the original wrapping are the indentations made by the wire.

| 45. Crooked knife |

1889
New England or eastern Canada
Painted wood, metal
5 ½ x 8 in. (14 x 20.3 cm)
RTCNA 330g

This crooked knife features a chip-carved technique that may derive from immigrant German wood-carvers during the latter part of the nineteenth century, who applied this style of decoration to boxes, large and small, and to mirror and picture frames. The knife bears the raised initials PP and a carved date of 1889, which accords well with the influence of German carving. It is bound in piano and picture wire. The presence of three heart motifs—one of them raised above another and the third perpendicular at the top—in a freestanding composition harks back to the heart symbols that the Scottish soldiers took with them into French Canada in the form of silver brooches and lockets as a pledge of loyalty to their loved ones back home. This motif was quickly adapted by the Montreal silversmith trade and is used today by contemporary Iroquois jewelers.

| 46. Crooked knife |

Late 19th century
Micmac peoples, Nova Scotia or northern New Brunswick
Wood, paint, metal, cord
6 ¼ x 8 ¾ in. (15.9 x 22.2 cm)
RTCNA 330a

This knife handle is, in my experience, unique in that it has at the top a raised device with an abstract triangular design bearing traces of paint that is apparently derived from the potato and wood stamps which decorated New England and Canadian splint basketry (see cat. no. 15). The Canadian dealer from whom I purchased this unusual "potato stamp" knife is quite sure that its origin is Micmac. To this day, Micmac farmers who settled along the northern border of Maine in the Depression era still use crooked knives to fashion the sturdy handles for their splint baskets. This example originated in New Brunswick or Nova Scotia. It is aesthetically pleasing in its slender angularity.

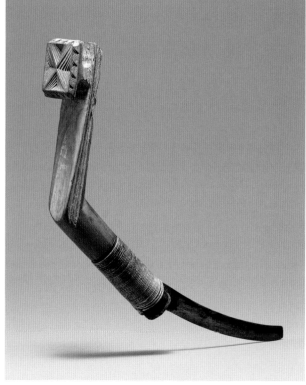

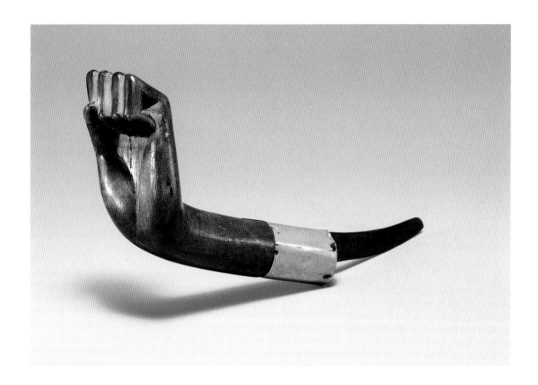

| 47. Crooked knife |

Late 19th century
Penobscot peoples, Maine
Wood, metal
3 ½ x 8 ½ in. (8.9 x 21.6 cm)
RTCNA 330C

Knives of this type, carved as a clenched fist, are traditionally associated with Penobscot carvers from the Old Town area of Maine.[1] The handle on this example may be seen as a metaphor for the "hands-on" philosophy of Indian traditional artists and as a symbol of the woodsman's ethos.

Crooked knives gave carvers the opportunity to explore non-Native motifs such as ships' figureheads, playing cards, and carved initials indicating ownership. In the twentieth century, they sometimes make reference to current events or trends—even to a favorite movie star (RTCNA 330f; not in catalogue). In the fashioning of canoes, such knives were used for cutting root lashings and as birchbark pieces to fill gaps and tighten ribs. Crooked knives were also used to carve pairs of hickory handles for the highly decorative New England and Maritime splint baskets (see cat. no. 17).

1. Speck 1940, p. 37, fig. 6.

48. Mukak with lid

Late 19th–early 20th century
Ojibwa peoples, Minnesota
Birchbark, spruce root, Native-tanned skin ties
10 ½ x 12 ⅜ in. (26.7 x 31.4 cm)
RTCNA 279

Folded and stitched mukaks, or birchbark containers, were ubiquitous in the Northeast Woodlands, including the Great Lakes region. Made by women, they were often, as here, fitted with lids. Besides serving for general storage purposes, they were often used as containers for maple sugar. Over the years, three of these scraped, figurated mukaks by this artist have come to light, of which this is perhaps the finest example. They are distinguished by a strong and idiosyncratic narrative element. The mukak in the Flint Institute of Arts, Flint, Michigan, dating to about 1900, shows a figure with arms akimbo, smoking a pipe; another figure is portaging a canoe on his head; and there are also several pairs of strutting birds.[1] The second example is in the Donald Jones collection, now housed in the Nelson-Atkins Museum of Art, Kansas City.[2] On the present mukak, the liveliness of the design is even more pronounced. There are several running figures. Geese squabble over a fish. Two herons testily confront each other. And two men flee from a supernatural horned being. On the opposite side, two chiefs debate the fate of a prisoner. The imagery is overwhelmingly concerned with confrontation, but the meaning of the scenes remains obscure. While some kind of ritual or story may be enacted here, a sort of Native American Aesop's fable, the figures and activities may be unrelated.

1. Flint Institute of Arts 1973, p. 80, fig. 364.
2. Not published.

| 49. Lidded box |

ca. 1890

Peter Dana Point, Maine

Incised birchbark

3 x 4 x 2¾ in. (7.6 x 10.2 x 7 cm)

RTCNA 301

This exquisite miniature trinket box was made by the best-known late-nineteenth- and early-twentieth-century northeast birchbark artist, Tomah Joseph. Until his time, Algonkian designs on birchbark were highly symbolic—C-scrolls or outlined quadrangles arranged to form interlocking, often curvilinear units. Passamaquoddy Tomah Joseph was among the first to add scenic and figural narrative scenes to his repertory of birchbark engraving, drawing on his own deeply rooted knowledge of Northeast Woodlands myths and legends.[1] His scenes of culture heroes are enlivened by a gently humorous and piquant style, which the art historian Joan Lester has aptly called "history on birchbark."[2] Tomah Joseph made illustrations of the stories he knew on all manner of birchbark objects, large and small—letter holders, sewing and tatting boxes, handkerchief and collar boxes, wall pockets, fireplace log holders, moosecalls, even umbrella stands. They range in size from a monumental (over fifty inches long) birchbark model canoe down to a trinket box as modest as this one.[3]

Characteristically, as on the lid of this box, he would engrave the word *seeps*, which means "ducks," next to a proud mother duck followed by a row of ducklings. This was not merely a picturesque device but a celebration of nature's bounty and the woodsman's life he loved. On this little box, he also engraved the Passamaquoddy phrases *kolele mooke* and *mikwid hamin*, signifying "good fortune" and "remember me." While his art was Tomah Joseph's most lasting contribution, he also played a significant role in the preservation of traditional woodland skills and served as a guide to visitors who wished to tour the Maine forests and

fish the lakes and streams. Indeed, he is known to have taught the young Franklin D. Roosevelt the art of canoeing at the Roosevelt family's Canadian summer home at Campobello Island, just off the northern Maine coast.

1. Leland (1884) 1992. When Charles Leland began, in the summer of 1882, to collect Passamaquoddy legends and folklore, his main source was Tomah Joseph, who also supplied drawings. Unfortunately, these were tampered with by Leland, who sentimentalized them.
2. Lester 1993.
3. Vincent, Brydon, and Coe 2000, pp. 94–95, no. T43.

IV

INDIAN FANCIES

Victorian Propriety

| 50. Trunk |

1840s

Micmac peoples, Nova Scotia or northern New Brunswick

Birchbark, wood, spruce root, porcupine quill

7 ⅝ x 12 ¼ x 9 ½ in. (19.4 x 31.1 x 24.1 cm)

RTCNA 300

By the turn of the nineteenth century, several tribes from the Canadian Maritime provinces had developed a marketable art for the growing Euro-Canadian population in Quebec City and Montreal and for visitors to Nova Scotia and New Brunswick. Among the most spectacular objects made were quill-decorated trunks, often with a curved lid following the example of Franco-English caskets and trunks, larger versions of which were familiar items in non-Native homes. Traveling cases and sea chests come to mind. Although this characteristic Micmac trunk is much smaller than the full-size European models, it remains one of the larger quilled Micmac art forms.

This tour de force of the quiller's art provides a repertory of mid-nineteenth-century Micmac designs at the height of the classic phase. The colors, which are vegetal, are still restricted to a blue (logwood), golden brown (bloodroot), and natural, and although faded today, they remain in harmonious, legible condition. The center cartouche of the lid bears the quilled initials MD. Whether these letters refer to the owner, who may have commissioned the piece, or to a surgeon or medical doctor is not known. The high quality of execution contributes to making this a treasure box worthy of containing the most precious belongings of a governor-general's wife or of a well-to-do colonial. To this day, the lid fits snugly on the box and the quills retain the original elegance of having been laid down with exceptional precision. Equally, it could have been taken back to England as a souvenir of adventurous times in the New World. Most extant examples have been found in England.

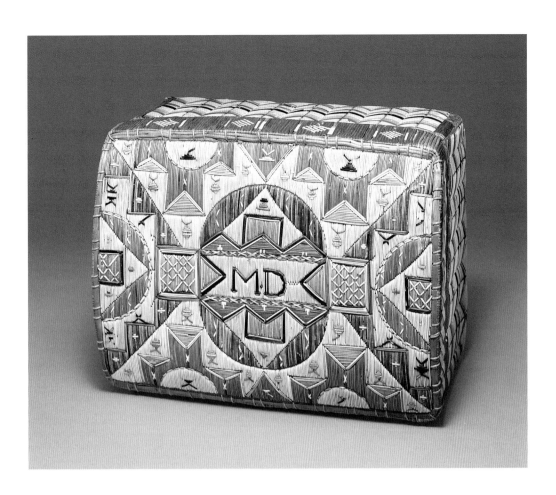

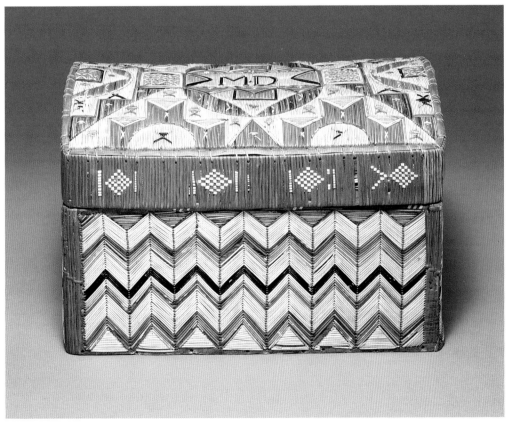

51. Lidded box with Huron pincushion

1820s or 1830s
Micmac peoples, Nova Scotia or northern New Brunswick
Box: Birchbark, wood, spruce root, porcupine quill
Height 2 ¼ in. (5.7 cm); diameter 3 ¾ in. (9.5 cm)
Pincushion: Silk trade cloth, porcupine quill
2 ½ x 2 ½ in. (6.4 x 6.4 cm)
RTCNA 670a, b

52. Lidded box

1840s
Micmac peoples, Nova Scotia or northern New Brunswick
Birchbark, wood, spruce root, porcupine quill
Height 3 in. (7.6 cm); diameter 4 ⅞ in. (12.4 cm)
RTCNA 290

The stylistic progression from the box shown at the top, made in the 1820s or 1830s, to the box shown at the bottom, made in the 1840s, is evident in the placement of the checkerboard pattern. The earlier of the two displays the pattern on the sides of the box and the lid, whereas the later one shows the pattern only on the sides of the lid; the repeat chevron motif adds an element of syncopation and rhythmic variety. The lid of the later box is divided into a number of salient patterns relieved by color variations that form a quadripartite system, each of the quadrants displaying an earth symbol. Two of these are surmounted by trees reaching skyward, and the two opposed panels are adorned with flying thunderbirds. The three-part quilled design on the lid of the earlier box has strongly geometric accents, which suggests that it is Micmac.

There was an active trade in such souvenir art between Canada and England from roughly 1800 through the 1880s. Most likely, many of these objects were bought directly by British and continental Europeans, but others were assembled for shipment and sold overseas.

I picked up the smaller box in a Devon antiques shop in 1977. Inside was a pincushion typical of small items made for trade. Unlike the box, the pincushion is of Huron manufacture, but they may well have been sold together. In any case, a pleasant surprise awaited me when I opened the box after I had left the shop.

53. Chair seat

Mid-19th century
Micmac peoples, Nova Scotia or northern New Brunswick
Birchbark, wood, porcupine quill
12 x 14 ½ in. (30.5 x 36.8 cm)
RTCNA 327

The Micmac peoples of Nova Scotia and northern New Brunswick developed one of the most attractive and picturesque of post-contact craft specialties. I refer to the vast repertory of quilled bark objects that were made between the 1820s and the late nineteenth century, of which quilled chair seats are typical. Chair seats were not always saddle shaped, like the present example, and they could be larger, with less curvature. They were set into chair frames often crafted by Canadian cabinetmakers, the backs of which also had quilled insert panels. It is rare to find completely quilled chairs for which the quillwork has survived in unworn condition. But, evidently, many of the panels were sold separately as souvenirs and, like this one, survived nearly intact. Despite some fading, this one retains its colorful appeal. The dyes are still vegetal, and the designs are classic, striking a balance between simpler, earlier quill designs and the more garish ones made later in the nineteenth century.

The regularity of such decorative schemes may betray the use of a compass and the protractor tools employed by surveyors and the colonial military. Certainly, such close attention to geometric motifs suggests a European influence. The sophisticated design scheme would suggest a date for this chair saddle in the mid-nineteenth century. To the best of my knowledge, elementary figural motifs of this kind have not thus far appeared elsewhere in Micmac quilling,[1] although Ruth Whitehead illustrates a petroglyph of a sharply triangulated figure that she characterizes as "in the Europeanized manner."[2]

1. Whitehead 1982, p. 52. It would appear that the seat panel shown in figure 78 is the same panel shown here. It was formerly in the Lance Entwistle collection, London, and was purchased from James Economos, Santa Fe.
2. Ibid., p. 137, fig. 274.

54. Dollhouse chair

1860
Micmac peoples, Nova Scotia or northern New Brunswick
Wood, birchbark, porcupine quill
7 x 4 ⅛ x 5 ⅛ in. (17.8 x 10.5 x 13 cm)
RTCNA 287

Micmac women excelled at quilling panels and seats for insertion into full-size chairs (see cat. no. 53).[1] Less commonly seen are miniature versions of such chairs, only a few inches high but quilled in a like manner and accompanied by tiny tables (here missing), also quilled. While these were made for children's dollhouses, adults were also delighted by their charm. Undoubtedly, this chair was part of a set. The toy frame is typically of midcentury Canadian manufacture, and while it lacks a quilled seat back, the heart shape of the open support preserves Victorian sentiment. Such pieces may also have served as salesmen's examples, and they recall other miniature items, such as the silver services that were part of the Victorian scene.

1. For one of the finest surviving full-size chairs, with the quillwork in excellent condition, though the chair frame is later than the date ascribed by the author, see Ewing 1982, p. 379, no. 464.

| 55. Pouch |

1800–1820
Micmac/Iroquois peoples, Quebec or Canadian Maritimes
Wool and cotton trade cloth, silk ribbon,
glass and cut-brass beads
6 ¾ x 6 ¼ in. (17.1 x 15.9 cm)
RTCNA 291

This exceptional and very early beaded pouch might have
been placed in a domestic setting as a decorative feature in
a corner cabinet. On festive occasions, it would have been
used as an ornamental accessory by the lady of the house.
This type of pouch initiates a plethora of such fancies that
become increasingly colorful and bold in design up until the
1890s. They were made by various Northeast tribes, such as
the Micmac, Maliseet, Mohegan, Huron, and Iroquois.

The present example has a delicacy of design that retains
a kind of eighteenth-century feeling. The motifs, multiple
borders and garlands across the top and a quatrilobe floral
element, act in concert with musical precision.[1] On the
reverse, the garlands change to looped swags and the central
motif becomes a series of chevrons, each of the triangular
lines of beads a counterpoint to the six-sided shape of the bag.

1. For a twentieth-century example of this same four-petal design as it
spread to the north coast of the Gulf of St. Lawrence, see the
Montaignais winter moccasins "of European inspiration" illustrated
in Simard and Bouchard 1977, p. 231. Lobed motifs figure in different
ways on the lids of Micmac quilled boxes and gaming pieces; see
Whitehead 1982, p. 138, fig. 276.

| 56. Pair of mittens |

ca. 1850–60
Cree or Cree/Métis peoples, Manitoba
Native-tanned skin, silk ribbon and thread
Each 9 ¼ x 5 ⅝ in. (23.5 x 14.3 cm)
RTCNA 505a, b

| 57. Panel bag |

ca. 1840
Cree/Métis peoples, southern Manitoba
Native-tanned skin, porcupine quill, glass beads, metal
13 x 7 ¼ in. (33 x 18.4 cm)
RTCNA 504

Both the pair of mittens and the panel bag shown here draw
on a common heritage—that of the Cree/Métis peoples of
Manitoba. In general, bags from the upper Great Lakes and
its prairie borders are descended from an earlier form that,
in its verticality, is ascribed to the eighteenth century. Most
of these rare vertical bags have survived in French collections,
having been brought by the French to the New World. In
the early to mid-nineteenth century, settlements along the
Red River valley in Canada, in the present-day Winnipeg–
Fort Selkirk area, developed two types of bag. The firebag,
which is purely Indian in origin (cat. no. 117), and the panel
bag. The chief decoration of the latter is a beadwork panel

at the bottom that originated among the Métis, peoples of mixed Indian and Scottish heritage. Métis bags like this one are as close to a European aesthetic as to a Native American one. The designs on the panel recall folk art with such subjects as weeping willows and vases of flowers, and the beadwork is more like stitchery, with a touch of the "sampler" about it. The doeskin panel is as soft as a European purse, and the delicately quilled floral motifs, while Indian in technique, have the mellifluousness of an arabesque.

Except for their somewhat later date, the Métis mittens could have accompanied the bag.[1] However, the chain-stitched flower embroidery and the ribbon appliqué cuffs owe something to the Ojibwa/Ottawa tradition as well as to the Cree/Métis.

1. Another highly decorated pair of mittens of the same type is in the Fenimore Art Museum in Cooperstown, New York. See Vincent, Brydon, and Coe 2000, p. 167, fig. T94.

58. Pincushion

Mid-19th century
Huron peoples, Wendake (Lorette), Quebec
Wool and silk trade cloth, glass beads, moosehair
Height 2 ½ in. (6.4 cm); diameter 9 in. (22.9 cm)
RTCNA 294

By the mid-nineteenth century, an element of whimsy enters into the fashioning of objects for domestic use. Their functions become increasingly subordinate to the Victorian demand for decorative display pieces that stand on their own as accessories for showy interiors. Huron artisans thus felt encouraged to exercise imagination over practicality. This large pincushion is an embodiment of this trend, leaving one to wonder where a pin would be placed in such an elaborately designed surface. An eclectic vocabulary developed that became as effusive as was necessary to meet the fantasies of non-Native consumers. In this particularly striking Huron example, it is possible to discern two different stylistic approaches. One reflects the efflorescence of late-Victorian taste. The other harks back to the "botanical" style of about twenty years earlier. Ruth B. Phillips notes these two styles in her pioneering study of nineteenth-century Eastern Woodlands souvenir art. She also cites a pincushion that is so close to the present example that it is either by the same hand or from the same Huron cottage industry.[1]

While the dripping looped fringes and eight-lobed border are beaded in the heavy piled Seneca/Iroquois style, the central floral motifs are embroidered against a red background, with moosehair in a noticeably more delicate Huron style. This contrast between the inner and outer fields pushes harmony and consistency to the limit, denoting the emergence of high Victorian flamboyance.

1. Phillips 1998, color section, pl. 33.

| 59. Letter case |

1835–40
Huron peoples, Wendake (Lorette), Quebec
Birchbark, silk trade cloth, moosehair
Each 7 ¼ x 10 ½ in. (18.4 x 26.7 cm)
RTCNA 303a, b

This domestic fancy and the two that follow (cat. nos. 60, 61) serve as an interesting commentary on the response of Huron artisans to the non-Native demand for souvenir art. One of the resources the convent-trained Huron women relied on to keep abreast of the market was a familiarity with British and European pattern books and fashion. This cross-cultural interchange is reflected in the similarity between English calling card cases and those made by French-Canadian Indian women. The English cases are of silk embroidery floss rather than moosehair, but both customarily include a floriated border with a flowering sprig in the center.[1] This compositional format and even the embroidery style are clearly related to the Huron letter case shown here. The spatial relationships in the English design scheme are maintained almost exactly in this larger Native-made version, although the feeling is quite different. The English version is "prettier," more sentimental; the Huron examples are more graphic, show greater technical and organizational mastery, and are more accurate in floral detailing, much like a botanical engraving from a generation or so earlier. The Huron artisan is closer to nature, which makes her statement more powerful, while the English prototype is more courtly, and answers to grace-and-favor.

1. Phillips 1998, p. 238, no. 6.42.

60. Tray

ca. 1860
Huron peoples, Wendake (Lorette), Quebec
Birchbark, moosehair
8 ¾ x 12 in. (22.2 x 30.5 cm)
RTCNA 323

Dating to about 1860, this single tray marks a stylistic progression from the earlier letter case (cat. no. 59) and acknowledges, to a greater degree, English design preference. Here, arabesque-like curlicues and blossoms flow rhythmically into the leaves. Observation of nature becomes less acute and more decorative, indicating a savvy awareness of the market for which it was produced. The sides of the tray are raised and angled at the corners, achieving a compartmentalization that is purely Victorian.

61. Pair of trays

Late 19th century
Huron peoples, Wendake (Lorette), Quebec
Birchbark, moosehair, cotton trade cloth
Each 8 ½ x 8 ½ in. (21.6 x 21.6 cm)
RTCNA 325a, b

This pair of square trays marks the end of the stylistic development seen in the preceding letter case and tray (cat. nos. 59, 60). The undulating borders are of high-style Victorian complexity, comparable to elaborate Rococo Revival nineteenth-century mirror frames such as were hung over many American and English mantels of the period. They encircle a number of standard motifs—the smoker, the perching bird, women at work. The smoker motif has been carried over from earlier in the century, but here has been simplified and made more formulaic (see cat. no. 62).

62. Card case

Mid- to late 19th century
Huron peoples, Wendake (Lorette), Quebec
Birchbark, moosehair, cotton trade cloth
4 x 2 ¾ in. (10.2 x 7 cm)
RTCNA 288

Card cases based on Euro-American examples were a staple, in fact part of the bread and butter, of northeastern American souvenir art.[1] Many were adorned with floral designs on cloth backing over birchbark. Others were quilled directly on the birchbark. The most elegant of this type were constructed from the soft, inner layer of the bark and finely stitched along the edge with cotton thread over bunched moosehair. Bird or porcupine quills were dyed and then used for the figural subjects. Representations of smokers with pipes were favorite motifs, repeated over and again. A bird in full song appears on the upper panel, while below, a gentleman enjoys a smoke. On the reverse (not shown) are two more pipe smokers, one seated, on the upper panel, and one standing below. All are wearing European-influenced dress.

The pristine condition of this small case, with colors surely as fresh as the day it was made, suggests that it was rarely used and carefully stored away. Cases such as these are difficult to date precisely, for they were made over a long period of time, from before the mid-nineteenth century almost to the beginning of the twentieth.

1. Phillips 1998, p. 239, no. 6.44.

63. Glengarry cap

ca. 1840
Huron peoples, Wendake (Lorette), Quebec
Wool velvet and silk trade cloth, silk ribbon, moosehair
4 x 11 ¼ x 6 ⅛ in. (10.2 x 28.6 x 15.6 cm)
RTCNA 324

While British sovereignty took hold in Canada following the French and Indian War (1754–63), French culture continued to thrive. The British Army included the Scottish Glengarry Regiment, whose dress uniform was distinguished by the unique form of cap seen here. Huron Indian girls, instructed by French nuns in French embroidery techniques, later adapted them as a field for their embroidery art.

Most of these caps were sold to British residents and visitors as souvenirs of their stay in Canada, and many were taken back to England and Scotland as reminders of their own heritage, with the exotic element of "Indianness" added. To this day, most of these caps are found in attics and antiques shops in the British Isles. This black velvet cap, for example, was discovered in the English countryside as late as the 1970s. The floral displays on the side panels and top reflect both the Huron closeness to nature and the tasteful elegance of the moosehair embroidery style at its apogee. The effect is softer and silkier than in the case of the earlier, embroidered black leather moccasins (cat. no. 128), also of Huron workmanship.

64. Cap

Late 19th century
Micmac peoples, Nova Scotia or northern New Brunswick
Cotton velvet, silk ribbon, glass beads
6 ½ x 10 in. (16.5 x 25.4 cm)
RTCNA 307

Traditional Micmac caps worn by women were cut on the pattern of a Breton cap. In the later part of the nineteenth century, an inspired Micmac woman at Richibucto, New Brunswick, departed from the standard shape and made a group of beaded caps composed of six panels, modeled after a European deerstalker. The type piece, made by Mary Ann Geneace, is at the New Brunswick Museum, St. John.[1] It is probable, but not certain, that she also made the cap shown here. Not only are the spade-shaped leaves strikingly similar, but the back panel is almost a duplicate in reverse. A beaded cross motif is on the visor of the New Brunswick cap, while this one shows a six-petal design to exactly the same scale in the same location. A small, floral beaded bag, in the Eugene V. Thaw collection, attributed to the Niantic or Mohegan tribe in Connecticut, has leaf designs and a flower petal almost identical to those on these two Micmac caps.[2]

1. Harrison et al. 1987, p. 47, fig. 38 (exh. cat. ed., p. 23, no. E.53).
2. Vincent, Brydon, and Coe 2000, p. 89, no. T679.

65. Mounted legging panels

ca. 1870
Eastern Cree peoples, Quebec
Wool trade cloth, glass beads, wood frame
19 ½ x 11 ½ in. (49.5 x 29.2 cm)
RTCNA 333

This pair of vertically mounted legging strips, beaded in eastern Cree floral style, evidently never fulfilled their intended function as Indian fancy wear. Rather, they were set side by side in a wood frame and adapted as a decoration for an English domestic interior. They quietly made their way to the same London antiques shop as the Slavey shelf valance (cat. no. 66) and were purchased in recognition of their reappearance as a Euro–Native American curiosity. The plainness of the frame indicates that it is either English or provincial Canadian in origin. The assemblage of frame and panels exemplifies a curious blending of the Old World with the New during the years of settlement. Its nostalgic appeal has only increased over the passing years.

| 66. Valance |

Late 19th–early 20th century
Slavey peoples, lower Mackenzie River
Cotton velvet, silk ribbon, glass beads
7 x 32 ¼ in. (17.8 x 81.9 cm)
RTCNA 500

Beaded and scalloped valances were typically made to decorate the wall shelves of traders' or trappers' living quarters in settlements along the lower Mackenzie River valley, which extends northward from the Great Slave Lake to the Barents Sea (Arctic Ocean). They added a welcome accent of warmth to the interiors of the log or board homes, whose occupants rarely ventured far afield—except to trade—in the desolate winter landscape of the frozen north. In her excellent study on northern Athabaskan art, Kate C. Duncan reproduces a photograph of a Hudson's Bay Company post manager and his wife in their Mackenzie River home, about 1906–12, with two Indian-made valances hanging from shelves on the wall.[1] Shelf valances were also produced by the Gwitchin Indians of Old Crow Village, Yukon, and Fort Yukon, Alaska. These were often enhanced by fringes and more complicated flower designs. But the combination of yellow, white, blue, and red beads seen here harmonizes in a way recognized more as Mackenzie Slavey than as Gwitchin, whose taste ran to pastel pink, lemon green, pearly white, and ice blue (see cat. no. 149).

This valance made its way to England, where it surfaced three years ago at Kensington, Church Street, in an antiquarian shop owned by John and Valerie Arieta, the same source for the mounted leggings acquired a couple years earlier (cat. no. 65). Despite the gentle relief of its colored floral beadwork, this modest attempt to add a note of gaiety to the bleakness of a harsh existence expresses the fragility of life in the Indian far north.

1. Duncan 1989, p. 103.

67. Lady's hat

1890–1920
Abenaki peoples (?), New Hampshire or adjacent Canada
Brown ash splint
Height 6 ½ in. (16.5 cm); diameter 12 in. (30.5 cm)
RTCNA 73

This fanciful tour de force of technical virtuosity shows the application of a medium once reserved for purely functional basketry, such as trunks and storage containers, to a lady's woven hat of brown ash splint. The Abenaki, who once inhabited south-central New England, were pushed northward by colonial incursion in the eighteenth century; they live today in southeastern Quebec, Maine, and New Hampshire. While they inhabited the backwoods, they made up for their quasi isolation by the exercise of a refined sense of decorativeness in their basketry.

An extraordinary example of the lengths to which Abenaki weavers could go is well illustrated in this almost overrefined, masterly rendition of a woman's fancy dress hat.

Was this hat made to be worn? Or was it a basket weaver's fantasy? The latter possibility is suggested by a diminutive hat, which came to light subsequent to this one's appearing on the market, that was of decorative value only and surely made by the same weaver. One could picture either of these two hats on a Victorian mantelpiece or this one displayed on an old-fashioned hat stand as a sort of visual pun. Ann McMullen dates the present hat to the beginning of the twentieth century and describes its attribution to the Abenaki as "certainly a good bet."[1]

1. Personal communication from Ann McMullen, June 2, 2002.

V

WEAPONS

Glorifying Combat

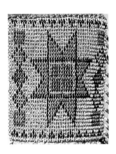

| 68. Club (skullcracker) |

1850–60
Assiniboine peoples, Montana or adjacent Canada
Stone, wood, rawhide, sinew, paint, feathers
23 ½ x 4 ½ in. (59.7 x 11.4 cm)
RTCNA 396

| 69. Club (skullcracker) |

1870–75
Central Plains Sioux peoples, North or South Dakota
Stone, wood, rawhide, sinew
26 ½ x 5 in. (67.3 x 12.7 cm)
RTCNA 397

Both these clubs were made for combat. They feature long handles completely encased in rawhide and are of uncompromising military aspect. The implacable, bellicose stare of the "face" club, embodies the bravery and belligerence of its warrior owner, who brandished it about 1850–60. Its large eyes and startling green paint (now much faded) announced confrontation that brooked no retreat. Originally, horsehair or feathers—or both—protruded from the terminal, enhancing the dynamic sweep of the design. Water was probably used not only to tighten the handle's grasp but also to make sure that the stone was held within a seamless grip. When the trader Bill Hawn of Santa Fe and Hawaii obtained this piece, he was told that it was unquestionably Assiniboine in origin and probably from the Fort Belknap Reservation. The reservation was settled by both Assiniboine and Gros Ventre tribes considerably after this object—a family heirloom—was made.

Like the Fort Belknap club, the Sioux example, at right, is also from the combat period, but probably later. The elliptical shape is typical of clubs from the Central Plains. The classic type is symmetrical, with a point at either end. This example is more complex. The elliptical portion is surmounted and almost obscured by a mountain-ram's head, with curving horns dovetailed into the stone, which rises out from the main body like a harbinger of the lethal impact to come. Atop the head is a casque of crystals—probably representing the sheep's wool—that shows a remarkably adaptive use of the geode (a hollow stone lined with crystal) from which the club is fashioned. The club was obtained from the Santa Fe gallery owner Forest Fenn, one of the first dealers to raise the acquisition of American Indian art to a level commensurate with that of other cultural endeavors. From time to time, he would unexpectedly bring forth objects from his monumental collection and randomly make them available. On one of these occasions, in 1990, I was fortunate enough to acquire this formidable weapon.

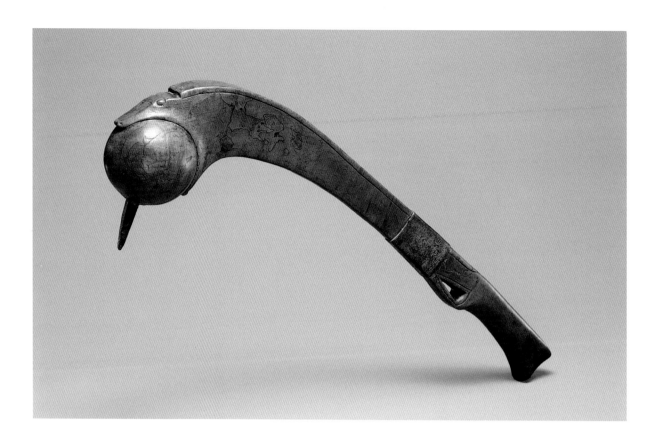

| 70. Ball-headed club |

Late 18th century
Western Great Lakes, collected in Minnesota
Wood, metal
18 ½ x 6 in. (47 x 15.2 cm)
RTCNA 268

Design and function are here integrated with a refinement that makes this ball-headed club exceptional. Many Great Lakes and Plains clubs are carved without a sense of balance or with the ball head proportionately outsize. Such carvings were fit for bludgeoning but not for rapier-like dispatch. This one is perfectly balanced for a quick, decisive thrust. It has a grim, purposeful beauty perfectly geared to express the values of a highly militarized society.

According to the Santa Fe dealer James Economos, who sold me this club in 1988, it was found in Minnesota. It is from the western Great Lakes area, probably at its juncture with the Plains. It is distinguished by a narrow, yet strong, profile—taut but slightly arched, to further its forward thrust—which served in aiding its wielder to reach the designated enemy. The ball

is tightly clenched in the gaping jaws of an otter; whether it is being gripped or disgorged is hard to say, so tenacious is the tension maintained. Feathers were once tied to the triangular hollow located just above the grip, not only to serve as decoration but also to increase the efficacy of the weapon by calling up supernatural powers. The iron spike that at its base splays into seven stars evokes the four cardinal directions and forms the circle of the universe, a subtle but effective way to call upon such powers. While the veteran collector Richard A. Pohrt Sr. has noted that there were probably Indian blacksmiths on the Plains, more often a non-Native blacksmith was tapped to forge the spikes for these clubs.[1]

1. Pohrt 1989, p. 96.

71. Pipe tomahawk

1840–60
Ojibwa peoples (?), Minnesota or Wisconsin
Wood, metal
18 x 10 ⅛ in. (45.7 x 25.7 cm)
RTCNA 275

For information on this pipe tomahawk, we again turn to Richard A. Pohrt Sr., who writes: "It is not certain when the pipe tomahawk was first introduced, but it appears to have been sometime during the first half of the eighteenth century. . . . There is a strong possibility that the pipe tomahawk was first manufactured by a blacksmith in America. . . . We also cannot discount the possibility that an Indian, who was familiar with metal working or serving as an apprentice to a blacksmith, first engineered the pipe tomahawk."[1] The use of this implement continued long after the colonial wars and was much used at tribal celebrations. Even today, commercial examples are made for Indian parade purposes. According to Pohrt, the pipe tomahawk, which was originally associated with close hand-to-hand combat, was no longer needed in warfare after about 1870,

when it became a parade and ceremonial symbol and was often larger in size than this one.

The present example is a transitional work. It is old enough—1840 to 1860—to exhibit the sturdy workmanship of earlier types and retains something of the early elementary style, but the constellation pattern hammered into the basal flange borders on the later, more decorative style. Several pipe tomahawks with similar celestial designs on the blade are known. In addition, the long wood handle is traditional in style—what an Indian friend of mine calls "straight stuff." The blade was perhaps fashioned by an Indian smith, or perhaps it was provided by a non-Native to a tribal band at its request.

1. Pohrt 1989, p. 96.

72. Knife case

ca. 1843
Ojibwa peoples, Minnesota
Native-tanned skin, glass beads, silk ribbon, wool yarn
12 ½ x 2 ¾ in. (31.8 x 7 cm)
RTCNA 238

This elegantly beaded knife case is nearly identical to a case in the Denver Art Museum that was included in the seminal 1965 exhibition "American Indian Art Before 1850," curated by Norman Feder.[1] The museum's case displays the date 1843 with the initials RDB embroidered at the top. Feder notes that the Ojibwa in the 1840–60 period commonly applied dates to their work.

In support of Feder's argument for an Ojibwa attribution, the initials RDB refer to a member of the well-known Boyd family still prominent in Isle, Minnesota, at the southeastern edge of Mille Lacs Lake. These two cases would appear to be by the same maker. The diamond and square devices along either border of the beaded panel shown here are akin to those on the Denver Museum's case, but the eight-pointed star motif differs slightly in that its center is not a bisected rectangle but rather a square with a cross of red beads that divides it into four squares.

1. Feder 1965, no. 24.

73. Dagger

1850–60

Tlingit peoples, southeastern Alaska

Wood, steel, abalone-shell inlay, ivory, Native-tanned skin

14 ¾ x 2 ¾ 1 in. (37.5 x 7 cm)

RTCNA 160a, b

The Metropolitan Museum of Art,

Gift of Ralph T. Coe, 2002 (2002.602.4)

Sheath

1850–60

Tahltan peoples, British Columbia

Wool and cotton trade cloth, glass, metal beads

26 ½ x 3 ⅛ in. (66 x 7.9 cm)

The Metropolitan Museum of Art,

Gift of Ralph T. Coe, 2002 (2002.602.5)

This dagger has long been associated with the accompanying Tahltan (Athabaskan) beadwork sheath. Both bear the same accession number, and they were auctioned together at Sotheby's, in 1998, by the collector-connoisseur Adelaide de Menil.[1] They were subsequently purchased from the Alaska on Madison Gallery in New York the following year.

Attribution of the dagger is certainly Tlingit. Bill Holm, in his book *Indian Art of the Northwest Coast,* describes it as either Tlingit or carved by the Tahltan at or near their community at Telegraph Hill, situated at the top of the mountain chain that separates the Alaska Panhandle from the interior of British Columbia.[2] The confusion arises from the fact that the Tahltan maintain crests and there is a long history of commerce and intermarriage between the two groups. It is suggested here that the dagger is in all probability Tlingit in origin and its pommel made from a walnut gun stock, as Bill Holm posits. In his monograph on the Tahltan,

the greatest early authority on Tlingit culture and the leading field collector of Tlingit art, George T. Emmons, states: "Spears, knives, bows and arrows were their weapons. Of these accoutrements nothing remains but the war knives and most of these, judging from the fine workmanship and elaborately carved ornamental heads, are of Tlingit manufacture."[3]

The cylindrical nostrils of the bear, the forward-curving eyebrows, and the upward slant of the abalone-shell inlaid mouth lend to the dagger an impressive aura of warlike aggressiveness. The sheath offers a totally different aesthetic, quiet and serene. The curvilinearity of the beadwork appliqué is in the finest classic Tahltan style.

1. Sotheby's, New York, December 2, 1998, sale no. 7228, lot 445.
2. Both the knife and the sheath are discussed in Holm and Reid (1975) 1978, no. 11.
3. Emmons 1911, p. 14.

74. Knife and case

ca. 1870
Assiniboine peoples, Montana or adjacent Canada
Native-tanned skin, rawhide, glass beads, porcupine quill
Knife: 9 x 1 in. (22.9 x 2.5 cm)
Case: 9 x 2 ¾ in. (22.9 x 7 cm)
RTCNA 674a, b

In the spring of 2002, I bought this northwestern Plains beaded knife sheath from the dealer John Molloy, of Santa Fe and New York. It was equipped with a hand-forged knife and a handle equally "home made," its parts joined by a socket made from a brass shell casing. While the majority of knives found with beaded knife cases are not the original, this one, if not the original, was probably made about the same time, circa 1870. The case's paired arrow or beaded triangular motifs in seven vertical registers are totally compatible with Assiniboine design, while the eccentric color harmonies of blue, mustard yellow, and white reinforce the unconventional Assiniboine taste in colors. The typically Assiniboine simplicity of design seems to point to a pre-reservation date, when the migration of the Assiniboine bands through the parklands of western Canada on their way to the Missouri River valley was on the wane.

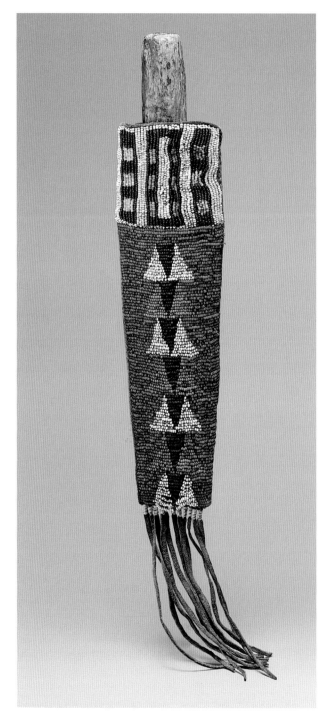

VI

RITUAL OBJECTS AND IMAGERY

Agents of the Spirit World

| *75. Objects from a man's business bundle* |

ca. 1790–1880s

Mesquakie or Potawatomi peoples, probably Tama, Iowa

Wood, birchbark, Native-tanned skin, glass beads, wool yarn, feathers, porcupine quill

Maximum height 12 ¼ in. (31.1 cm)

RTCNA 230a–f

Objects from the Great Lakes area quite often appear on the ethnological art market as individual pieces, outside the context for which they were made. In their isolation, their meaning as affiliated interacting symbols of religious or spiritual significance is fragmentary at best, and often lost altogether. While these six objects from a medicine bundle, preserved together in England, may not form a complete set, they nonetheless afford us invaluable insight into the ways objects in business bundles might have been assembled. The

objects would have been packaged together in a wrapper, now missing. Anyone who has been fortunate enough to open the back of a small Buddhist bronze and see the sutras and tracts within come to light will understand what unwrapping the contents of a bundle would have meant in the spiritual context of Native American tradition.

Each of the objects in this business bundle served to aid a different aspect of a man's search for prowess in male affairs. The most immediately striking is a charm bag woven with red and white glass seed beads, with a dramatic underwater panther design in red against a white field. The vertical horns of the panther signify his supernatural role, and having his cooperation would have assured spiritual power for the owner. The small wood doll, clearly male, symbolizes success in love; the birchbark cylinder to the left originally fit over the body like a sheath. The figure's great age is attested by the fact that extensive wearing of his cylinder in ceremonial usage has effected a change in the patina. The wool yarn charm bag no longer has its original contents, but the miniature vertical feather insignia symbolizes chiefly status or preeminence in leadership. It is the oldest object in the bundle and may well date to the eighteenth century. The panther charm bag may date to as late as the 1880s.

76. Bowl and bag from a medicine bundle

1850–60

Winnebago peoples, collected in Winnebago, Nebraska

Bowl: Wood, diameter 5 in. (12.7 cm)

Bag: Wool yarn, Native-tanned skin ties

3 x 3 ¾ in. (7.6 x 9.5 cm)

RTCNA 229a, b

A number of small, crafted bird-effigy bowls for personal healing used as containers for medicine, dating well back into the mid-nineteenth century, surface occasionally from the Indian Great Lakes and Prairie regions. This one, with a rich patina, was accompanied by a twined bag of extremely early date. When the late James Howard, a noted Oklahoma anthropologist whose specialty was Prairie and Plains culture, was in London at the "Sacred Circles" exhibition in 1976, he described to me a curing medicine bundle he might be willing to part with. Upon his return he wrote to me, offering one from the Nebraska Winnebago. "It belonged to the late Mrs. Green Rainbow, a native herbalist. This outfit

contains two items that, though utilitarian, are exquisite objets d'arts in their own right. The yarn bag is done in the very finest twine technique, with very delicate colors. The wooden medicine bowl has a a stylized bird's head as a handle, reminiscent of the Mississippian archaeological culture."[1]

Professor Howard had acquired these objects, together with accompanying medicine pouches, from a Mr. Sterling Whitesnake in 1964. They had been found by Mr. Whitesnake hidden behind a wall when he moved into a dwelling about two miles east of Winnebago. He found, in addition, an otter-skin medicine bag that Mrs. Green Rainbow also owned and which she probably used in a Winnebago

medicine ceremony that is related to that of the Ojibwa Midewiwin medicine lodge. As Professor Howard observed, bowls of this type recall late, pre-contact Mississippian ceramics, thus suggesting a continuity from prehistoric times to the recent past not often cited in Great Lakes literature.

The motifs on the yarn bag are a mainstay of Winnebago design. They also embellish the pair of Winnebago woman's moccasins in this catalogue (cat. no. 131), on which there is a similar beaded pattern of discrete triangles and diamonds layered in registers across the front.

1. Personal communication from James Howard, 1976.

| 77. Charm bag |

ca. 1875
Ojibwa peoples, Minnesota or adjacent Canada
Wool yarn, plant fiber
7 x 8 in. (17.8 x 20.3 cm)
RTCNA 231

In the late nineteenth century, the Great Lakes tribes developed a technique of weaving commodious bags from spools of commercial wool yarn. The technique traveled quickly, and they were soon made in locations from Minnesota all the way down to Oklahoma. In a sense, they are the Great Lakes and Prairie equivalent of the Plains possibles bag (see cat. no. 125). Miniature versions were made to hold personal charms. The most elaborate were executed in fine beadwork and many depict the mythical underwater panther (see also cat. no. 75). These supernatural creatures dwelt in the streams and small lakes of the Midwest. They could wreak havoc with their gaze, but if subdued, they could be powerful allies. This whole bag is, in effect, a conceptualized panther, as the overall diamond pattern that frames the panther image on the front and entirely covers the back represents a panther's spots. Held in the hand, the bag was a talisman of personal power for its owner.

| *78. Staff* |

Mid-19th century
Potawatomi peoples, Wisconsin
Wood, Native-tanned skin, deer dewclaws
12 x 3 in. (30.5 x 7.6 cm)
RTCNA 319

While medicine staffs from the Three Fires (the Ojibwa, Potawatomi, and Ottawa peoples) are usually rather plainly carved, with a flat, featureless animal image at the top, greater care was taken among the Potawatomi, who made handsome three-dimensional staffs, also known as ritual shaking sticks. This example, one of the very few graced with a delicately rendered human face, probably represents a manitou, or guardian spirit. It has an attached leather collar, tanned by rubbing animal brains into the stretched hide to soften it, from which hang split thongs laced through deer dewclaw rattles. The head is set off by roach headgear, and the hairline and top of the head show traces of old paint. This venerable staff was used primarily as a musical instrument to accompany ceremony and song, as shaking it activates the sound of the dewclaws.

It is one of a pair known to have belonged to a Potawatomi chief. The documentation states that Odie Munn, who, with her father, operated a trading post at Rhinelander or Tomahawk, Wisconsin, sold it to the collector Richard McCallister (the year is not known).[1] Its mate is in the collection of the Wisconsin Historical Society, Madison.

1. Personal communication from Toby Herbst, Santa Fe, 2002.

| 79. Miniature club |

ca. 1860
Penobscot peoples, Maine
Painted root
7 ⅓ x 3 ⅛ in. (19.1 x 7.9 cm)
RTCNA 281

This tiny, but fully realized, miniature club may once have been part of a religious bundle of objects invested with spiritual power. It is a facsimile of the full-size root club originally used by northern New England tribes for combat, and later for ceremonial purposes. After the upper New England shores and rivers became a noted destination for vacationers in the late nineteenth century, the full-size club was developed into an elaborate Indian symbol, which was offered to outsiders but was also used by Native Americans at parades and patriotic celebrations as preferred regalia. Selling these clubs became a road to economic survival for the Passamaquoddy and the Penobscot of Maine. Still masterfully carved today, the large versions remain an important display at tribal celebrations.

In size this miniature club is unique. Indeed, it may be the only northern New England medicine charm of its type extant. It came to light unexpectedly in a Santa Fe antiquarian shop, The Rainbow Man, in the late 1980s.

| 80. Prescription stick |

Early 19th century
Prairie Potawatomi peoples, Kansas
Incised wood, paint
1 ⅝ x 6 in. (4.1 x 15.2 cm)
RTCNA 235

James Kagmega gave me this small Potawatomi prescription stick not long before he died. A noted Potawatomi culturalist, he also served in the U.S. Army as a German interpreter during the Second World War. He stayed at my apartment in Kansas City on a number of occasions, when he would arrive, unannounced, like a materialized spirit.

When I visited James Kagmega at his home in Mayetta, Kansas, in the late 1970s, on one of the last occasions I saw him, he took this prescription stick out from underneath his bed and presented it to me. Undoubtedly, it had belonged to his people for many years and may be one of the oldest on record. A full-size pair of prescription sticks from the same

tribe are today in the Nelson-Atkins Museum of Art, Kansas City.[1] James kindly identified these sticks when I first visited him, about 1972.

The esoteric information on such a stick is not the business of outsiders. The plant forms here seem to appear to signify the ingredients of medicine recipes. Other sticks have dots or striped, polelike designs that indicate the intervals between prescriptions; they probably also contain mnemonic indications for songs or litanies.

1. Coe 1976a, p. 99, no. 162.

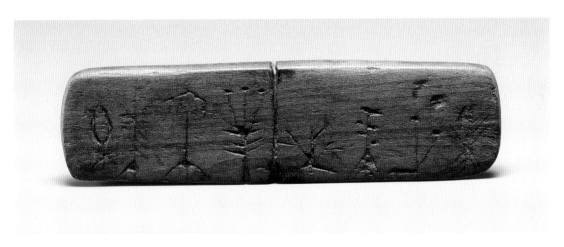

81. Tupilak

1900 or earlier
Eskimo peoples, eastern Greenland
2 ½ x 5 ¾ in. (6.4 x 14.6 cm)
Painted wood, bone inlay
RTCNA 622

In the 1880s, a group of Danish ethnologists exploring eastern Greenland came across the sad village of Angmagssalik, now called Tasiilaq. Most of the inhabitants had been killed off by starvation and disease. Those who remained were asked to make carvings, visual evidence of their culture, so that it could be seen and appreciated by the outside world. Among the earliest carvings that have survived is a group of small tupilak figures of dark wood. Most of these are today preserved in the Danish National Museum, Copenhagen.

The only figure in the group known to have come to the United States is this one, which was originally brought to light in the late 1970s or early 1980s by the London dealer-conservator Marvin Chasen, who found it at one of the London ethnological street markets in Portobello Road, Bermondsey, or Camden Passage.

Tupilak spirit monsters circulate unseen, but to eastern Greenland Eskimos they are incarnations of evil. Evidently, figures such as this one were made for the ethnologists to render visible the tiny tupilak monsters. Since then, eastern Greenland carvers have made scores of these little creatures for sale to tourists and other visitors. Often, they are of ivory and can occur in sets. Later tupilaks are equipped with bases. As a whole, the later varieties are more self-consciously artistic than the rare, early examples such as this one, so stark and threatening in appearance.[1]

1. For an example of a tupilak carved in 1957, see Meldgaard 1960, fig. 56.

| *82. Effigy puppet* |

Late 19th century
Yup'ik peoples, Kuskokwim/Yukon River delta, western Alaska
Painted wood, shell bead inlay, commercial cord
15 ½ x 3 ½ in. (39.4 x 8.9 cm)
RTCNA 608

This charming puppet is a classic example of the theatrical apparatus with which the Eskimo *angakok* (shamans) of western Alaska impressed an audience in performances that typically took place inside the *kashim,* or village dance house.[1] The shaman, in a trance state, would operate the puppet by moving the detached handle, vividly illustrating his own mythical journey to the bottom of the sea and his subsequent ascent to the real world on the back of a seal ally. On his return from his trance state, the shaman would tell of the wonders he had seen, thereby reinforcing his command of shamanic powers right in front of his attentive audience. On this puppet, the shaman can readily be spotted atop the supernatural seal.

There is a certain whimsical sense of fantasy evident in this charming puppet that would have softened the seriousness of the performance. The entertainment served not only to retain the audience's attention but also to curry its appreciation of the shaman's supernatural powers, thus securing future business. Only an expert shaman could continue to captivate his onlookers and supplicants and in this way keep up with his rivals. Rather than eliciting fear and trepidation, as did shamans in other parts of the far north, those of Alaska created a generally benign, almost folksy theater, exemplified by this representation of the shaman himself, carried endlessly through oceans and skies on the back of his seal familiar.

1. A model *kashim,* with a ceremony in progress, is illustrated in Collins 1973, p. 93, no. 132.

83. Tamanous pole

Late 19th–early 20th century
Salish (Quinault, Quileute, or Klallam) peoples,
Olympic Peninsula, Washington
Painted wood
122 x 14 x 13 in. (309.9 x 35.6 x 33 cm)
RTCNA 598

One of the least studied areas of Northwest Coast sculpture, deserving of more attention than it has heretofore been accorded, is the impressive corpus of tamanous poles and boards from the northern Olympic Peninsula shore extending along the west coast southward as far as the Quinault and Quileute tribal areas. Little is recorded about the meaning of these monumental sculptures. The nineteenth-century missionary Myron Eells, during his long service among the Puget Sound Indians, described them as receptacles "in which the spirits are believed to dwell; or which [are] sometimes used in performing their incantations."[1] But he was never more specific about their meaning. Even the translation of the word "tamanous" remains elusive. This pole is rotted along the back of the head, neck, and shoulders, which may indicate that it was placed against the outside of a longhouse, under the projecting eaves that channeled water and decay. Tamanous poles were the personal property of individuals. The owner was safeguarded by the protective tamanous spirits who lived within and who protected him against illness and danger.

The relief-carved, clownlike face on this pole relates directly to other representations of guardian spirits or power figures also from the Salish area of the Northwest Coast. Above the face, a spirit bird thrusts upward. Its swelling form reminds one of ceremonial handheld rattles from the same area. Greatly enlarged for theatrical impact, the ascending guardian bird brings this monumental sculpture to an unexpected visual climax.

The pole dates well back into the nineteenth century. It was bought by Mr. and Mrs. Marc A. Franklin of San Francisco from James Flury of Seattle, who stated that he had purchased it from a private institution, Marsh's Free Museum, in Long Beach, Washington. In turn, Marsh was said to have acquired it from the "original owner" in the 1950s, along with a full-size canoe whose location is now unknown.[2] The Canadian artist Paul Kane (active ca. 1850) made a painting of a similar carving attributed to the Klallam Indians near Port Angeles, Washington. Thus, it is also possible that the north coast of the Olympic Peninsula was the site of origin.[3]

1. Ruby and Brown 1976, p. 62.
2. Invoice from Marc A. Franklin to Ralph T. Coe, 2001.
3. Sturtevant and Suttles 1990, p. 538, fig. 3.

84. Transformation puppet

Late 18th–early 19th century
Tlingit peoples, southeastern Alaska
Bone, sinew, abalone-shell inlay, plant fiber
Height 6 ½ in. (16.5 cm)
RTCNA 147

This small, articulated transformation puppet is thus far unique in the entire corpus of Tlingit art. Aggressive in its iconography, it is a chilling tour de force of manipulative artistry. With gritting teeth and bony sockets in its skull, the masked face is as haunting as it is macabre. The tiny abalone-shell eyes peer at us intensely, emerging from a world suspended between life and death. The exquisitely crafted rattles in each hand are miniatures of full-size rattles used during a shamanic performance.

The puppet must have been held in the hand at the back. By pulling the sinew strings, the shaman-operator would open the chest cavity to reveal a tiny raven sprouting mysteriously from the ribcage. It, too, has abalone-shell eyes and a provocative beak that could inspire trepidation. Further pulling of the sinew apparatus would again draw the raven upward until, finally, a minutely carved, delicately scaled human face mask deep inside the body cavity would climax the performance. The mask is, in effect, a minuscule shaman's face mask, a sine qua non for Tlingit curative sessions. Like the Tlingit ladle (cat. no. 85), the puppet is crowned by an octopus. The suckers, like a train of snakes, drape from the head and over the shoulders and back, a serpentine element that served to center the power of the shaman's trance. This work is comparable aesthetically to the finest miniature ivory carvings of medieval and Renaissance Europe, medieval prayer diptychs and Renaissance plaquettes.

But rather than addressing the humanistic traditions of the Western world—unless it is the Northern European concept of the skeletal dance of death—it awakens us to the dark world of shamanism.

This figure was discovered a decade ago by a rancher in Wyoming. It was shipped to New York in a fragile tin box along with two very mediocre Acoma pots that the owner chose to pack more carefully. This was a once-in-a-lifetime discovery. The recipient, the New York dealer Eleanor Tulman Hancock, showed it to me in 1994. Carelessly pushed into a cramped Rich's candied ginger tin container, it arrived partly dismembered. A New York conservator painstakingly reassembled it piece by piece with almost no loss.

Peter T. Furst, who used this figure as the centerpiece of a lecture he gave on shamanism for Recursos de Santa Fe in the spring of 2002, states apropos this puppet, "Skeletanization and the shaman contemplating his own skeleton are at the very forefront of shamanic ideology and practice. That this figure represents a shaman is obvious from several of its characteristics: the two rattles in its hands, the tiny mask finally revealed at the very back of the chest cavity when it is fully opened, thus displaying the shaman's inner essence, and the skeleton mask the figure itself is wearing."[1]

1.   Personal communication from Peter T. Furst, 2003.

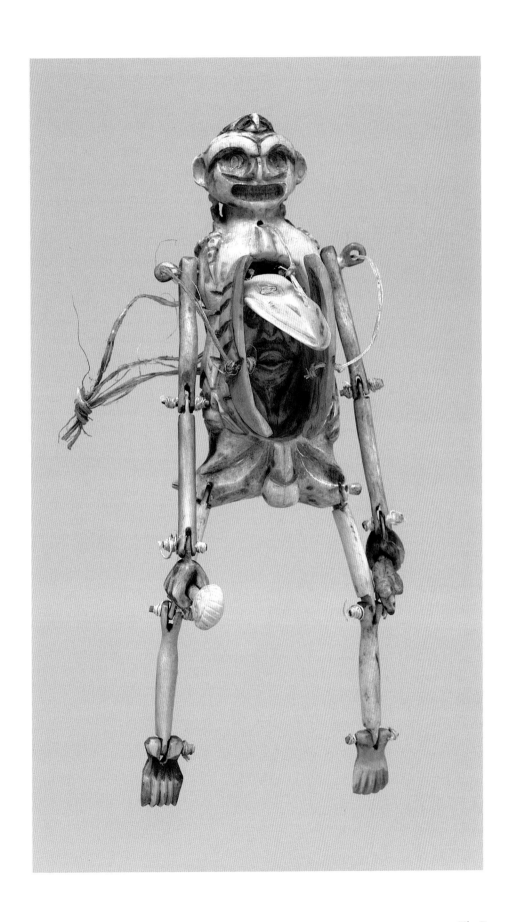

85. Ladle

ca. 1860
Tlingit peoples, southeastern Alaska
Wood, horn
19 ½ x 3 ¾ in. (49.5 x 9.5 cm)
RTCNA 668

This well-carved Tlingit ladle retains shamanic powers, principally contained in the rows of tentacles ascending upward above the octopus's head. These ensured that the curer's presentation of the medicinal potion to his supplicant was effective and awe inspiring. The octopus suckers encircle a single, small standing figure framed within another surround of tentacles. The handle of this ladle is of particular interest in its departure from the standard handles with tiny animals stacked in totemic style. A ladle with a handle such as this one was destined for special use. So bulky is this handle that it could have been grasped only where it joins with the spoon proper. The ladle was therefore too awkward to be used for ordinary feasting or food consumption but was reserved for the dispensing of shamanic potions. Stylistically, it appears to date to about 1860. The handle is affixed to the ladle with three old wood plugs.

VII

MODELS

Paradigms of Culture in Miniature

86. Totem pole model

ca. 1820–40

Tlingit peoples, southeastern Alaska

Stained and painted wood

30 x 4 in. (76.2 x 10.2 cm)

RTCNA 148

Carved from a single flat board, this totem pole model, with its extremely shallow relief, resembles a rattle panel also made by the Tlingit, in the Peter the Great Museum of Anthropology and Ethnography, St. Petersburg.[1] The panel has similar schematic zones of design, and though not carved in relief, its similarly archaic graphic style also suggests an early date, perhaps even earlier than 1820–40. While the rattle panel shows several sections of one animal depicted on each side, the present carving exhibits five interlocking but carefully separated animals in an archaic style. The fully developed use of the primary, secondary, and tertiary formlines of a full-blown Northwest Coast totemic carving are barely hinted at here. Indeed, the crown of the upper face is expressed only as a series of black squares. The colors are a berry stain and charcoal black, evidence of a more restricted palette than that seen later in the nineteenth century. The bear (the third motif from the top) wears slat armor that went out of use about 1840, also an indication of an early date. Perhaps this pole model was carved for a Russian patron, as it was made well before Alaska was sold to the United States, in 1867. At any rate, it belongs to the incunabula of totem pole models.

It came to light in a shop that I visited on Madison Avenue, in New York City, where it was identified rather vaguely as "southern" in origin. Later that day, as I was walking through an exhibition at The Metropolitan Museum of Art of paintings by the nineteenth-century American still-life master William Harnett, I suddenly made a connection between the geometric style of the paintings and the regimented linearity of the slat armor on the pole model. Realizing that this archaic form of armor was a strong indication of an early date, I raced back to the shop and bought the piece on the spot.

1. Fitzhugh and Crowell 1988, p. 87, fig. 95.

87–90. Group of totem pole models

1875–1890

Haida peoples, Haida Gwaii (Queen Charlotte Islands),
British Columbia

Following pages, left to right:

87. 1875–1885
Stained and painted wood
27 x 4 ½ in. (68.6 x 11.4 cm)
RTCNA 157

88. 1885–1890
Wood, abalone-shell inlay
24 ⅛ x 4 ⅜ in. (61.3 x 11.1 cm)
RTCNA 158

89. ca. 1890
Wood, horn inlay
26 ⅛ x 5 ¼ in. (66.4 x 13.3 cm)
RTCNA 210

90. ca. 1900
Painted wood
a. 20 ¾ x 4 ⅛ in. (52.7 x 10.5 cm)
b. 19 ½ x 4 in. (49.5 x 10.2 cm)
RTCNA 198a, b

The totem pole model on the left (see following page) has the fullness of form characteristic of Haida carving. The painted surface is heavily varnished. The carvings show, from top to bottom, a bear with a frog in its mouth, a bear clenching its own long tongue, and a bear grasping a fishtail. The talons of a now-absent eagle that once surmounted the pole are still visible at the top. Like the two adjacent examples, this model demonstrates the classically Haida method of blocking out individual animal forms section by section, thus adding a strong sculptural element of plastic restraint. This measured approach is noticeably absent in the Heiltsuk example from Bella Bella (cat. no. 93). I bought this model in 1992, in Santa Fe. The missing eagle did not prevent me from buying it, as its formal qualities were sufficient to offset its incompleteness.

The second pole to the right, perhaps slightly later and embellished with inlaid abalone-shell eyes and hockers (paw joints), demonstrates another aspect of classic Haida style. The animal forms are delineated as much by rather shallow incised outlines as by deep carving. Northwest Coast totem pole models run the gamut from direct reference to poles that existed to mythological and specific crest references to pure invention. Here, three dignified bears are represented. Because they seem too mature to represent the mythical bear cubs of the Bear Mother legend, they are probably the product of the carver's fancy, an outgrowth of what Carol Sheehan has termed "Haida non-sense" in her book on Haida argillite art.[1] While a very competent and pleasing work from a formal point of view, the linear incising represents a decorative element that has crept in, making this model slightly more commercial in tone than the previous example. It was auctioned at Sotheby's in 1986, attributed to the Tlingit. Relegated to the section on miscellany at the back of the catalogue, with only a tiny illustration on the very last page, it nevertheless intrigued me.[2] It was bid in by a Santa Fe dealer and soon hanging on the wall of his shop. I bought it from him almost immediately.

The center totem pole model represents, from the bottom, a raven grasping the tongue of a bear that is crowned by a segmented, highly abstracted hat. The hat shields the body of a seal, whose front and back flippers are shown across the front and at the sides. The elegance of and refined detailing on this pole indicate that the artist who produced it was first and foremost a carver of the compact, hardened coniferous shale rock called argillite. Another stylistic characteristic of this artist's work is the compass-drawn holes for the eyes, the marks of which are often found on argillite carvings, particularly plates. The segmented hat displays four potlatch rings (see cat. no. 91), and an unusual feature is the prominent, framing flange that extends along the edge. One may assume that the eclectic mix of compositional devices on a pole model like this one, seemingly thrown together for effect rather than referring to a specific totem pole or crest, were reassembled to attract a non-Native market.[3] The feeling, however, is entirely indigenous, because the compositional elements are drawn strictly from the traditional Haida repertory.

Several other objects appear to have been made by the carver of this pole model. One example is a small wolf's head in argillite, meant to be affixed as a handle on a slate box. The box was bought on the Northwest Coast, in 1881, by Captain Adrien Jacobsen, who collected on behalf of the group that eventually formed the Museum für Völkerkunde, Berlin.[4] A carved wood feast dish sold at Christie's in 1996 is also attributable to the same hand,[5] as is another totem pole model carved of alder wood. That pole was sold at Seahawk Auctions, in Burnaby, British Columbia, in 2001.[6] It is to be hoped that further research will give this neglected artist a name and a larger corpus of work. He belongs to the late period of Haida carving, around the turn of the twentieth century, when carvers specialized in such for-sale items as canes and powder horns.

I acquired this pole in 1956 in exchange for the very first pole model I bought, in 1955, from the Carlebach Gallery in New York (see fig. 4 on p. 15). It had a noticeable coating of varnish that helped to give it a rich, dark patina. A small spot was removed from the flange, which proved to be aged soot over the varnish. This would suggest that the pole may have been near a stove or fireplace, perhaps before it left Native lands, the pole having been varnished, rather than painted by the carver.

It is not often that one comes across a matched pair of totem pole models as those seen on this page. Such pairs were likely made to adorn a curio collector's cabinet or mantelpiece, and, as is usual in such for-sale items, they comprise a potpourri of crest-derived imagery. At the top of the pole on the right is a face in the round surmounted by a typical Haida hat with three rings denoting the owner's status or the potlatch feasts that he has hosted. This element on a full-size totem pole is generally referred to as a "watchman." Pole models that are better conceived than this pair are more unified in composition. That effect is achieved by formal articulation by carving rather than, as in this case, the continuous outlining of limbs, eyebrows, wings, eye sockets, sides, and base in black paint. Here, some details are accented by pale green and vermilion swabs that appear to have been applied rather hastily. Nevertheless, one cannot deny the decorative charm these pieces exert as a fantasia on Haida themes. The animal imagery includes an eagle and a bear, a long-beaked bird—

either a curlew or a heron—a beaver holding a stick, and a bear with a frog in its mouth. In these images, we begin to see the transformation of traditional crest motifs into a tourist-oriented formula.

1. Sheehan 1981, pp. 67ff.
2. Sotheby's, New York, December 3, 1986, sale no. 5522, lot 420.
3. Sheehan 1981, p. 66.
4. Drew and Wilson 1980, p. 265.
5. Christie's, New York, June 5, 1996, sale no. 8426, lot 132 (with reference to another bowl by the same hand in the Landesmuseum, Hannover, Germany).
6. Seahawk Auctions, Burnaby, British Columbia, November 2–4, 2001, lot 777, illus.

Charles Edenshaw, Haida, 1839–1920 (?)

| *91. Totem pole model* |

ca. 1890
Old Masset, Haida Gwaii (Queen Charlotte Islands),
British Columbia
Argillite
16 ¼ x 3 ¼ in. (41.3 x 8.3 cm)
RTCNA 182

The carver of this masterly totem pole model was the celebrated late-nineteenth-century Haida artist Charles Edenshaw. Edenshaw served as cicerone for the noted linguist and ethnologist John Swanton when he visited the Haida town of Masset to do research for his definitive account of Haida myths, published by the Smithsonian Institution in 1905. One of the most prominent chiefly longhouses in Masset was the Monster House, as it was locally known. It was famed for its monumental totem pole, which told the story of the great flood, common to many cultures. Placed at the front of the house, the pole went straight up the center. Edenshaw's model, which he probably carved a number of years before he met with Swanton, is a free variation of that pole.

The columnar shaft consists of three sections. The middle section represents a tall hat that comprises six identical male figures, one set above the other, three at each side. There are seven incised rings at intervals across the hat-shaft, each of which signifies a successful achievement or potlatch feast. At the flared base of the hat is a bust of the owner or a chief. This effigy forms the base of the pole. A raven perches at the very top, leaning outward to inspect the small climbing figures as they flee the primordial flood.

In the Haida version of the myth, the survivors do not enter a vessel, as in the account of Noah's ark in the Bible, but climb to high ground for safety. The use of conflated imagery—the chief's hat as a pole—is typical of the synergy with which Haida artists could invest their compositions, so that the sum of the parts is greater than their individual effects would be.

Robin K. Wright, curator at the Burke Museum of Natural History and Culture, University of Washington, Seattle, has described this pole, citing several characteristics

of Edenshaw's carving style: "The rounded, medium width formlines; open, nearly centered eyelid lines; eyesockets that slope out immediately below the lower eyelid line; and cross-hatched tertiary space bordered by a double engraved tertiary line. The single hatched background areas behind the figures on either side of the hat rings is also typical of Edenshaw's argillite model totem poles. The arrangement of the figures on [the] pole is similar to a number of full-sized totem poles in Haida villages that represent versions of the flood story."[1]

On my first pilgrimage to Masset, in 1967, I was told to look up Chief William Matthews (Chief Wiha), who "knew a lot about the old days." Chief Matthews's childhood home had been the original Monster House, and he lived in a frame house that had long ago replaced it.[2] He and his wife were kind enough to welcome me into their home. After a fine meal, we went outside and Chief Matthews, pointing to a depression in the ground, said, "Our [Monster House] pole is now in an English museum. And the young people here—do you think they give a chief like me respect. . . . No. They only want to go to the movies." He seemed saddened but resolute, as he recalled the privileges of the old traditional life of which he was the end of the line. Chief Matthews died in 1974. In 2002, nearly half a century after I met him, I visited his grave by the shores of Masset Inlet, to pay my respects. (See also cat. no. 92.)

1. Robin K. Wright in Sotheby's, New York, November 28, 1989, sale no. 5939, lot 207.
2. MacDonald 1996, p. 185.

Charles Edenshaw, Haida, 1839–1920 (?)

| 92. Totem pole model |

ca. 1885

Old Masset, Haida Gwaii (Queen Charlotte Islands),

British Columbia

Argillite

26 ¼ in. x 4 ⅝ in. (66.7 x 11.7 cm)

RTCNA 678

It is a rare event when a "lost" major argillite totem pole model by Charles Edenshaw comes to light. In a widely published photograph of this artist, he is pictured with, among other works, two argillite totem pole models.[1] The whereabouts of one of these poles remained unknown until it suddenly appeared on an eBay Internet auction. There, it attracted the attention of the Santa Fe dealer Taylor A. Dale, who recognized diagnostic similarities between the pole in the photograph and the image on eBay that seemed undeniable. He immediately called me, and I raced down to his gallery. The enlarged photographs that we requested from eBay confirmed that the two poles were indeed one and the same. The bid we submitted was successful.

Of the Haida carvers working in argillite in the late nineteenth century a number were masters, but Edenshaw was gifted with the most articulated sense of technique and balance of design. His style is clearly indicated by the controlled and harmonious manner in which the widely differing figural elements on this model interlock and recombine so that all its motifs continuously swell and recede in one unified crescendo. This sophisticated approach to sculpting has been analyzed by Bill Holm: "As is characteristic of Edenshaw's model poles, each figure interrelates with those adjacent to it by means of grasping claws and overlapping limbs."[2]

A sphinxlike figure with plaited hair and feline ears authoritatively crowns this totem pole model. She holds at each side a copper, symbol of wealth, rectitude, and power, and kneels aggressively over a female humanoid shark (so identified by the labret inserted in the lower lip), a variation on a crest that belonged to the Edenshaw family. The third image from the top is an owl with a frog in its mouth. And the face below the owl is that of an eagle surrounded by a ruff. The general configuration of this last face identifies it as unmistakably by Edenshaw, as it relates to several frontlets by or attributed to this artist.[3] The pole is an extraordinary feat of Edenshaw's imagination. (See also cat. no. 91.)

1. For a reproduction of this photograph, see MacDonald 1996, p. 220, pl. 159.
2. Holm 1983, p. 111, no. 189.
3. See R. Wright 2001, p. 237, fig. 5.5, and Abbott 1981, p. 187, figs. 29, 30.

93. Totem pole model

ca. 1900
Heiltsuk peoples, Bella Bella, British Columbia
Painted wood
49 x 5 ½ in. (124.5 x 14 cm)
RTCNA 156

Heiltsuk carved totem pole models, in the past misidentified as Kwakwaka'wakw, have heretofore remained underappreciated for their true contribution to Northwest Coast Indian art style. I first saw this pole many years ago, at the now defunct Bonnefoy Gallery in New York. Sometime later, it turned up unexpectedly in Santa Fe. When I saw it again, it seemed to me to reflect the idiosyncratic stylistic eccentricities indicative of Heiltsuk origin. These include an openwork structure, face masks with belligerent expressions, exaggerated beaks, and postures that connote aggression or hostility. This exaggerated manner does not typify all Heiltsuk art, to be sure. But further evidence of the pole's attribution came to light with the recent exhibition and catalogue organized by the Royal Ontario Museum, Toronto, of the collection of Dr. Richard W. Large, a nineteenth-century missionary and medical superintendent in the town of Bella Bella.[1] In that collection are two totem pole models that, one way or another, conform to the overstated characteristics cited here and are almost certainly by the carver who made the present example.[2] Other Heiltsuk carvings, such as houseposts and water ceremony boxes, can also reflect this style, which breaks with the conventions of classic Northwest Coast Kwakwaka'wakw formalism.

1. M. Black 1997.
2. Ibid., p. 44, nos. 20, 21.

| 94. Canoe model |

1860–70
Tlingit peoples, southeastern Alaska
Painted wood
3 x 26 x 4 in. (7.6 x 66 x 10.2 cm)
RTCNA 146

One of the reasons I aquired this otherwise typical Tlingit canoe model from the northern sector of the Northwest Coast was that it appears to be one of the very few such models, if not the only one, that is not only painted but decorated with relief-carved designs on the stern and prow. Certainly, the carver was more than casually involved in the design embellishments. The bird representations are inverted—on the bow section the bird elements are depicted upright, while on the stern, complementary images are upside down.

While the Tlingit peoples relied on cottonwood logs to make smaller fishing canoes, most of their largest and most impressive canoes were actually acquired from the Haida peoples, who traded their canoes to the other Northwest Coast peoples from Vancouver to the Copper River in Alaska.[1] Thus, this example may well be considered a Tlingit-made model depicting a Haida-made original. The flatness of the relief hints, however, at a Tlingit style of interpretation. Evidently, Haida canoes were sometimes painted or repainted by their Tlingit owners. George T. Emmons photographed a large Haida canoe owned by a Sitka Tlingit that may very well have been repainted.[2]

1. Emmons 1991, p. 85.
2. Ibid., p. 88, illus.

Late 19th century
Quinault peoples, Olympic Peninsula, Washington
Painted wood
6 ¼ x 32 x 7 in. (15.9 x 81.3 x 17.8 cm)
RTCNA 206

While a fair number of tribal canoes from the Pacific coast of the Olympic Peninsula have been preserved, practically none are known with the specific iconograph, of animals and a spirit mask seen on this model. A bear, whale, and seabird are represented on both sides. The very high, massive sternpost not only served to accommodate the maskette, it also gave the lines of the canoe an exceptional thrust and strength, suitable for Pacific Coast travels in open water. In comparison with canoes of the central and northern Northwest Coast, Salish canoes were usually equipped with a snoutlike prow and a vertical stern, constructed on a fairly simple pattern. The Canadian anthropologist Wilson Duff has suggested that this profile may be a survival, on the Northwest Coast, of an early influence from the Arctic

Eskimo/Aleut.[1] In view of the recent reassessment of the relationship between the arts of the northern Northwest Coast and the supposedly less sophisticated art of the southern Salish tribes in Washington State, canoes such as this one have gained new interest as harking back to origins now obscured by a layering of subsequent cultural developments. The Quinault and Quileute peoples from the southern part of the Olympic Peninsula, together with the Makah and Klallam tribes at the northern end of the peninsula, have recently revived this canoe type in modern renditions. This reasserts its place in the overall scheme of northern Pacific maritime architecture.

1. Duff 1981.

| *96. Canoe model with sail* |

ca. 1890
Kwakwaka'wakw peoples, Vancouver Island or adjacent mainland, British Columbia
Painted wood, plant fiber
9 ½ x 26 ½ x 5 ½ in. (24.1 x 67.3 x 14 cm)
RTCNA 152

The connection between the canoes of the southern coast and those of the central coast north of southern Vancouver Island may be seen in the generic similarity between the hull of this Kwakwaka'wakw model and that of the Quinault example (cat. no. 95). The present model is clearly more complex, with a stern and bow that are now fully evolved; nevertheless, there is an echo of the Salish sternpost in the flattening that occurs at either end, which allows a miniature carved eagle to be placed at the bow or stern, according to whim. This model would seem to be one of the most complete southern Kwakwaka'wakw canoe replicas known. It has a large square minutely woven sail, a diminutive kerfed storage box, and an open box stove complete with stones to be heated. Other equipment include a paddle, hunting bow, bailer, harpoon spear, adz, and roll of bark. There are two lively thunderbirds painted on either side of the canoe, as if they were flying very low over the water. The chiefly occupant, in full regalia, is clothed in a button-type blanket and wears a traditional painted conical cedar bark hat. There is even a Native cordage halyard attached to the sail so that he can alter his course. Five thwarts can serve as seats, with one, now missing, at the prow. The dignitary seems to be on an important mission, supervised and perhaps even guided by the eagle. Surely the maker of this model outdid himself in depicting his love of craft detail and the art of canoe building. A date at the end of the nineteenth century is not unlikely.

97. Kayak model with hunter

1840–50
Aleut peoples, Aleutian or Pribilof Islands, Alaska
Gutskin, fur, painted wood, sinew
4 x 12 x 2 in. (10.2 x 30.5 x 5.1 cm)
RTCNA 597

During the Russian occupation of the Aleutian Islands, hundreds of delicately constructed kayak models were made for non-Native consumption. There are twenty-seven of these very early Aleut models in the Etholén collection of the National Museum of Finland, donated by the Russian-Finnish admiral Adolph Etholén in 1846.[1] The present kayak model with hunter would appear to be closely associated with this group. Six of the Etholén examples are two-person bidarkas, and the remainder, one-person kayaks that conform closely to the present model. The exquisite frame construction is here clearly visible through the transparent seal-gut covering. The fabric and interior framing are rendered with admirable accuracy, with all the delicate finesse associated with an elaborate airplane model kit. One can easily speculate that a model-making industry seems to have been involved here, with many of the parts made in multiples, down to the equipment with which this little kayak was once furnished. Only a miniature float, carved and painted to scale, has survived on this model's afterdeck. Theoretically, it would be possible to reassemble the deck equipment if the cache of harpoons, visors, spears, atlatls, and iron hooks made for this kayak could ever be found. When this kayak model left the Aleutians remains unknown. It was acquired from Bill Parkinson, a San Francisco *marchand amateur* and collector, by the dealer Taylor A. Dale, of Santa Fe, who sold it to me in 1999.

1. Varjola 1990, pp. 173, 212–13.

Sarah Novalinga, Inuit, b. 1979

| 98.Kayak model with hunter |

1998
Belcher Islands, Hudson Bay, Nunavut
Seal and fish skin, fur, synthetic fabric, metal, wood,
sinew, plant fiber
6 ½ x 39 x 8 in. (16.5 x 99.1 x 20.3 cm)
RTCNA 650a, b

Kayaks from the eastern Canadian Arctic differ from those of western Canada and Alaska in that their hulls are covered with dark sealskin and do not convey the same transparent effect (see cat. no. 97). The profile of this kayak is typically triangular at midsection, and the stern and bow sharply project far forward and aft, somewhat in the manner of a Venetian gondola. Both lines and construction facilitate skimming lightly over the water. The acquisition of this kayak model was my reward at the end of a two-day train trip north from Winnipeg to Churchill, Manitoba, an isolated town on Hudson Bay, home to polar bears, Athabaskans, and Inuit alike.

Anyone who has read the well-known Canadian author Farley Mowat's account of this same journey, which he made a number of times, starting as a youth, will experience the same sense of Arctic isolation and dreaming as I did while the train trundled slowly northward from prairie to forest to swampy sub-Arctic scrub, and finally to the stony sub-Arctic

itself.[1] It is one of the first locales one reaches where genuine central Arctic goods can be found for sale. A focus point for such opportunity is the Arctic Trading Company, in Churchill, managed by Penny Rawlings. When I arrived, she had two kayak models that had been there for some time; of the two, I purchased the larger, by Sarah Novalinga, who comes from the isolated Belcher Islands, off the western coast of Quebec, in Hudson Bay.

Sarah Novalinga told me that she was taught traditional crafts at Sanikiluaq by a non-Native schoolteacher, who was, in turn, trained by "our elder here." Her faceless hunter comes complete with a fishing spear, hook, and pike; a float for attachment for the catch; a double-ended paddle; and a light, fish-skin game bag. There is a tiny basket on the deck, also by this artist and possibly made for this model, that Penny Rawlings suggested I add as an integral feature. The cockpit is outfitted with a raised fish-skin liner to protect the hunter from water and spray, as the draft of a full-size kayak

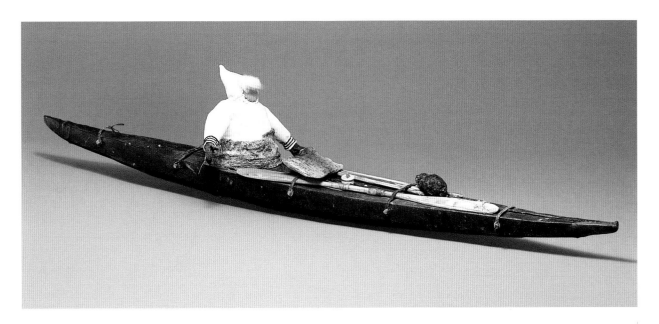

is very shallow. There are five straps attached at various points on the deck for carrying extra freight. The design and finish of every component are consonant with the spare simplicity of the Arctic environment. Variants of this minimal aesthetic in kayak models can be found to the east along the Ungava Peninsula, farther east in Greenland, and as far south as the Labrador Inuit communities above the Gulf of St. Lawrence.

1. Mowat 1952.

99. Canoe model with two dolls

ca. 1860
Micmac peoples, Nova Scotia or northern New Brunswick
Canoe: Birchbark, wood, porcupine quill
4 ¾ x 22 x 4 ¾ in. (12.1 x 55.9 x 12.1 cm)
Dolls: Silk, cotton, and wool trade cloth, glass beads, resin
Height 7 in. (17.8 cm); 7 in. (17.8 cm)
RTCNA 298a–c

Since about 1820, birchbark canoe models by the Maritime Micmac peoples were chiefly made as souvenirs for British soldiers, civil servants, their families, and other souvenir hunters seeking "red Indian" keepsakes. Romantic associations led to such purchases, but later generations have come to treasure these mementos not only as indices to a past culture but also as works of refined technical beauty in their own right.

The early-nineteenth-century Micmac canoe models were quilled with single rows of simple chevron designs applied to the entire length of the canoe, which emphasized the swelling lines of the canoe profile with an artistic license not found in full-size examples. This model represents a later phase. It comes with a pair of resin dolls and is decorated with only a modest, single row of quilled triangles stretching from stem to stern just below the gunwales. This style is characteristic of canoes made in the Victorian period, approximately 1860. The resin figurines are clothed as male and female, and the style of dress is everyday rather than ceremonial. The swelling curvature of the bow and stern tell us that this type of canoe was intended for fairly deep water.

| *100. Canoe model with accoutrements* |

Before 1845

Maliseet peoples, New Brunswick

Painted birchbark, wood, plant fiber, bird quill, silk trade cloth

Canoe: 2 ½ x 16 x 3 ¼ in. (6.4 x 40.6 x 8.3 cm)

Implements: maximum length 12 in. (30.5 cm)

RTCNA 295a–i

Although the London open-air antiques markets, such as Portobello Road, Bermondsey, and Camden Passage, no longer offer a large selection of Native Canadian ethnological arts, as late as 1976 it was still possible to come across rarities such as this Maliseet birchbark canoe model with its accompanying miniature equipment set still intact.

This model came to light during the time the exhibition "Sacred Circles" was on view in London. As the curator, I was approached a number of times by Londoners and, occasionally, American visitors who were kind enough to offer me objects they had found in the London markets. Leyland and Crystal Peyton, who had an eagle eye for spotting works of ethnic interest from many cultures, came

across this rare, unusually well equipped canoe model from New Brunswick. A letter that accompanied the model stated that it had been in an English country house since 1845, having been brought to England by English visitors to French Canada, and that it had been made by the Maliseet of New Brunswick.

Because the Maliseet were nominally a riverine people, living in several settlements along the verdant St. John River separating New Brunswick from Maine, their canoes tended to be lighter in construction than those of the Micmac and other Maritime peoples, whose canoes had to withstand harsher offshore conditions. This model follows the Maliseet aesthetic for lightness of form and delicate articulation of integral canoe parts such as thwarts and gunwales. The fishing and hunting accoutrements that have been added give this particular model a completeness of its own. Along with a gun, paddles, and spears, there are even two rolls of birchbark, miniature versions of larger rolls provided in full-size canoes to make quick repairs en route.

Jo Polis, Penobscot, active 1870s

101. Canoe model

ca. 1875
Indian Island/Old Town, Maine
Incised birchbark, wood
2 ½ x 13 x 2 ⅞ in. (6.4 x 33 x 7.3 cm)
RTCNA 299

This attractive birchbark canoe model is engraved with the signature "Jo Polis" on the bottom of the hull. Also present are the initials OT, which presumably stands for Old Town, Maine, immediately adjacent to Indian Island, the home of the Penobscot peoples. The model is an early example of a type of souvenir birchbark work made specifically to attract summer tourists visiting the state of Maine, offering them an authentic, Indian souvenir and providing Indians with much needed supplementary income.

But who was Jo Polis? As well as being the maker of this canoe model, he also crafted a larger one now in the Peabody Essex Museum, Salem, Massachusetts.[1] Both models were engraved by scraping the outer layer of bark to reveal the lighter, inner layer. Using this technique, Polis departed from the traditional symbolic patterned designs to create drawings that specifically illustrate scenes of Indian life. Indeed, he may have been the first to practice drawing on birchbark, perhaps basing it on older rock engravings by New England and Canadian maritime artists. If this is the case, we may surmise that the scene on the bottom of this model, a moose being chased by two Indians on snowshoes, denotes the kind of narrative art that the better-known carver Tomah Joseph would soon develop into a paradigm of Northern Woodlands Victorian souvenir art (see cat. no. 49). Quite possibly, Polis was Tomah Joseph's mentor.[2] This tempting possibility has yet to be confirmed, and the modest corpus of Polis's birchbark work awaits further investigation.

1. Monroe 1996, p. 170, illus. lower right. The annotation reads, "Miniature Canoe, Penobscot artist, 1878." (The illustration is, unfortunately, nearly indecipherable.)
2. I wish to thank Joan Lester for calling my attention to Jo Polis.

102. Canoe model

1920s or 1930s
Central Algonkian peoples, Ontario
Painted birchbark, wood, plant fiber
5 ⅝ x 26 x 6 ½ in. (14.3 x 66 x 16.5 cm)
RTCNA 328a, b

A later stage in the Northeast canoe model repertory is represented by this model from the 1920s or 1930s. Collecting it reminded me of the time when, as a boy during the Second World War, I was at camp on the Temagami Lakes in northwestern Ontario. The Ojibwa guide, who was taking a group of us across a string of heavily forested lakes, would carve by the campfire at night, crafting a canoe model very similar to this one. The model was ostensibly being made for me, although I never received it. What I would give for that model today!

I was fortunate enough to find this Ontario version of a similar canoe in 1991. It is central Algonkian in type, although it is not wholly traditional in construction, as nails, rather than spruce lashings, are used to attach the gunwales to the hull. The picturesque scraped designs portray young moose, not old enough to have grown antlers, swimming through the water as though accompanying the canoe. These images are consistent with those on models made for visitors to fishing camps, such as the ones I visited in my youth. The full-size canoes, made for two passengers, were usually between twelve and seventeen feet long, with plenty of room for a third passenger and camping supplies.

ca. 1890
Central Plains Sioux peoples, North and South Dakota
Native-tanned skin, paint
22 x 30 ⅜ in. (55.9 x 77.2 cm)
RTCNA 417

The military scenes portrayed in a series of vignettes across this tipi model closely parallel the style of action drawing that developed on the Plains to preserve the histories of actual warfare and noble exploits of prominent warriors. These were painted both on full-size tipis and on hides. One of the precursors of this spirited style is to be found in winter counts, the pictoral chronicling of important natural and tribal events.

During the 1870s, Indian warriors were imprisoned in U.S. government camps. Tipis were banned, but the Indians were encouraged by soldiers and even journalists to develop what is loosely referred to as ledger-book art. The drawings were made in ledger books provided to the artist as a means of recording events, much as winter counts had served that purpose earlier.

This tipi model must have been made by one of the major Plains ledger-book artists. Stylistically calligraphic in its translation of equine and hand-to-hand combat, the narrative retains the same vitality as the day it was painted. On the right flap, seven heads of slain enemies are depicted together with a quirt and a tomahawk. Accented in a vibrant red, the heads have undoubtedly been scalped. The left flap shows three hands, symbols of leadership in raids or battle. On the main field, three riders on horses are shown in combat. One rider, not visible behind his shield, slumps over the side of his horse; in front of him a warrior stands poised to fire a gun, the crown of his head bleeding from a wound. On a second horse, vividly colored yellow, a rider in full feather-bonnet regalia holds aloft a tall lance. He, in turn, charges a warrior who is firing a gun. Two solar symbols are painted on either flap, and just below the smoke hole at the top a warrior is shown striding toward another warrior who sinks to the ground.

While the artist seemingly placed these vignettes at random, there is a fine balance maintained by the alignment of the horses and the rhythm governing the depiction of lances, guns, warriors, and headdresses. Later on, in the early twentieth century, such images were often mannered and stereotyped, particularly those made for sale to outsiders.

| 104. Tipi model |

Late 1860s–1876
Blackfoot peoples, Montana or Alberta
Native-tanned skin, paint, glass beads, cotton trade cloth, metal, horsehair
24 x 43 in. (61 x 109.2 cm)
RTCNA 420

Blackfoot tipis from the northwestern Plains were traditionally decorated along the lower rim with images of the sun and moon, providing instant recognition of a common tribal affinity. The rows of moons along the bottom edge of this tipi model conform to that convention. The Blackfoot have a deeply held belief in celestial deities, the sun and his wife, the moon—here represented by the yellow circles in blue triangles. At the top, a three-striped rainbow, a yellow sun, and yellow, red, and white stars create a realm of light, the beam of which—probably representing the Milky Way—bisects the center field. To the left is a mythical eagle from whose red head and green body lightning dramatically radiates.

This scene is the owner's dream vision, which served to protect the family. The tipi model thus encodes a very personal message displayed for all to see.

The use of what is most likely thick buffalo hide indicates that this model probably dates from the end of buffalo days, but before canvas tipis became the standard. Because of its use of Native materials, including earth paints and an early form of decorative dangle made from wrapped thread, this powerfully nostalgic object may be dated to between the late 1860s and 1876, when the Plains Indians were required by the U.S. government to relinquish their free, roaming life and submit to the confines of the reservation.

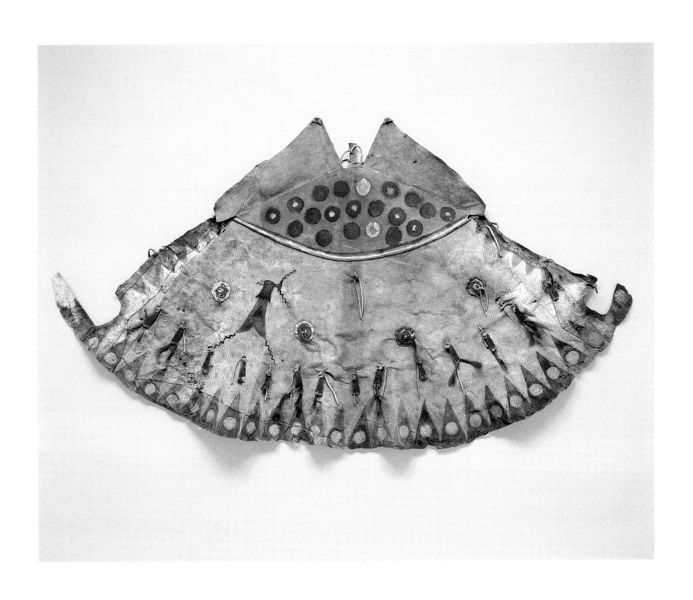

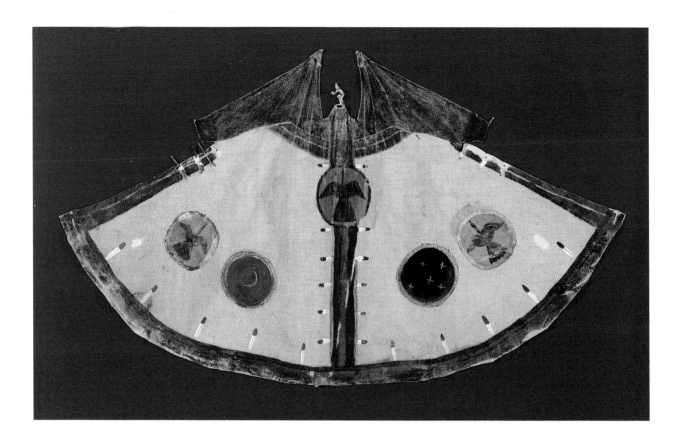

105. Tipi model

ca. 1915
Kiowa or Comanche peoples, southwestern Oklahoma
Cotton trade cloth, paint
22 ½ x 41 in. (57.2 x 104.1 cm)
RTCNA 529

This muslin tipi model is the latest in date of the three examples in this collection (see cat. nos. 103, 104). The symbols on the tipi follow in the tradition of the large scenes that were commissioned, from the late 1860s up to the beginning of the twentieth century, by traders and military personnel to decorate the walls of their quarters.

The theme denotes a personal connection to a family who were members of the Native American Church (NAC), a visionary religion with Christian associations. The sect emerged in the Southwest and was based in part on the consumption of peyote (it is sometimes called the Peyote Religion) in redemptive services that extended over many hours, often throughout the night. The "church" was usually a tipi, stored away and raised only for services.

Five painted medallions decorate the surface of this tipi model. At the left, a mythical water- or messenger bird carries prayers up to the heavens; next to it is a representation of the moon. At the right, two more roundels, depicting stars and another messenger bird, serve to balance the composition. The red stripe dividing the two halves signifies the good red road, the path of righteousness and integrity of those who gather to worship. Along the path, a spirit bird carries the prayers of the congregation heavenward. The form of the bird derives from the anhinga, a Southern species of waterfowl.

In contrast to the dramatic depictions of heroic exploits on many tipi models (see, for example, cat. no. 103), this one is notably imbued with a calm spirituality. The roundels seem to float, creating a silvery tranquillity that accords well with the message of brotherliness and rectitude expressed in the rituals of the Native American Church.

VIII

SMOKE OFFERINGS

Pipes and Tobacco Bags

106. Tobacco bag

1860–70

Assiniboine peoples, Alberta or Saskatchewan

Native-tanned skin, wool trade cloth, glass beads

32 x 6 in. (81.3 x 15.2 cm)

RTCNA 409

This tobacco bag is a fine example of the longitudinally organized type made both by the Cree and neighboring Assiniboine peoples who settled in Saskatchewan and Montana after leaving the eastern Plains. The elongated proportions, lack of fanciful adornment, simplified motifs on the beaded panels, and use of blue beads for trim—reminiscent of old style upper Missouri River beading—point to a pre-reservation origin. The tight enframement of the central beaded panel with concentric borders indicates the influence of mid-nineteenth-century Plains design. And the centered "meat-rack" pattern, on one side, and the vertically connected blue-beaded diamonds, on the other, look forward to the unconventional Assiniboine treatment of such motifs, especially later on during the reservation period. The tubular beads on the red borders of the central panel on both faces are called luster beads and occur earlier than the bugle beads, also tubular, used in the 1890s. The combination of colors is also Assiniboine in its acerbic harmony and is not unlike the brightly juxtaposed, high-pitched tones of a Fauve painting by Matisse or Vlaminck. This oddball sense of color would develop greater complexity as Assiniboine beadwork matured at the end of the nineteenth century and the beginning of the twentieth. The carrying strap near the top of the bag on both sides is distinguished by a pair of red stroud roundels with a blue bead surround, indicating an influence from the tradition of firebags of the Cree and the Cree/Métis of Canada from the 1840s (cat. no. 117). The abstract, multicolored patterning reflects the Assiniboine delight with highly syncopated visual effects.

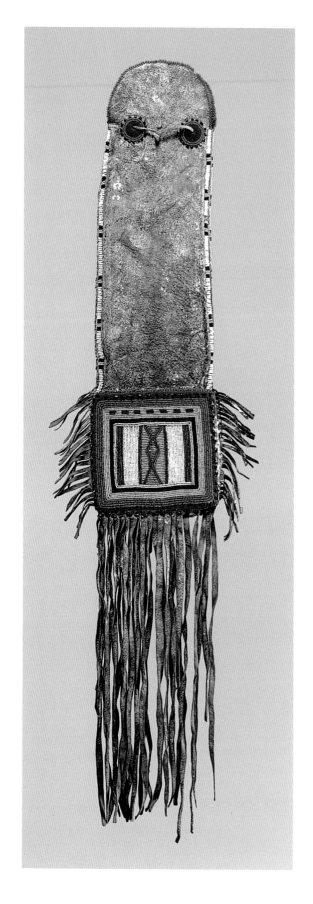

| 107. Tobacco bag |

Late 1890s
Assiniboine or Gros Ventre peoples,
Fort Belknap Reservation (?), Montana
Native-tanned skin, metal, horsehair, porcupine quill, glass beads
40 x 7 in. (101.6 x 17.8 cm)
RTCNA 418

There can be no question about the generally northwestern Plains origin of this beaded tobacco bag, a number of its details point specifically to either an Assiniboine or a Gros Ventre tribal origin. Most likely, it was made on the Fort Belknap Reservation in Montana, where both the Assiniboine and Gros Ventre peoples live, the Assiniboine at the north end, the Gros Ventre in the small communities of Hays and Lodgepole at the south end, about twenty-five miles away. There has always been a good deal of cultural interchange between these two tribes. Assiniboine characteristics on this bag include the eye-catching deep blue field of the beaded panel and the slightly off-center position of the hourglass motifs. Also typically Assiniboine are the mountain motifs immediately above the panel, which are of slightly different sizes, again providing a pleasing asymmetry. The deep russet color of the beads at either side of the hourglass motifs is a shade favored at the Fort Peck Reservation, in northeastern Montana, home to both the Assiniboine and Sioux peoples. This coloration could indicate a Sioux influence, although a classic Sioux design would not display this kind of offbeat manner.

Joyce Growing Thunder Fogarty

Assiniboine/Sioux, b. 1950

| 108. Tobacco bag |

1977

Native-tanned deerskin, paint, glass beads,

porcupine quill, trade cloth

40 x 8 in. (101.6 x 20.3 cm)

RTCNA 442

When I first visited the James Fogarty family in 1982, they were camped out in a trailer near the Montezuma Castle National Monument in Camp Verde, Arizona. Joyce Growing Thunder Fogarty, James's wife, had already made, at my request, a war shirt for the exhibition "Lost and Found Traditions."[1] During this visit, a large beaded tobacco bag that hung on a wall inside the trailer caught my eye. The subject, a warrior on horseback, seemed to hint at a personal story. And indeed, there was a family history.

In 1977, during the American Indian Movement (AIM), the Fogartys lived on the Fort Peck Reservation, at Oswego,

west of Poplar, Montana, which was Joyce's original home. Joyce's family's land allotments had at that time been leased by the Bureau of Indian Affairs to ranchers living off the reservation (this arrangement continues today). The Fogartys, together with members of their community, lobbied for the right, so long denied, to farm their own land. The Bureau cooperated only reluctantly and eventually all but ceased to cooperate at all. Ultimately, the project failed. This tobacco bag was Joyce's personal statement of protest, the only one she could make. The Fogartys generously agreed to sell it to me. I have lent it back to them on a number of occasions, as it is still a family treasure.

The subject matter is more ironic than would at first appear. A mounted warrior is shown parading in the tradition of victory dancing. He appears as a triumphant warrior—a dandy in full regalia, with his horse's tail and his lance lavishly decorated with eagle feathers. The horse fairly prances with pride. But the American flag, so prominently displayed, is upside down, an international signal of distress adopted by the American Indian Movement as an emblem of protest. This elegantly beaded panel is so beautifully composed and so harmonious in color that its message—of glory and defeat, economic ruin, and the political clashing of cultures—can be easily overlooked (see also cat. no. 156).

1. Coe 1986, p. 141, no. 167.

109. The Messiter pipe

ca. 1840

Yankton Sioux peoples, eastern South Dakota or adjacent Minnesota

Wood, bird and porcupine quill, horsehair, wool trade cloth, glass beads,

animal skin, paint, feathers

2 x 31 in. (5.1 x 78.7 cm)

RTCNA 392

The Messiter pipe was collected by Charles Alston Messiter (1841–1920), a sports hunter who traveled extensively, particularly in Africa and North America. His collection was kept at the family home at Barwick House in Somerset until 1969. Technically, what is most interesting about this resplendent pipe stem is that it combines porcupine with bird quillwork. The style accords well with a Yankton Sioux attribution. The Messiter pipe is distinguished by a particular blue-green quill dye, which is also specifically characteristic of Yankton Sioux art.[1]

A date for the stem of about 1840 or earlier would seem appropriate; it may have been collected at the time of the uprising of the Sioux living in the Minnesota River valley, which began in 1862. A similar pipe stem (with bowl), also embellished with a small white beaded roundel on the top of the stem, is in the collection of the British Museum, London.

The pipe stem was auctioned at Sotheby's in 1982 and acquired by Alexander Acevedo, of the Alexander Gallery in New York City.[2] In the Sotheby's catalogue, it was identified as Blackfoot. It was subsequently acquired by the Masco Corporation (Manoogian collection). I bought the pipe in 1999. Its spartan yet elemental power seems to express the very core of Plains Indian warrior spirituality in the heyday of buffalo days, before the intrusion of outside settlers.[3]

1. Personal communication from Bill Plitt, 2002.
2. Sotheby's, New York, April 24, 1982, sale no. 4842y, lot 284.
3. Along with other major pieces from the Messiter collection, the pipe was included in the slim, but important, exhibition catalogue *Akicita: Early Plains and Woodlands Indian Art from the Collection of Alexander Acevedo;* Southwest Museum 1983, p. 34, fig. 39.

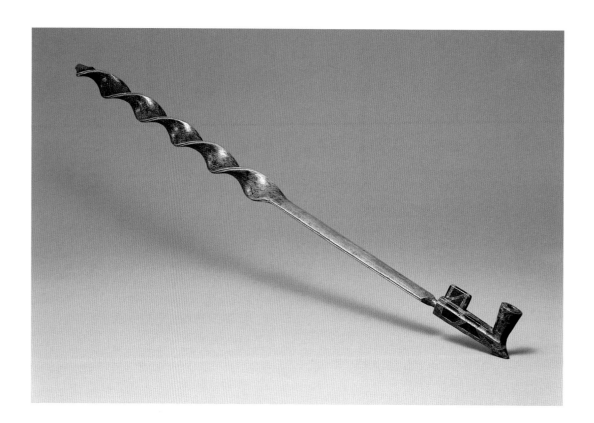

110. Pipe bowl and stem

1840–50
Ojibwa or eastern Plains peoples
Western Great Lakes–eastern Plains
Wood, lead
Bowl: Height 2 ½ in. (6.4 cm)
Stem: Length 34 in. (86.4 cm)
RTCNA 243a, b

There is a popular misconception that pipe bowls and their stems were always made as a pair. But, in fact, they were carved individually by different artisans and were often traded separately. A replacement—which generally maintained the same regional or tribal style—was made when there was breakage or when the pipe was given as a gift.

After I acquired this lead-inlaid wood pipe bowl, I was eager to pair it with an appropriate stem. Ideally, this would be in the twisted-stem style, from about 1840, and made by either a western Great Lakes Ojibwa carver or possibly a Sioux artist from the adjoining eastern Plains, as the pipe bowl was clearly made about that time and in this border region. The problem was solved when the Masco Corporation put on the market a twisted pipe stem that met these specifications.

Here, the severity of the close-grained maple burl bowl, accented by tight-fitting metal appliqué, joins a virtuosic example of stem carving. Both patience and great skill were required to push the heated rod through the entire ash stem, taking great care not to puncture it.

111. Pipe bowl and stem

ca. 1840
Great Lakes or eastern Plains people
Western Great Lakes–eastern Plains
Painted wood, metal, silk ribbon
2 ¼ x 23 ¾ in. (5.7 x 60.3 cm)
RTCNA 266a, b

This pipe and bowl are stylistically consistent, although the stem may be of birch, rather than the usual ash, and the bowl of maple. The stem is embellished with a segmented pattern, and two garrulous muskrats on the bowl shake their hairy coats as if just emerging from the water, lending the piece a humorous, slightly zany quality. The resist-branded dots along the top of the stem and the striations of the muskrats' fur add a subtle stylistic refinement. The muskrats are not merely decorative. Their demeanor brings to mind the trickster Iktome, who is often comically represented looking over his shoulder as he clings to the bowls of Sioux pipes. But if a specific narrative is intended, it has been lost to time.

ca. 1885
Ojibwa peoples, Minnesota
Bowl: Catlinite, chlorite, lead
4 x 7 ¾ in. (10.2 x 19.7 cm)
Stem: Wood, glass beads, metal
2 ⅜ x 22 ¾ in. (6 x 57.8 cm)
RTCNA 246a, b

This pipe and bowl were found at Mille Lacs, Minnesota, and probably come from the local Ojibwa band still active there. The bowl is distinguished by the use of black chlorite together with red catlinite and lead inlays. This is a typical Ojibwa combination, although red-and-black inlaid pipe bowls are also found among the eastern or Minnesota Sioux and the Wisconsin Winnebago, which can make attribution difficult. This pipe, however, with its classically heavy, prowlike form would appear to be of a Great Lakes origin.

I acquired this pipe from the trader Sherman Holbert, of Fort Mille Lacs. Sherman, a walking encyclopedia of Indian lore, went to school with his Ojibwa neighbors long before there were any paved roads around the lake, let alone the casino that scars the land. In the 1960s, he bought this pipe from an Ojibwa woman. Sometime later, he lent it back to the tribe for a ceremony. When it was returned, it contained some unburned sage, which had been blessed, and she instructed that it not be removed. It remains there to this day.

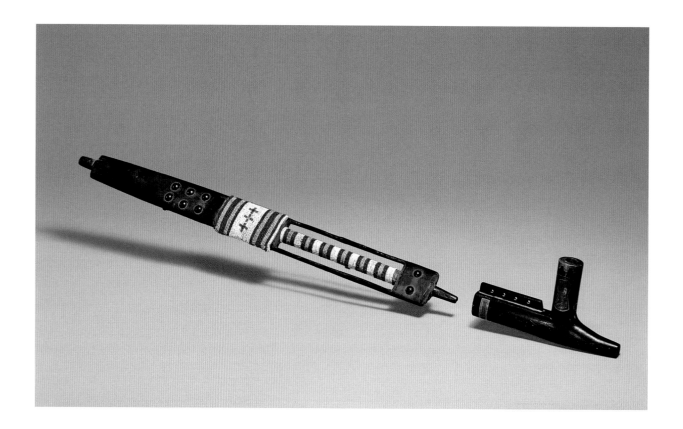

113. Pipe bowl

ca. 1840
Eastern Sioux peoples, Minnesota or eastern Dakota
Catlinite, black stone, metal
2 x 4 ½ in. (5.1 x 11.4 cm)
RTCNA 395

114. Pipe bowl

Late 19th century
Central Plains Sioux peoples, North and South Dakota
Catlinite
5 ¼ x 6 ½ in. (13.3 x 16.5 cm)
RTCNA 385

The round, wheel-like form that distinguishes this unusual pipe bowl signifies an eastern Plains origin. It also indicates a date fairly early in the nineteenth century, since the type went out of fashion for the most part after 1850. A more specific basis for this date is the fact that by 1840 there was a military presence at Fort Snelling, in what is now Minnesota. (The fort is still partly intact and immediately adjoins the Minneapolis–St. Paul International Airport.) The pierced comb of the pipe bowl displays an amorous scene that would have been considered quite titillating in its day and would certainly not have been openly displayed. Moreover, the pipe shows no evidence of having been smoked. One wonders if it was made for sale to a U.S. Army officer by an enterprising Native American artist. A very good place for such a sale would surely have been Fort Snelling.

There is a group of catlinite pipes produced toward the latter part of the nineteenth century with a very distinctive, easily recognized motif that were apparently made by the same master carver. The animal imagery of all these pipes would seem, considering their spiky teeth and winglike head projection, to represent a supernatural horse. Three close variants, in the Minnesota Historical Society, St. Paul, and in two private collections, suggest a progressively elaborate stylistic development. The present pipe is more elementary in composition, with a strong, succinct articulation of the features, and the head is crowned by a winglike comb, in a rather eccentric treatment. The Minnesota Historical Society example is more ornate, has a more prominent comb, and was designated a "dragon head" by Norman Feder.[1] The pipe in one of the private collections is more routine in feeling, like the repetition of an already familiar subject. And the example in the other private collection is joined to a long narrow, jointed stem, also in red catlinite, that is pure fantasy and nearly impossible to smoke. It seems to be a late production made specifically for sale. The present, more massive version has been thoroughly smoked and used. The concept of the supernatural horse lives still today on the Plains.

1. Feder 1971b, p. 70, no. 73.

115. *Pipe bowl*

1815–20
Haida peoples, Haida Gwaii (Queen Charlotte Islands),
British Columbia
Argillite
2 ½ x 3 ¾ in. (6.4 x 9.5 cm)
RTCNA 180

This argillite Haida pipe bowl is one of a relatively small group of pipes, all of them rather simple and archaic in style, that belong to the incunabula of Northwest Coast argillite carving. The pipes by no means replicate one another, but most of them are small and without the stylistic complexity that developed in Haida carving after 1820. The present example dates to between 1815 and 1820. The exfoliation of the original surface on the bowl proper, which may have resulted from exposure to heat, is perhaps an indication of use. The killer-whale image that constitutes the greater part of the bowl—note the truncated fin behind the head—is an early depiction of this clan symbol in Haida art. The whale seems to spring out of the water, in an arched configuration still seen in Haida art today.

Such pipes may have been smoked at funerals around this time, though argillite carving soon became exclusively a trade art. The compact pipe design was superseded by a far more convoluted scheme of interlaced and interconnected animal imagery, in which an elaborate decorative style, derived from European motifs, was explored and function became virtually irrelevant. After 1840, there was a partial return to purely Haida motifs, which were then juxtaposed and combined with this new manner to produce an almost phantasmagoric representation.

I X

B A G S

Beauty, Mobility, and Symbols of Authority

116. Prestige bag

1800–1820
Potawatomi or Menominee peoples, northern Wisconsin
Native-tanned and dyed skin, porcupine quill, wool strap
9 ¾ x 7 ½ in. (24.8 x 19.1 cm)
RTCNA 254

Northwestern Great Lakes prestige bags such as this one were originally associated with the once-powerful Black Religion and were based on European shot pouches worn by the military. Early bags of this type, which developed just prior to the middle of the eighteenth century, were less vertical in format and often decorated with underwater panthers and bold geometric designs.

The next generation of bags, which would include the present example, dates from the very end of the eighteenth century and were in use until after the first quarter of the nineteenth century. They were made primarily by the Potawatomi and Menominee peoples, who lived in northern Wisconsin. In form, if not in size, they point the way toward the full-size bandolier bag (cat. nos. 118, 119) of the Great Lakes region made in the late nineteenth century. These earlier, smaller bags, however, were made to be hung from the shoulder or carried by hand. They tended to be less bold and more decorative in design. The quatrefoil that here centers the composition has survived into our own times.[1]

The dark color of black-dyed skin was obtained by soaking the skin of a deer in a tannic solution of oak galls and walnut hulls, along with iron filings or similar metallic residue. The red quills are dyed with natural bloodroot, and there are traces of commercial blue dye.

1. For related examples, see Penney 1992, p. 70, and Flint Institute of Arts 1973.

117. Firebag

ca. 1820

Ojibwa or Cree peoples, southern Manitoba or Saskatchewan

Wool, silk and cotton trade cloth, glass beads, metal buttons

21 x 9 ¼ in. (53.3 x 23.5 cm)

RTCNA 664

Bags such as this one are of Canadian origin. They are called firebags, probably because they were used to carry equipment for starting a fire, among other things. The main feature, a rectangular, loom-beaded panel with bilaterally split abstract geometric designs on a white field, hangs below a cloth or skin pouch.

The beaded areas on later firebags tend to be more elaborate, although this would not strictly apply—as in much of Native American art—because, as techniques were passed down from generation to generation, older and more advanced designs could be combined and occur contemporaneously. (This is one reason for the difficulty in dating works.) One clue to the date of this firebag are the cloths used on the upper, pouch portion. The red and blue stroud and the black velveteen patch are early nineteenth century, as is the coarse gray suiting common on early-nineteenth-century military trousers and jackets. The pair of red baize eyelets at the top is also early military issue. At a later date, the drawstrings and, later still, two wool yarn braided straps were attached. This example could be of western Ojibwa or even Plains Cree manufacture, and an acceptable location would be southern Manitoba or Saskatchewan. The bold, striking patterns on their ground and the archaic power of the composition tend to favor a date early in the nineteenth century, about 1820.

| 118. Bandolier bag |

1875–early 1880s
Winnebago peoples, Wisconsin
Wool and cotton trade cloth, wool yarn, glass beads, metal button
34 ½ x 12 in. (87.6 x 30.5 cm)
RTCNA 224

Bandolier bags from the upper Great Lakes region are sometimes hard to classify, but one good indication of Ojibwa attribution is a beaded face design with X motifs. The full-size bandolier bag, as seen here, replaced the smaller bags of the early nineteenth century (cat. no. 116). The discretely organized interlocking beaded design of this bag displays a quiet, overall patterning. The even quality and the avoidance of overaccentuation in favor of a serenity and sense of control point to a date midway in the development of late-nineteenth-century Great Lakes bandolier bags—between 1875 and the early 1880s. The X motif is here, but fragmented and reassembled into a discontinuous design. Both the Menominee of northeastern Wisconsin and the Winnebago, who lived on farms in the central region of the state rather than on reservations, were accomplished progenitors of this looser style. The Menominee, however, tended to repeat small design units over and over again, with a feeling for syncopated visual effect. The complexities of attribution are settled here, however, by the fact that the straps are offset, thus overlapping the bag proper at each side. Because this feature is clearly a Winnebago preference, it is safe to attribute this classically balanced bag to a Winnebago beadworker perhaps living in the area of Wisconsin Dells, or in one of the farming communities such as Tomah or Wittenberg, where tribal members maintain farms to this day.

| 119. Bandolier bag |

ca. 1870
Ojibwa peoples, Minnesota
Wool and cotton trade cloth, wool ribbon, glass beads
39 x 11 ¼ in. (99.1 x 28.6 cm)
RTCNA 596

There are many variants on the Ojibwa X motif noted in catalogue number 118. Here, for example, the Xs are separated by a strong cross element. The continuity of the motifs is broken, and they play a secondary role. The dominant upper-register stroud panel, with its solid red color, indicates a fairly early date, about 1870. A decade later, this panel becomes less prominent and, ultimately, all but disappears. The beaded face panel, on the other hand, becomes more pronounced by stages and by the turn of the twentieth century is often fully pictorial, culminating in bouquetlike still-life scenes.

The most interesting feature of the bag is also its most subtle, namely, the two center tabs embellished with vertical rows of ten paired tiny ascending thunderbirds. Figures are rarely seen on bandolier bags, and they are generally limited to thunderbirds and human figures.[1] Here, the once prominent reference, during the eighteenth and early nineteenth centuries, to an important religious icon—the supernatural thunderbird—is now marginalized.

1. Pohrt 1996, p. 17.

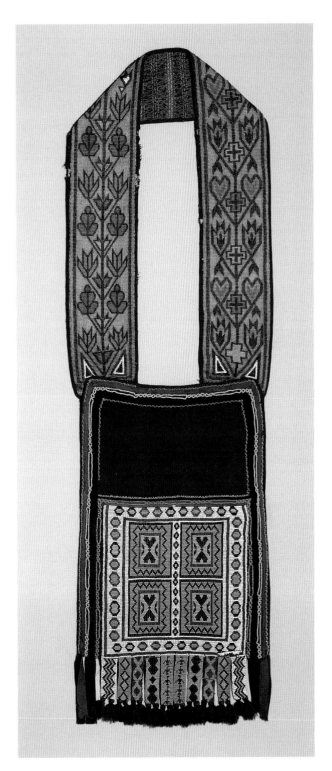

120. Flat bag

Late 19th–early 20th century
Warm Springs peoples (?), Oregon
Cotton and wool trade cloth, glass beads
16 x 12 ⅝ in. (40.6 x 32.1 cm)
RTCNA 606

The impressive design of this fully beaded bag is enhanced by the symbolism of its motifs. Later flat bags were often more picturesque and less astringent in content (see cat. no. 122). Against a rich blue background float four singular images, most notably an eagle ascending sharply with upstretched wings toward a morning star. Below the eagle are two eagle feathers that denote this particular bag as paraphernalia for the Feather Religion, which was widespread in the Plateau region after 1904. This faith was inspired by the dreams of the Klickitat prophet Jake Hurt, and it advocated a life of moderation within the context of traditional tribal values. The Feather Religion formed a parallel to other revival faiths such as the Plains Ghost Dance, the Prairie Faw Faw Religion (see cat. no. 146), and the Dream (Smohalla) cult of the Puget Sound area. All these religions, in one way or another, were concerned with the revitalization of Native American values, which were increasingly being lost to white cultural dominance.

Through dreams and dance, these cults invoked the past and hoped to bring about the return of buffalo days. Far from being warlike in their practices and beliefs, their pursuits were spiritual and peaceful. The eagle on this bag has no association with U.S. patriotism; its connotation here is purely Indian, both as a spiritual messenger and as an icon of the Universal Creator.

121. Flat bag

Late 19th–early 20th century
Yakima peoples, central Washington
Cotton and wool trade cloth, glass beads,
Native-tanned skin straps
12 ¾ x 9 ¾ in. (32.4 x 24.8 cm)
RTCNA 516

A note inside this flat bag states that it was made by the Yakima, a major tribe of the central region of Washington State. The Yakima are famed for these beaded carrying bags, which have a seemingly endless repertory of subject matter. Such bags are still carried by Plateau women at ceremonial occasions. I once attended a snake dance in the village of St. Ignatius, in the far northeastern corner of Montana. There, several hundred Flathead Indian women performed in a complex interweaving zigzag pattern. They carried at their sides colorful flat bags, which seemed to flash in the sunlight as they twisted and turned.

The overlay stitch on the front of this bag is executed in contour beading, a specialty of Plateau beaders and seen on the most prized examples. Echoing the leaf and strawberry motifs, the blue beaded background, like concentric ripples of water, lends a dynamic, wavelike energy. The fine quality of beadwork demonstrated here only hints at the great variety of bead-decorated cradleboards, cuffs, vests, moccasins, and dresses made by the numerous peoples who live in the intermontane area, a northern plateau region between the Cascade Mountains and the Rockies.

A period of great unrest ensued in the 1840s, after the Oregon Trail opened paths of settlement into what was then known as the Oregon Country, and little by little Native Americans were forced into reservations. In 1863, the U.S. government established two reservations in Idaho, one for the Shoshone, in the south, and one for the Coeur d'Alene and related peoples in the north. The Coeur d'Alene were settled at the village of Plummer, near the Washington State border, and they have remained there ever since.

The Coeur d'Alene are noted for their small version of the beaded flat bag. A number of these bags, of which this one is a prime example, are characteristically octagonal in shape. The designs on this double-faced bag form a jewel-like vignette. On one side (not shown), a svelte yellow horse prances on a blue field delicately relieved by random specks of red and black beads, as if galavanting through a mythical sky. The white bead above the horse is probably the maker's signature. On the reverse (seen above), a more topical program is followed. Here, two eccentrically colored doves are presented one above the other. The green dove has just snatched a seed, which it holds in its beak, indicated by three light blue beads, while the purple dove, eyeing the seed, surreptitiously prepares to pounce. The maker who executed this bag was a keen observer of bird life, as anyone who has witnessed a dove preparing to pounce would surely confirm.

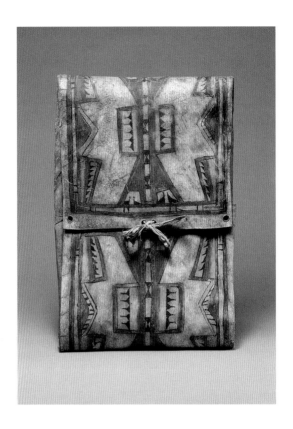

123. Child's envelope parfleche

ca. 1875
Cheyenne peoples, Oklahoma
Rawhide, paint, Native-tanned skin ties
16 ½ x 11 ¼ in. (41.9 x 28.6 cm)
RTCNA 387

Although children's parfleches are small in scale, they maintain the monumental quality of the finest proportioned designs used on full-size adult examples. This parfleche (a container made of rawhide) reproduces a classic Cheyenne pattern best described in the monograph by Gaylord Torrence: "The distinctive character of Cheyenne parfleches emerges from the power of the drawing. The images possess a sense of tension and a precise linear structure deriving from the artists' emphasis on fine, brown-black outlining, which is the primary activating element of the paintings. This effect of line is frequently enhanced by the placement of small black units throughout the design [which] establish shifting focal points and rhythmic directional movements."[1] Each half of the parfleche has a central motif composed of half triangles abutting a rectangle. These elements are, in turn,

accented by hourglass devices and ball finials, so that the whole of each half unit can be read either as a single format or as one that is separated in two. The customary border enframes the composition. Thus, a perfectly balanced design of positive and negative elements is created by the harmonious juxtaposition of open and closed forms.

This rare child's parfleche, most likely one of a pair, almost certainly originated among the southern Cheyenne of central western Oklahoma. The attribution is supported by the fact that much of the material culture of the northern Cheyenne of Montana was destroyed by the U.S. Army at the Dull Knife Massacre in 1879, and most of the traditional arts of the Cheyenne survived in the south.

1. Torrence 1994, p. 105.

124. Pair of envelope parfleches

1880–85
Brulé Sioux peoples, South Dakota
Rawhide, paint, Native-tanned skin ties
a. 22 ½ x 13 ⅜ in. (57.2 x 34 cm)
b. 22 ¼ x 12 ⅞ in. (56.5 x 32.7 cm)
RTCNA 603a, b

Central Plains parfleches in envelope form were customarily made in pairs, one placed on either side of a horse, although often they do not survive together. This pair, made by the Brulé Sioux, employs bright commercial pigment and displays a boldness of pattern that marks them as originating in the late nineteenth century. More specifically, they belong to the period 1880–85, when prominent diamond motifs were combined within a format generally divided into two distinct registers. The upper and lower registers would have a pair of motifs, each of which would, in turn, be provided with a wide border, usually red or yellow, as an overall framework. Later on, toward 1900, the outer borders become wider and more dominant, and the optical effect even more dynamic.[1] This present pair of envelopes may thus be placed squarely in the middle of this increasingly bold and abstract development.

1. For this type of Sioux envelope, dating to about 1900, see Torrence 1994, p. 96, pl. 14. For a comparative pair, see ibid., p. 94, no. 13.

| 125. Pair of possible bags |

ca. 1900
Sioux peoples, North and South Dakota
Native-tanned skin, porcupine quill, metal
a. 12 x 17 x 3 in. (30.5 x 43.2 x 7.6 cm)
b. 12 x 16 x 3 in. (30.5 x 40.6 x 7.6 cm)
RTCNA 413a, b

The brilliant coloration and harmony of design on this notable pair of Lakota Sioux possible bags (so named because they could carry anything possible) reflect the desire of the Central Plains Sioux to reassert their cultural heritage after 1875, when they were relocated to reservations. The bags are related in design to the envelope parfleches (cat. no. 124), but they are more refined and technically sophisticated. The quilled horizontal red bands have their origin in the parallel lines of red quillwork that often decorated full-size wearing robes and tipi liners. One can imagine the clout that these bags would have lent to a rider as he paraded at such celebratory occasions as the Fourth of July or Indian Days, events that provided a stage from which to display symbolically the military prowess once confirmed in battle.

X

MOCCASINS AND CLOTHING

Dressed for Honor, Pride, and Nobility

126. Pair of moccasins

ca. 1808
Seneca peoples, New York
Native-tanned skin, porcupine quill
Length 10 ½ in. (26.7 cm); width 4 in. (10.2 cm)
RTCNA 675a, b

This pair of moccasins, dated to about 1808, is among the earliest Eastern Woodlands moccasins whose history can be closely followed. The leather from which they are fashioned is very soft, and there are no beads to distract from the discreet quillwork. They give us an impression of what, quill-decorated moccasins might have looked like before the intrusion of European influence and materials.

On the inside of each moccasin is a somewhat worn inscription, reading, "RJD from SDP," and loosely attached to one of them is a handwritten label as follows: "Presented to Susan Dutton Powell by a Squaw of the 'Seneca Nation'— about the year 1808—Her father Thomas Dutton having charge at that time, of the 'Indian Reservation' under the care of Philadelphia Yearly Meeting of Friends. Devised by S. D. Powell to R. J. Dutton." To simplify a complicated family account, Thomas Dutton (1769–1869), a Philadelphia Quaker, married Sarah Jones on November 24, 1791, at the

Radnor Meeting of the Society of Friends. One of their seven children, Thomas (b. 1803), married Hannah Ridgeway in 1837, and they had three children. Their son Rowland Jones Dutton (b. 1832) is of special interest to us because he is the gentleman whose initials are inscribed inside these moccasins.

How did they come into the Dutton family? Thomas Dutton's daughter Susanna (b. 1795) was the girl presented with the moccasins by the "squaw" of the Seneca Nation, about 1808. Thomas Dutton had been asked by the Philadelphia Yearly Meeting of the Society of Friends "to undertake the management of a farm at Tunesassa, in Cattaraugus County, New York, adjoining a Reservation on the Allegheny River belonging to the Seneca Nation of Indians. This farm had been purchased . . . under a concern for the improvement and gradual civilization of the Indians by giving them instruction in farming, as well as school education."[1] If the

| *Moccasins and Clothing*

year 1808 is used as a criterion, Susanna was thirteen years old when the moccasins were gifted to her, probably as a welcoming gesture to the family's assuming responsibility for the farm. At the publication of the Dutton family history in 1871—but commemorating the one hundredth birthday of Thomas Dutton Sr.—Susanna was still living in West Chester, Pennsylvania. Perhaps on this occasion she gave the pair of moccasins to her nephew Roland Jones Dutton.

At any rate, they eventually passed to the same collector who also owned the pair of child's moccasins (cat. no. 129), and thence to the dealer John Molloy, who brought them to my attention. (For a somewhat later pair of Seneca quilled moccasins, see cat. no. 127.)

1. Cope 1871, p. 57.

127. Pair of moccasins

ca. 1830
Seneca peoples, New York
Native-tanned skin, porcupine quill, glass beads, silk ribbon
Length 9 ¾ in. (24.8 cm); width 4 ½ in. (11.4 cm)
RTCNA 309a, b

These brilliantly colored Seneca moccasins, in their elaboration of quilled decoration, are a stylistic successor to the pair previously described (cat. no. 126). The earlier pair has Y-shaped quilled projections around the cuff that may represent feathers. Here, the device has metamorphosed into a more controlled, three-pronged motif, of which there are five on each side. The cuff is wider, and the quilled border is bolder. The blue silk cuff border is now embellished with small white seed beads. In the earlier pair, the cuff terminates abruptly above the heel. While the quillwork extending down the vamp is basically meant to conceal the frontal seam, it later becomes a completely independent element, with multiple stripes and a delicate wavy line of overlay quills framing the vamp motif.[1]

These moccasins have a well-documented history. They were collected by a German nobleman, Baron Johann Friedrich Kraus, during his travels in America in the 1830s. In Buffalo, New York, he also collected two related pairs of Seneca moccasins. The three pairs entered the Speyer collection, one of the most notable collections of American Indian material acquired in Europe between the First and Second World Wars. (The collection was subsequently bought by the Canadian National Museum, now the Canadian Museum of Civilization, Quebec.) But it was the early travelers to the interior of America, such as Prince Maximilian zu wied and Prince Paul, duke of Würtemberg, who initiated in the 1820s and 1830s the German interest in Indian cultures, particularly those of the Prairies and the Plains.

These moccasins were one of two pairs sold at Seahawk Auctions, Burnaby, British Columbia, in June 2000.[2] The consignor provided notes made by his great-grandfather Baron Alexander Kraus that read, in part, "My father, Johann Friedrich Kraus, was born on the island Ahl, in the River Lahn, close to the Baths of Ems, where my grandfather, Jacob Kraus, owned an iron foundry. I had also another brother, Fritz, who was 10 years older than me, and who, after traveling in the United States of America, where he visited also the Indians, brought me two pairs of shoes of Buffalo skin, embroidered with Porcupine stings (which I still own). He died (at the age of 25) within three days in Frankfurt, on the 25th of September, 1835, of typhoid fever." It is clear from this account that Fritz Kraus was the original collector of both pairs.

1. For a comparable pair, see Grimes, Feest, and Curran 2002, p. 97, no. 25.
2. The present pair was lot 1223; the accompanying pair was lot 1224.

128. Pair of moccasins

1790–1815
Huron peoples, Wendake (Lorette), Quebec
Native-tanned and dyed skin, deer and moosehair, porcupine quill, silk ribbon, metal
Length 10 ½ in. (26.7 cm); width 4 ½ in. (11.4 cm)
RTCNA 302a, b

This stunning pair of Huron moccasins is one of the oldest to survive and may well date to the end of the eighteenth century. The highly elaborate design includes such exquisite attention to detail as fully quilled circles within half circles instead of the usual half circles alone. The finesse of the floral designs in the primary panel of the cuffs and the evenness of the closely spaced stitching create the effect of an imaginary garden. The tendrils and unfolding blossoms that extend downward across the vamp display an unusual rhythmic harmony, and the device of the matching parts against the dark tones of the walnut-dyed leather reflect an earthiness that is essentially Northeast Woodlands in character. Heavily worked moccasins such as these were purchased by Europeans directly from the makers or through the local convent. Their high style would have precluded daily use, and they would have been costly even at the time they were made. In England, they might have been displayed prominently in what eventually became known as Indian corners. This usage may well have determined why the present pair remains in pristine condition. In their commingling of the Native American love of nature and the French love of refinement, they represent the encounter between the Old World and the New.

129. Pair of child's moccasins

1810–15
Wyandot or Shawnee peoples, western Ohio or southern Ontario
Native-tanned skin, sinew sewn, ornamented with thread, silk ribbon, white glass beads
Length 4 ¾ in. (12.1 cm); width 2 ¼ in. (5.7 cm)
RTCNA 236a, b

This tiny pair of child's moccasins is notable for its delicate tailoring, of a perfection in keeping with adornment for a loved child. One can almost feel the snap of minuscule scissors trimming the silk into cuff appliqués. The blue and red panels are divided horizontally by neatly cut rows of white silk diamonds. An exquisite attention is paid to details: the narrow strip of green silk at either end of the panels; the outer blue panel sewn to the cuff in just barely visible red thread; the inner cuff sewn in a complementary white; the pairing of the glass beads on the rim. The construction is single seam, with a double row of petite white beads that conceal the seam running down the vamp.

As to the origin of these moccasins, Ruth B. Phillips provides an acceptable solution in her monograph on the important collection of Great Lakes material culture assembled in the early nineteenth century by Major Jasper Grant. Grant served at Fort Malden in Amherstburg, Ontario, from 1806 to 1809. In 1902, his collection was deposited by his grandson in the National Museum of Ireland, Dublin, where it remains to this day. Two pairs of moccasins published by Phillips exhibit the same tailoring and rows of tiny diamonds as those pictured here. They are attributed either to the Wyandot, Shawnee, or Iroquois. The Wyandot and Shawnee were active around the Fort Malden area, where Grant was posted; it would thus seem fitting to attribute the present pair of child's moccasins to one of these two western Ohio tribes.

1. Phillips 1984, p. 44, nos. 33, 34, illus. p. 70.

130. Pair of woman's moccasins

ca. 1840
Huron peoples, Wendake (Lorette), Quebec
Native-tanned skin, wool and cotton trade cloth, silk ribbon, glass beads
Length 9 ½ in. (24.1 cm); width 3 ¼ in. (8.3 cm)
RTCNA 669a, b

This festive pair of Huron moccasins displays a well-known beadwork design seen also in Huron pouches of this period. It includes a Europeanized central floral motif with two green leaves on both the vamps and the cuffs. Other Huron moccasins from the same period were even more cross-cultural. The Native parts are sewn over a European suede slipper with a hard sole, suggesting that the moccasins were destined for a non-Native or Métis girl to wear to an elegant soirée. In addition, the sole would have had a square toe, a reminder that round-toed shoes did not come into fashion until after the mid-nineteenth century, thus supporting a date of about 1840.

The Huron were vanquished by their cousins the Iroquois in the seventeenth century. Relocated by the

Franciscans from the area around Lake Simcoe, north of Toronto, to a safe haven on Christian Island, Ontario, they eventually settled in the village of Lorette, very near present-day Quebec City, where they live to this day. About fifteen years ago, in a reassertion of their Native American heritage, the Huron renamed the village Wendake.

131. Pair of woman's moccasins

1880–1900
Winnebago peoples, Wisconsin
Native-tanned skin, glass beads
Length 9 ⅜ in. (23.8 cm); width 3 ⅜ in. (8.3 cm)
RTCNA 237a, b

One of the most easily recognized types of moccasins was traditionally made by the Winnebago of Wisconsin. Each moccasin is cut from a single piece of buckskin, and the vamp is completely concealed by an enveloping single cuff, leaving only the toe exposed. Across the flap are three diamond motifs, each subdivided into nine facets, against a background of six horizontal stripes. Along the bottom edge of the flap and extending around the back is a narrow border—one side green, the other side blue—offset by beaded triangles in white and yellow. The overall design and construction of these moccasins is classically Great Lakes in conception. The result is as stylish as it is striking. The syncopated arrangement of triangular motifs can also be found on the miniature Winnebago woven bag (cat. no. 76).[1]

1. For another example of a Winnebago bag with the triangular motif, see Kahlenberg 1998, p. 251, colorpl. 259.

Wabuse (Mrs. Joe Hill)

Ojibwa, active 1970s

| 132. *Pair of woman's moccasins* |

1975

Mille Lacs Ojibwa Indian Reservation, Minnesota

Native-tanned skin, cotton velvet, glass beads

Length 11 in. (27.9 cm); width 3 ¾ in. (9.5 cm)

RTCNA 240a, b

This pair of pointed-toe moccasins was purchased in 1984 at Fort Mille Lacs village, Onamia, Minnesota. The village is actually a group of rusticated log buildings near the Mille Lacs Ojibwa Indian Reservation, a center for fine objects of the Ojibwa culture established many years ago by the trader Sherman Holbert. Sherman introduced me to a good many Ojibwa traditionalists. Among them was Mrs. Joe Hill, whose Indian name is Wabuse. In 1975, Wabuse made this pair of beautifully fashioned, old-style moccasins in the pointed-toe style popular among the Ojibwa from about 1880 to 1920. The cuffs and vamp are faced with deep-set, black cotton velvet, again in the old-style manner. The sparkling floral design, in green, white, blue, and yellow beads, is Wabuse's own variant on a classic Ojibwa theme.

133. Woman's skirt and blouse

ca. 1914–18
Winnebago peoples, Wisconsin
Cotton velvet, wool and cotton trade cloth, glass beads,
paillettes, buttons, silk ribbon
a. Blouse: 22 ¼ x 17 ½ in. (56.5 x 44.5 cm)
b. Skirt: 35 ½ x 26 ½ in. (90.2 x 67.3 cm)
RTCNA 247a, b
The Metropolitan Museum of Art,
Gift of Ralph T. Coe, 2002 (2002.602.8a, b)

This cotton velvet skirt and blouse carries the same emphasis on fashionable appeal that one finds in the nearly contemporaneous Osage woman's wearing blanket (cat. no. 148). It was made by the Wisconsin Winnebago, and is of Great Lakes rather than Prairie origin. There is an indirect but palpable influence of turn-of-the-century Anglo fashion at work here, but such pronounced color combinations remain purely Midwestern Indian in taste. The ensemble was probably made about the time of the First World War. It is a transitional piece, pointing back to the late-nineteenth-century Winnebago floral design vocabulary but also presaging the greater freedom of postwar flapper-era fashion. This dressy outfit showed up in 1982 at Parson's Trading Post, in the resort area of Wisconsin Dells.

| 134. Hood |

1840–50
James Bay Cree peoples, Quebec
Wool and cotton trade cloth, glass beads
26 x 11 in. (66 x 27.9 cm)
RTCNA 308

This type of beaded, rectangular cloth hood marks the apogee of the northeastern woman's hood not only with regard to size and length but also for complexity of decoration. The present example displays, within each bordered register, beaded tendrils that flow in parallel cascades of flowers and vines, almost like musical notations. The elaborate design is offset by the undecorated panel that extends up the center of the hood to the crowning tassel.

The James Bay Cree were undoubtedly familiar with the Micmac and Maliseet Atlantic Coastal beaded hoods that initially derived from French Canadian Breton-style caps. But because they lived far inland, along the southeastern shore of James Bay, they were sufficiently isolated to develop their own style, an oblong rather than partially curved hood profile. The height of the hood ensured that it could be prominently seen from far away.

This particular hood descended through the family of Donald Alexander Smith, Lord Strathcona (1820–1914), governor of the Hudson's Bay Company from 1889 until his death in 1914.[1] The Hudson's Bay Company, chartered by Charles II in 1670, became not only synonymous with the development of the transcontinental fur trade in Canada but served as a de facto agency of the British Empire in North America. Lord Strathcona was responsible for shifting the emphasis of the company toward the development of retail stores as much as trading enterprises, notably a chain of large department stores in the major cities of Canada. He was also heavily involved in the development of railways, both in Canada and the United States. Strathcona's collecting of Canadian Indian art went unnoticed until this hood was auctioned in 2000, eighty-six years after his death, at which time I acquired it.[2]

1. Newman 1985, p. 180.
2. Christie's East, New York, May 17, 2000, sale no. 8383, lot 187.

135. Cap

1850–60
Naskapi peoples, Labrador
Wool trade cloth, silk ribbon, thread
Height 10 ½ in. (26.7 cm); diameter 7 in. (17.8 cm)
RTCNA 501

Like the James Bay Cree hood (cat. no. 134), this cap was collected by Donald Alexander Smith, Lord Strathcona. When it was auctioned at Christie's, New York, in May 2000, it was identified as a Cree/Métis cloth-embroidered toque.[1] But it is certainly of Naskapi origin.

Both the Montagnais and the Naskapi peoples made similar high-crowned, multipaneled caps with panels of alternating red and black. These were worn only on important occasions. The Naskapi type is generally taller and more elegant in its subtle use of appliqué along the bottom edge. While the Montagnais and the Naskapi are culturally very similar, close enough to allow them to share a village twenty-five miles east of Goose Bay, Labrador, they consider themselves separate politically, and their arts can differ in detail, as can be seen by comparing this cap with the one following.

1. Christie's, New York, May 17, 2000, sale no. 8383, lot 189.

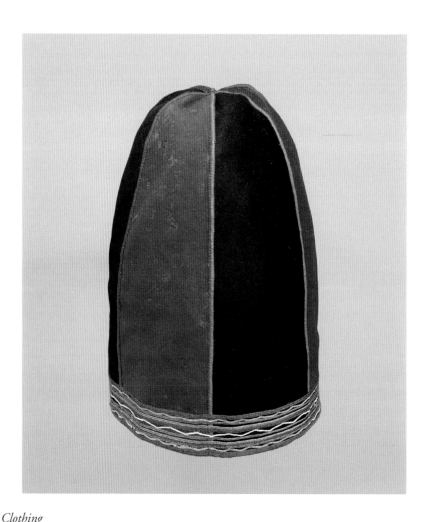

Marie-Jeanne Bacon, Montagnais, active 1980–90s

| 136. Cap |

1997
Gulf of St. Lawrence, Quebec
Cotton velvet, cotton cloth, silk thread
Height 8 in. (20.3 cm); diameter 8 in. (20.3 cm)
RTCNA 310a

Although I had been in Labrador in search of works for the "Lost and Found Traditions" exhibition, I had never visited the north shore of the eastern part of the Gulf of St. Lawrence. In July 1995, I finally motored as far as the Canadian naval base of Sept-Îles. On the way, I passed a sign for the large Montagnais village of Betsiamites, one of nine extant villages of the Montagnais tribe in Quebec, and I drove down the sloping coast road to the village. There, I discovered on the main street a small, neatly run shop marked Artisanat Opessamo. Inside were two charming ladies who had just finished making several classic, multipaneled Montagnais women's caps, embroidered with traditional motifs of mountains, suns, moons, and canoes. Looking at these freshly finished caps, I felt transported back to the nineteenth century. I purchased two of them: a woman's model (shown here), made by the proprietor, Marie-Jeanne Bacon, and, upon my return from Sept-Îles, its companion, a man's model with ear projections tucked in at the top. According the Canadian Telephone Information Service, the shop is now no longer listed, and my attempts to obtain Marie-Jeanne Bacon's birth date by long distance ended with a broken phone connection with the Betsiamites town hall records office.

137. Glengarry-style cap

ca. 1880
Iroquois peoples, southern Ontario or Quebec
Wool and cotton trade cloth, silk ribbon, glass beads
4 ½ x 12 x 5 ½ in. (11.4 x 30.5 x 14 cm)
RTCNA 314

This Glengarry-style Iroquois cap is shown to complement the earlier Huron Glengarry cap (cat. no. 63). The floral patterns here are heavier and less fluid than those of the elegantly refined Huron cap from about forty years earlier. There is also a difference in medium—heavy beading rather than the more subtle moosehair stitchery—and a more garish use of red cloth, far more assertive visually than its restrained predecessor. Here, the design elements are more pronounced, and the bulk of the cap requires bolder floral motifs. This comparison provides a good example of how traditional arts change over time.

Canadian Indian Glengarry-style caps are generally known in Great Britain because so many are seen in antiques shops, suggesting that they must have been a popular export item. This cap turned up unexpectedly in an antiques stall in Bath, in 1977, and I bought it specifically because of its rare, red background. The characteristics of the cap would indicate a date fairly late in the nineteenth century, about 1880.

138. Cradle cover panel

1800–1820

Eastern Sioux peoples (?), Minnesota or eastern Dakota

Native-tanned skin, birchbark, porcupine quill, metal cones

10 x 14 ⅛ in. (25.4 x 35.9 cm)

RTCNA 605

This early Sioux quilled panel originally served as a coverlet on the lower part of a cradle. Though part of an ensemble, it was made independently, and counts among the distinguished examples of early Plains quillwork that have survived. Two complete cradles, with most of their decoration intact, are in museum collections. A baby carrier on a newer frame, perhaps somewhat later in date, is in the Peabody Essex Museum, Salem, on deposit from the Maine Historical Society, Portland, where it is given as early nineteenth century.[1] The cover on that cradle, as reproduced, illustrates how the present panel would have served as part of a two-part wrapping for the baby. It is decorated with thunderbirds and anthropomorphic manitou-like designs rather than with deer, as here, but the dyes used are the same.[2] The second cradle belonged to the nineteenth-century American painter George Catlin and is now in the National Museum of Natural History, Washington, D.C., while the third is from another early collection, that of Nathan Jarvis, and is now in the Brooklyn Museum of Art.[3]

Here, five deer in two registers are depicted in striking silhouette, marching in procession above and below a row of diamond motifs with cross-shaped centers, which refer to the four directions of the universe. A pleasing design contraposition is achieved by having the deer look backward instead of facing forward. The deer are framed by bloodroot-colored borders that effectively redirect our attention inward.

Interestingly, the quills of this cradle cover panel are wrapped around birchbark slats rather than the usual rawhide, an unusual feature that may hint at a northern origin. The

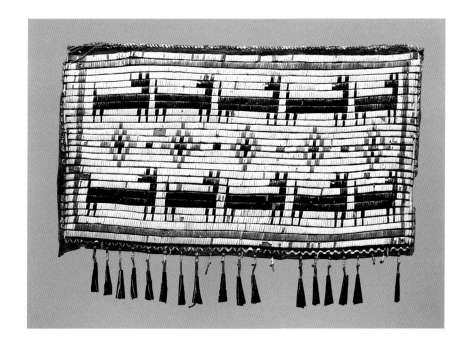

profiles of the deer at the far right are shorter than the others, perhaps suggesting that the quillworker miscalculated the space available or that it is fawns that are represented. The archaic simplicity of the design reflects early Plains quillwork at its best. One can imagine the sound of the metal dangles along the fringe tinkling when the cradle was shifted and attracting the attention of the baby within.

1. Grimes, Feest, and Curran 2002, p. 202, no. 91.
2. The figural designs hint at the relationship between the eastern Sioux and the Great Lakes Ojibwa. During the 1750s, the Ojibwa invaded the region in which the Mille Lacs Lake Ojibwa now live. They lit bags of gunpowder and dropped them down the Sioux lodge smoke holes, and the Sioux retreated down the Rum River. A band of Sioux still live south of Minneapolis in Prairie Island, and the Ojibwa remain in contact with them.
3. Feder 1964, pp. 28, 53, no. 29, fig. 38.

139. Roach

Mid-19th century
Eastern Plains or westernmost Prairie peoples,
Minnesota or the Dakotas
Deer- and horsehair, feathers, rawhide, wool trade cloth, metal,
porcupine quill
14 x 15 in. (35.6 x 38.1 cm)
RTCNA 444

This venerable roach, worn on top of the head of a qualified warrior or ceremonialist, conveys to this day the militancy that marked the Plains warrior zeitgeist before these peoples were confined to reservations, prevented from following the lifestyle that was their legacy. While the use of roaches has continued to this day, confinement led to a more decorative display and a conception of design that has lost its powerful, stark presence. This one still retains, subliminally, the bellicose aura of the person who might have worn it in buffalo days. The very essence of Plains military glory, it lent dramatic import to victory in earlier times.

The general concept of the form spread from East to West, having perhaps derived from the comblike hairstyle that distinguished warriors of the Iroquois Confederacy, notably the Mohawks.

140. Roach spreader

Late 19th century
Oto or Osage peoples, southeastern Nebraska
or eastern Oklahoma
Incised elk antler, pigment
8 ¼ x 2 ¼ in. (21 x 5.7 cm)
RTCNA 264

Roach spreaders are flat, spatulate shaped, and set within a roach (cat. no. 139) to help it retain its shape and to keep the fringelike surround standing upright. Some of the most accomplished and elegant roach spreaders were produced by the Prairie peoples bordering the Great Plains. Both the Oto, in southeastern Nebraska, and the Osage, in western Missouri and eastern Oklahoma, adopted some of the practices and customs of the Indians on the Plains, specifically the buffalo hunt. The large size of this roach spreader would indicate Plains custom, while the figure portrayed wears a Prairie-style turban. This would point to either an Oto or an Osage origin. It is one of the ironies of Native American cultures that such exceptional engraving skill was concealed within the roach when it was being danced. The jauntily attired chief depicted here is clothed in stylish regalia—German silver armlets, a bear-claw necklace, and a fur-trimmed turban with feathers—and appears to be naked to the waist.

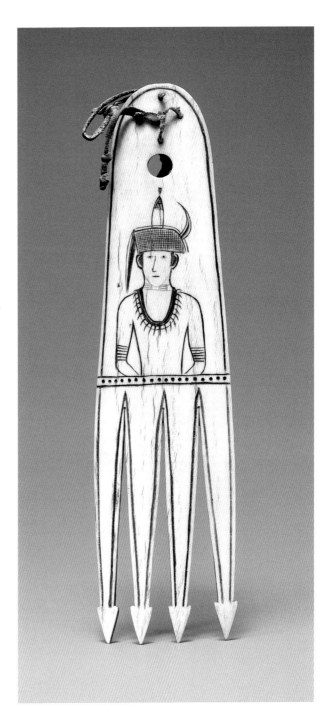

141. Leadership shirt

ca. 1860–65

Arikara peoples, upper Missouri River, North Dakota

Native-tanned skin, paint, porcupine quill, human hair,

ermine, feathers, silk ribbon

39 x 53 in. (99.1 x 134.6 cm)

RTCNA 439

This type of Plains shirt was awarded only to tribal leaders who had demonstrated qualities of leadership. Popularly known as war shirts, they are more accurately described as leadership shirts, since, unlike war shirts, it is not scalp locks that dangle from the sleeves. Rather, for this purpose tribal women would offer their hair, which was wrapped in fringe and then sewn onto the shirt in recognition of the wearer as their leader. Such shirts were probably used not so much for evoking war as for display at tribal meetings, oratory, and victory dancing. The ermine tails, called weasel tails to this day, served to reinforce the sense of flashing movement when the shirt was in use. The quilled floral motifs on the bib at the neck display a decorative play and delicacy of design that originated in the eastern Plains, rather than in the upper Missouri River region, where this shirt was actually made.

The three northwestern North Dakota tribes—the Arikara, the Mandan, and the Hidatsa—all made shirts of this type after the 1850s. This example is firmly identified as Arikara. It is difficult to date because of the superb preservation of its quilled colors, but it would probably range between about 1860 and 1865. Shirts such as this one were worn by upper Missouri and other northwestern Plains dignitaries when they met with government officials in Washington, D.C. In this context, they were considered by their owners visual equivalents of "Indian constitutions," in other words, paradigms of the law—natural, spiritual, and temporal. The hind legs of the deer that provided the hide for this leadership shirt hang down at each bottom edge, incorporating the whole of the animal and thus imbuing the wearer with spiritual power.

The shirt was originally purchased by the rancher Tom Barber about 1910 at a trading post in northern Montana. His son later remembered that his father's family, who lived in the East, had sent his father to Wyoming. There, he learned to participate in Native American ceremonials and became a student of their lore. This shirt was always stored under Tom Barber's bed, packed away in a trunk. Once a year, he would take his treasure out to inspect for insect damage, but by nightfall it was back once more in its trunk. This explains its remarkably pristine state of preservation. The overlay quillwork is the most complex and demanding of any technique employed by the Plains Indians, and the decoration of a shirt such as this one was a major undertaking.

| 142. Pair of moccasins |

Late 19th or early 20th century
Kiowa peoples, Andarko area, southwestern Oklahoma
Native-tanned skin, dye, glass beads
Length 10 ½ in. (26.7 cm); width 4 in. (10.2 cm)
RTCNA 380a, b

This pair of moccasins exemplifies the classic traits of southern Plains moccasin design. The Kiowa, southern Cheyenne, and Comanche of southwestern Oklahoma and Texas made some of the dressiest and most elegant of all Plains moccasins. The distinguishing hallmarks include the long configuration; the abundant, one-sided fringe that adds an element of luxury to the appearance of the vamp; a double train of buckskin and additional fringe that adorn the back, providing a note of grace to the step of the wearer; the restrained accents provided by the faceted and seed beads; and the small round tongue reduced to a circular, buttonlike medallion, which centers the whole composition. A diagnostic trait of Kiowa authorship is the way in which the hard cowhide sole projects marginally as a flange. Also characteristic is the rich yellow of the fringe and soft buckskin. The noted connoisseur of Plains art Joseph Rivera collected these moccasins. I acquired them from him about 1998.

143. Girl's cape

1890–1900
Blackfoot peoples, Montana
Glass beads, cotton trade cloth, metal bells, Native-tanned skin ties
11 x 22 ½ in. (27.9 x 57.2 cm)
RTCNA 416

This little girl's cape was made during the reservation period, when gingham dresses and other types of European clothing were infiltrating Plains Indian life. It is revealing that except for the buckskin thongs, all the materials used to fashion it are of non-Native origin, yet the effect is totally Indian. The horizontal, barred design is, however, in the Blackfoot tradition of full-size beaded dress yokes, here all the more concentrated in its visual effect for being scaled down. On festive occasions, young girls would be decked out in a cape like this to reclaim their "Indian-ness," which, in retrospect, adds a note of poignancy. The tubular beads came from what is now the Czech Republic and were in common use on the Western Plains at the turn of the century. They are strung on commercial string. The tent-canvas backing was likely smoked sometime during its previous incarnation as part of a tipi.

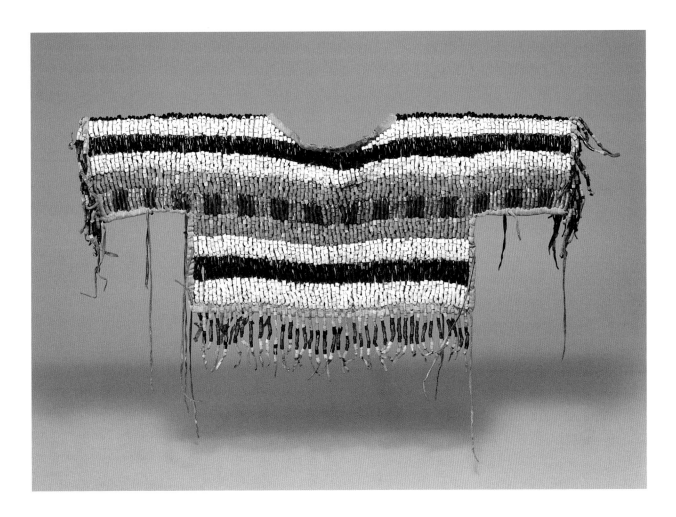

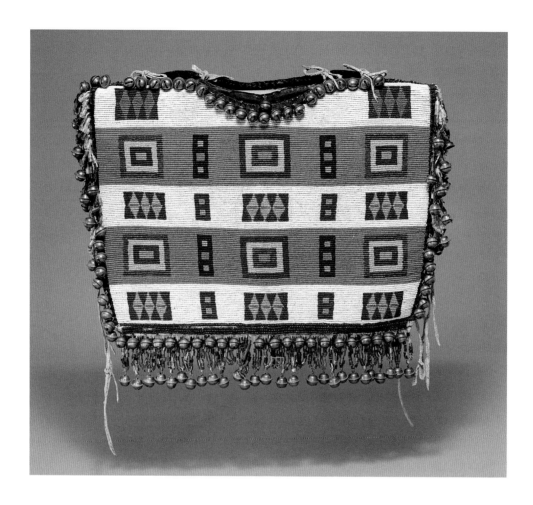

144. Girl's cape

1890–1905
Stoney peoples, Alberta
Glass beads, cotton trade cloth, metal bells, Native-tanned skin ties
13 ½ x 15 in. (34.3 x 38.1 cm)
RTCNA 399

The design on this young girl's cape is partly composed of a series of beaded rectangles within rectangles placed longitudinally in bands, or registers, across the garment. When the band is white, the rectangles contain a row of diamond-shaped feather symbols. When the band is blue, they contain the concentric squares in two alternating color progressions. This subtle shift in color pattern creates a visual dynamic that is characteristically Assiniboine. While these rectangles are also seen in the designs of the Central Plains Sioux, here they are repeated in a strikingly original composition that was once termed, in Canada, Western Sioux. The Western Sioux—or, as they are called today, the

Stoney Indians—are actually an Assiniboine tribe isolated at the base of the Canadian Rockies. The word Assiniboine translates as "stoney," or "people of the stones."

The lower part of this tiny cape has been backed with muslin rather than the original canvas. Perhaps the little girl grew, or the cape was gifted to another child who was slightly older. This may be why the red beads of the bottom addition are bugle beads rather than seed beads, which are smaller. The hawkbells and bugle beads may also be a later addition. Such alterations and changes are not uncommon and should be considered an integral part of Indian costume. (See also cat. no. 156.)

145. Pair of moccasins with beaded soles

ca. 1890
Sioux peoples, North or South Dakota
Native-tanned skin, glass beads
Length 9 in. (22.9 cm); width 3 ¾ in. (9.5 cm)
RTCNA 377a, b

While Plains moccasins that were beaded across the soles used to be referred to as "burial moccasins," there is clear evidence that they were not typically used for this purpose. This pair shows wear on the exposed buckskin and tongue, commensurate with a good deal of use. Not only is there wear on the cuffs, but there are also traces of dirt between the rows of lazy stitching along the sides and heel. Numerous other examples of sole-beaded moccasins also display significant damage on the bottom consistent with heavy use. Certainly, this pair was worn only on special occasions and may have served a number of ceremonial purposes. They could have been worn at an adoption ceremony, where the honored recipient was traditionally seated on a blanket, or at an important occasion such as a medicine bundle opening, which, on the Plains, was often conducted in a specially erected tipi. The owner of the bundle and, in this case, his wife, would sometimes be seated straight-legged facing the participants, so that the soles of the moccasins were visible.

The line of red beads that encircles the division between the sole and the body of these moccasins can be seen on Sioux beaded cradle covers of this same period. The checkerboard pattern is a classic Central Plains convention, here rendered with clarity and distinction.

146. Faw Faw coat

ca. 1900
Oto-Missouria peoples, Oklahoma
Wool and cotton trade cloth, glass beads, silk ribbon
39 x 70 in., (99.1 x 177.8 cm)
RTCNA 527

Indian resistance to European-American hegemony is generally considered to have been concluded by the time of the suppression of the short-lived Ghost Dance revival among the Plains and Prairie tribes and end of the Battle of Wounded Knee, in 1890. However, religious cults that kept traditional customs and beliefs alive continued to be practiced.

One of the cults that flourished after 1890 was under the leadership of William Faw Faw (Waw-no-she), an Oklahoma Oto-Missouria who lived near Ponca City. Adherents to his religion were costumed in war regalia decorated with design schemes derived from eccentric floral and equine motifs shared by the Osage, Iowa, Oto-Missouria, Mesquakie, Sauk and Fox, and Winnebago tribes. These reinterpretations evolved into abstract combinations of floral and curvilinear devices, horse heads (occasionally full profiles of the entire body), stars, and here, rows of abstracted buffalo skulls, linked in continuous patterns just above the bottom hem. The embellishment is most elaborate on Native-made Prince Albert–like coats, of which this is an example. Observant Faw Faw cultists also wore shirts, leggings, and breechclouts, decorated moccasins, and turbans; they sewed epaulets on their coats and carried bags similarly adorned with outlined beadwork patterns. The repetition of the design created zones of brilliant rust red, navy blue, yellow, lavender, light blue, and green, all outlined in white. The fleur-de-lys device, repeated twice, may have derived from spontoon tomahawks.

This particular coat was once in the collection of the Philbrook Museum of Art, Tulsa, Oklahoma.[1] The decoration is less complicated than that of more dramatic coats, some of which may have been made by William Faw Faw's wife.[2] Faw Faw paraphernalia was emblematic of the desire to return to the past grandeur of Native American life, which had, by this time, been irreparably lost.

1. Wade 1986, p. 81, fig. 63.
2. A detailed account of the development of the Faw Faw beadwork style is recounted in Wooley and Waters 1988.

Georgeann Robinson, Osage, 1917–1986

147. Man's dress outfit

1965–70
Pawhuska, Oklahoma
Wool trade cloth, silk ribbon, glass beads, sequins
Leggings: 34 x 13 in. (86.4 x 33 cm)
Breechclout: 56 x 12 in. (142.2 x 30.5 cm)
Trailer: 16 x 12 in. (40.6 x 30.5 cm)
RTCNA 511a–d

According to tradition, the Osage fell to Earth from the stars. Each of the three Oklahoma Osage towns, or *gentes* (clans), Hominy, Fairfax, and Pawhuska, holds its own summer celebration to commemorate this myth of celestial origin. The apparel worn during the yearly celebrations is treasured by Osage families and worn with great care. It is stored away in trunks when not in use and shown only to special guests. This man's dress outfit includes leggings, a breechclout, and a trailer, and was commissioned from the late Georgeann Robinson by an Anglo acquaintance who regularly attended the annual dances.

Georgeann Robinson was the best-known tribal ribbon appliqué artist of her generation. She was also the sister of the Osage dignitary Andrew Gray (see cat. no. 148), and for many years she ran the Red Men Shop in downtown Pawhuska. Her work is noted for its clarity of design, tight stitch, and strict interpretation of favorite Osage motifs. The tradition of fine costuming continues among the Osage due in no small part to her example.

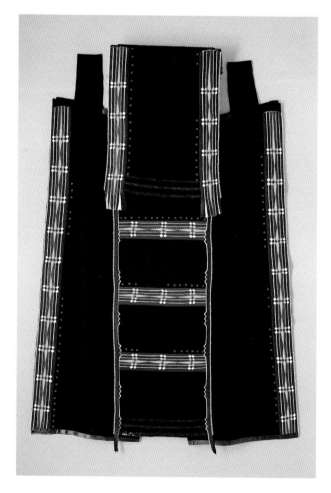

148. Woman's wearing blanket

Early 20th century
Osage peoples, Oklahoma
Wool and silk trade cloth, glass beads
60 x 67 in. (152.4 x 170.2 cm)
RTCNA 509
The Metropolitan Museum of Art, Gift of Ralph T. Coe, 2002 (2002.602.7)

Large wearing blankets with silk ribbon appliqué borders developed in Oklahoma around the turn of the century, particularly among the Osage and Oto peoples. They reached a peak in production during the height of the oil boom in Oklahoma, in the 1920s and 1930s. Osage families made fortunes from the oil on their lands, and their lifestyle became increasingly comfortable. Accompanying this extravagance was an elaboration in dress that marks a high point in Osage couture, and beautifully patterned wearing blankets such as this one became de rigueur. They are still worn by prominent Osage women at important occasions. Draped across the back, they are folded across the shoulders. The beaded hand symbols on this example, a special feature not always included, signify friendship.

The Osage trader and tribal council member Andrew Gray showed this blanket to me in 1978, displaying it casually across the trunk of his car at the Pawhuska dance ground. "I've got something here you might be interested in seeing," he said, in typically understated fashion.

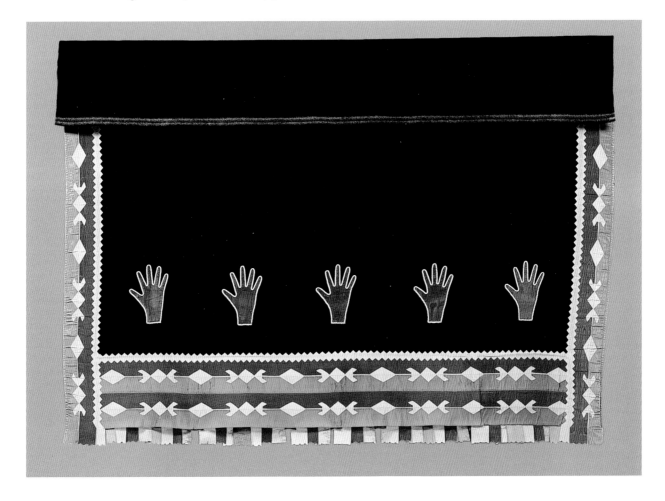

Alice Frost, Gwitchin, active 1960s–1980s

| *149. Baby strap* |

1985–87
Old Crow, Yukon Territory
Native-tanned skin, glass and plastic beads, wool tassels
5 x 48 in. (12.7 x 121.9 cm)
Width approx. 48 in. (121.9 cm)
RTCNA 486a

In 1988, I was using the Native-owned laundromat in Dawson City, Yukon (of Klondike fame), when I noticed above the row of machines a beautifully beaded Athabaskan baby strap of superior quality. I inquired and, to my delight, learned that it was for sale. In case there was any doubt as to its function, the legend "Baby" was spelled out at the center of the strap against a snowy white beaded background, as if to proclaim a mother's joy over her newborn. The design shows hearts on a tendril that abut each letter and blossom and that terminate in two pink and gold beaded petals at either end. Gaily colored wool tassels are suspended below. A darker pink is also used on the pair of blossoms on either side of the legend, the latter executed in light blue beads. The strap seems made to accommodate an infant of either gender. The prominence of baby pink fairly proclaims, It's a girl! The word "baby" is in blue, announcing, It's a boy! The strap is by the late Alice Frost, a respected elder from Old Crow, Yukon Territory, a traditional Gwitchin community accessible only by air.

Baby straps such as this one have been made since the last century, and probably earlier, by northern Athabaskan women to honor a christening or to show off their child on special holidays. They are slung over the mother's shoulder and tied around the waist at the front. The weight of the baby anchors the strap comfortably on her back. Later, the strap can be hung in the child's room or in the living room, to be admired by visitors. As the child grows older, it remains his or her property. When I visited a home in Fort McPherson, where I had gone to commission a strap from the daughter of the family, Joanne Charlie, her mother displayed in the front hall the several decorated baby straps of all her children, suspended vertically one after another. She pointed out to me her son William's baby strap. William was standing by her and was somewhat embarrassed to be singled out, as he was by then a young man, well into his midteens.

150. Tablita with attachment

Late 19th–early 20th century
Hopi Pueblo, Arizona
Painted cotton cloth, wood
Tablita: 19 ¼ x 14 ½ in. (48.9 x 36.8 cm)
Attachment: 18 ½ x 5 in. (47 x 12.7 cm)
RTCNA 629a, b

Pueblo tablitas are perhaps the most arresting dance headgear from the Southwest. Constructed of wood and cotton cloth, they are flat structures placed over the heads of women dancers and are often depicted on katsinas (see cat. no. 162). Tablitas appear at the Zuni and Rio Grande Pueblos, and at the Hopi Pueblo, where this one originated.

While modern tablitas are made of non-Native materials such as orange crating or plywood, this fine old example is fashioned by stretching muslin tightly over a hollow wood framework. This type of tablita is in the form of a castellated cloud terrace. The stepped elements are suggestive of the traditional steps that lead up to the entrance of a kiva, usually an underground religious chamber into which one descends by ladder. Dancers in ceremonials would proceed in lines across the village plaza with tablitas fitted over their heads, enhancing the rhythmical cadence of their stately movements. The phalliform motifs are prayerful symbols of increase, and the central feature is a rainbow, with raindrops spreading outward as if by capillary action. The katsina-like attachment was placed behind the dancer's head, completing the ensemble. Representing an ear of corn protruding from its husk, it "sprouts" cloud and rain motifs. Together, the tablita and its attachment symbolize abundance and encapsulate the continuance of life.

151. Feathered headband

ca. 1835
Maidu or Wintun peoples (?), California
Flicker feathers, commercial cord
4 ½ x 21 in. (11.4 x 53.3 cm)
RTCNA 621

Headbands made from flicker feathers are a characteristic adornment of the Pomo, Maidu, and other northern California peoples, both coastal and living inland in the central valley. In 2001, I was privileged to attend a nighttime ceremony at Indian Grinding Rock State Historic Park, at the traditional lodge that is often used by the Maidu community. It was an astonishing sight. Two rows of four to six male dancers facing one another moved in measured steps toward and away from the central fire. In the dark, illuminated lodge, the headbands, worn across the foreheads of the dancers, glowed with ethereal splendor. Their light, thin construction is repeated in other north-central California dance accoutrements, such as ear ornaments and abalone-shell pendant necklaces.

The headbands I saw that night were much like the present example, which I had found forty years earlier, in 1960, at Willis Tilton's Indian Relics, in Topeka, Kansas. It was rolled up in a tight bundle, two inches in diameter, and tied with a string. I bought it for $2.50.

Craig Bates, curator of the Yosemite Museum at Yosemite National Park, suggests that the headband is roughly contemporaneous with those collected about 1835, now in the Peter the Great Museum of Anthropology and Ethnography, St. Petersburg.[1]

1. Personal communication from Craig Bates, about 1990.

XI

DOLLS AND FIGURINES

Mirrors of Tribal Identity

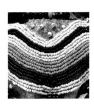

152. Female doll with child

Late 19th century
Eskimo peoples, Greenland
Native-tanned skin, paint, wood, cotton trade cloth
12 x 4 ½ in. (30.5 x 11.4 cm)
RTCNA 615

Greenland, the largest island in the world, was a colony and then a province of Denmark until 1979, when it was granted home rule. A continuing interest in the vibrant Eskimo arts of Greenland is still maintained in Denmark, and a number of European painters have been inspired by the dreamlike environment of this remote and barren land. There are no forests in Greenland, but rather ice caps and ice fields, with dwarf trees found in the southern coastal areas.

This wood-carved doll with movable arms was made in eastern Greenland. A charming feature is the little baby, her head encased in a traditional hood, who peeks out from behind her mother's head. A late-sixteenth-century watercolor by the English painter and cartographer John White, which shows an Eskimo woman of Baffin Island carrying her child in much the same way, points to the changes in style that have evolved over the centuries.[1] Most notable is the fact that only sealskin was originally used for clothing. This doll no longer wears the apron in the front or a "tail" on the back. These elements have been eliminated as concessions to European tailoring, evidenced also in the cut of the tunic, with its decorative pocketlike patches. The headband seen inside the still traditional cowl is modern. The boots seem to be modeled on European waders.

The fine detailing of this Greenland doll is seen in the above-the-knee boots, with center bands of appliqué and tiny colored strips of dyed seal leather topped by a semiroundel. The latter motif is one of the most easily recognized Greenland designs. Dolls of this form are still being made, but they tend to be more eclectically costumed, with bits of European cloth and Japanese silk. These dolls, while they have gained in decorative effect, have lost their simplicity and are no longer an expression of a harsh Arctic life.

1. Sturtevant and Damas 1984, p. 467, fig. 3 (right). The same watercolor is illustrated in color in Burland 1973, no. 29.

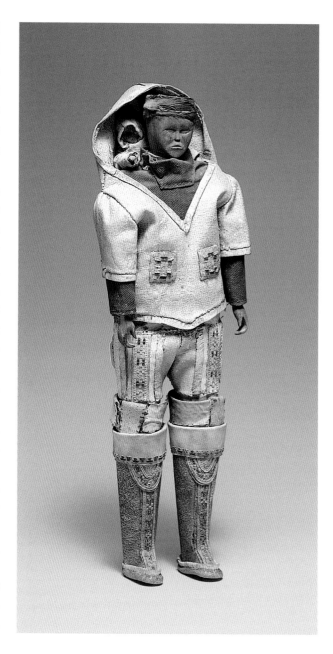

153. Mother and child doll

1870–80
Seneca peoples, New York
Corn husk, cotton and wool trade cloth, ribbon,
Native-tanned skin, glass beads, silk ribbon
10 ¾ x 5 in. (27.3 x 12.7 cm)
RTCNA 677

Dolls made from a corn-husk core are a specialty of the Iroquois, most notably the Seneca, south and east of Buffalo, New York. This prime example is at once Victorian in its dressiness and unmistakably Iroquois in the design of the beading on the skirt and cradle, the distinctive blue frock coat, and the frank dependence on a corn-husk core. Were it not for the consummate skill of the maker, such a doll might appear fussy and overly decorative, but taste and manual skill here strike a balance between overall harmony and exquisite detail. The openwork beaded collar is overlaid with necklaces and festoons that hang off the figure's left shoulder to join a beaded purse carried against the frock coat. The skirt is a jewel of traditional Iroquois beaded motifs of cascading flowers and trees of life. A notable exercise of the couturier's art in miniature is the skill by which delicate details are made to set off the broad areas of solid color, such as, in this example, the blue of the coat and the dense black of the skirt. Suspended on the mother's back and tied across her chest is a carved wood cradle, in which, wrapped in a plain blanket, sits a bonneted, corn-husk-faced tiny baby.

One wonders what inspired such a lovingly made object as this. Surely it cannot have been used for play, but must have been meant for a regal display of female dignity. It should be remembered that the clan mothers of the Iroquois Confederacy to this day occupy a position in decision making above that of the Haudenosaunee sachems (Iroquois chiefs) and even have the power, if necessary, to remove a dignitary from office. Fine Seneca corn-husk dolls in the same tradition as this one are still being made today.

154. Female doll

Early 20th century
Seminole peoples, Florida
Wood, cotton trade cloth, beads
12 x 6 ¼ in. (30.5 x 15.9 cm)
RTCNA 341

Dolls made by the Seminole peoples in the late nineteenth and early twentieth centuries seem to have been fashioned from rags and cloth.[1] Exactly when they came to be fitted with carved and painted wood heads is not clear, although we know that dressed wood dolls were made in the first decades of the twentieth century. But it would certainly seem that this doll is an early example. Seminole dolls in general are often referred to as patchwork dolls, yet this one, with its elegant, simple cape, shows no indication of having been made by a sewing machine patchwork technique. Rather, both skirt and blouse cape were neatly hand sewn out of strips of fabric joined horizontally at the edges. The blouse cape, draping freely from the shoulders, is typical of a Seminole lady's costume from the 1890s to the turn of the century, and there is a pronounced Caribbean flavor that reflects the cultural ambience of the geographic locale. The necklace is restricted to a single strand of tiny beads, very different from the layered, multiple strands on Seminole dolls made after the First World War. Although the paint on the head has greatly eroded, one can still see that it represents the close-cropped hairstyle of the day. The period dress, however, is not necessarily a definitive indicator of date, as often these dolls are clothed in earlier fashions. In this case, we can rely only on the evidence of wear and the simplicity of style. Merrill Domas, until recently a dealer in Native American art in New Orleans, obtained this doll in Kentucky before selling it to me.

1. MacCauley 1887. See also Munroe 1909.

| *155. Female doll* |

Late 19th century
Blackfoot peoples, northern Montana or Alberta
Native-tanned skin, glass beads, hair, wool trade cloth,
commercial leather, metal
10 ¼ x 6 ¾ in. (26 x 17.1 cm)
RTCNA 665

Certain Plains dolls appeal because of their kindly, maternal aspect. This rather petite Blackfoot example fits that criterion exactly and shows just enough wear so that one can easily imagine the affection it inspired when clutched by its young owner. This is a very personal creation and certainly not initially made for sale. It was, for many years, owned by the Oklahoma collectors Hans and Sigi Pannwitz and dates to the late nineteenth century.

A fair number of dolls from the Plains are of the "no face" type; their features are blank and the child could read into the doll the features of her choice. This is not the case here, where the figure's painted cheeks and beaded eyes and mouth give her an individual character all her own. Her dark hair is arranged in heavy braids, and she wears her very best brass disk belt. There is also a girlish aspect here that may actually be unintended. The dress, with beaded stripes forming the yoke across the bodice, is not only classically Blackfoot but is usually worn by a mature woman, as though the little girl were emulating her mother. The striped design appears also on a full-size girl's cape (cat. no. 143).

Joyce Growing Thunder Fogarty
Assiniboine/Sioux, b. 1950

| *156. Female doll* |

2000
Cotton cloth, glass beads, commercial leather, metal bells,
human hair, feather, ribbon, shell
19 ½ x 9 in. (49.5 x 22.9 cm)
RTCNA 400

During our many years of friendship, Assiniboine/Sioux Joyce Growing Thunder Fogarty and her husband, Jim, have often been guests at my house in Santa Fe, to say nothing of our camping throughout the West and together attending dances and ceremonies. They are tolerant of my foibles and count among the best of my teachers. Every once in a while, when visiting my home, Joyce would glance over at the girl's beaded cape from the Stoney Indians of Morley, Alberta (cat. no. 144). "Those people are my relatives, too," she would say, "because Assiniboine means Stoney. Someday, I'm going to make you a doll wearing that cape."

The gestation of this piece from conception to completion was an extended process, taking perhaps three years. This way of working is not uncommon among Native American artists, and it is one reason that exact dating, which can depend upon elastic circumstances, is very difficult.

In 1985, Joyce won the first of three Best of Show awards at the premier contemporary Indian art market, held annually in Santa Fe. This market is recognized as the most important in the country for Native American achievement in the arts. It was the first time that a doll maker had been so honored.

Joyce maintains a staunch adherence to the high standards of her forebears, to which she seems to have a unique key. Many well-known crafts artists have gained recognition for a specialty. But whatever Joyce chooses to undertake—be it a horse mask, a cradle, a knife case, or a war shirt—becomes an icon of Plains culture. As she works directly out of the Assiniboine tradition of the 1880s, it is little wonder that she chose a specifically Assiniboine cape on which to model this personal interpretation, an homage to her past. (See also cat. no. 108.)

157. Male doll

Mid- to late 19th century
Inland Tlingit peoples, Yukon or northern British Columbia
Native-tanned skin, wood, paint, human hair
7 ⅜ x 4 in. (18.7 x 10.2 cm)
RTCNA 676

Less well known than the coastal Tlingit is the small community of Tlingit peoples who live in the interior of British Columbia, east of the high coast ranges. They share many Northwest Coast traditions, such as crests and button blankets, and are also influenced by the adjacent Athabaskan cultures.

This small but powerful doll, its wood face vigorously carved in Northwest Coast style, nevertheless is dressed in what is clearly an old-style Athabaskan tunic, with pointed hems both front and back. The quiver case slung over the doll's shoulder is also Athabaskan, not Northwest Coast, in form.[1] But while trade relationships should not be discounted between coastal Tlingit bands and interior Athabaskans, it would seem more appropriate to attribute this doll to the inland Tlingit. The features of the face are Tlingit in style. The joined eyebrow that spans the forehead is like that of a miniature Northwest Coast mask. The doll was a rare find, which came to my attention only this past year, in 2002, having been in the distinguished Native American doll collection of Joel and Kate Kopp of New York.

1. Duncan 1989, pp. 42–45, figs. 2.19, 2.20, 2.21.

158. Figurine

1879
Zuni Pueblo, New Mexico
Painted ceramic
4 ⅜ x 2 ¼ in. (11.1 x 5.7 cm)
RTCNA 632

159. Figurine

1879
Hopi Pueblo, Arizona
Painted ceramic
5 ½ x 2 ¼ in. (14 x 5.7 cm)
RTCNA 633

Any history of the beginnings of tourist art from the Southwest would have to cite figurines of this kind, for they were the very first commissions made for outsiders by the Hopi and Zuni Pueblos. In 1879, the anthropologist James Stevenson, representing the Smithsonian Institution, made a trip through the Southwest and bought from these two pueblos a number of figurines. Little did Stevenson know what he had set into motion. By this act he opened the gates to the reciprocal relationship between Native Americans and outsiders in trading art that has long been a major component of art made in the Southwest. Thus was initiated an important chapter in Southwest culture in an appropriately quiet way.

The figurine at the top was acquired, probably by exchange, by the dealer James Economos, from whom I bought it in the early 1960s. It represents a Zuni maiden, recognized as unmarried by the whorls on either side of her head. The figurine at the bottom, from Hopi Pueblo, is more ambitious in production; the skirt overlaps the legs, and the *manta* was made separately and then attached at the shoulders and along the skirt. This figurine was acquired from the Santa Fe dealer Martha Struever by John Molloy, also of Santa Fe, who sold it to me in the spring of 2000. The Hopi figurine is more animated—she gesticulates, and her face, which shows modeling, is more expressive. Comparing these two figurines, one begins to see a transition from inanimate sculptural representation to representation imbued with a sense of movement.

XII

KATSINAS

Messengers of the Gods

160. Long-horned katsina

Late 19th century
Hopi Pueblo, Arizona
Painted cottonwood, feathers, fur, shell, imitation pearls,
bones, Native-tanned skin
13 ½ x 8 ¼ in. (34.3 x 21 cm)
RTCNA 643

Katsinas (*katchin-tihu*) are messengers to the gods and representations of the gods on Earth. They dwell in the San Francisco Peaks north of Flagstaff, Arizona. Appearing in the Hopi Pueblos during a months-long season, they return once more to the mountains after the July Home Dances. Small versions of katsinas are given to children, traditionally at the time of the Bean Dance, a festival that celebrates nature's yearly renewal. Typically hung from a nail in the home, they assume a spiritual animation and are used as an instructional device for the young.

Hopi katsinas of the late nineteenth century, such as this one, are generally blocky in construction. They have a modular immobility that imparts a restrained, unworldly dignity. In recent years, katsinas have been carved in more lifelike poses, with attention to gesture and movement. They also tend to be conceived as independent works of art, removed from their original function as intimate icons for the young.

This long-horned katsina has a long and venerable history. At some time in its life, its late-nineteenth-century origins were obscured by repaintings and refittings. The most significant replacement is the long horn itself.

ca. 1910
Hopi Pueblo, Arizona
Painted cottonwood, feathers, cotton velvet
10 ½ x 5 in. (26.7 x 12.7 cm)
RTCNA 642

According to the art historian Barton Wright, the velvet-shirt katsina probably originated in Moenkopi after 1900.[1] An outlier community situated between Tuba City and Hotevilla, Arizona, Moenkopi counts both Hopi and Navajo among its inhabitants.

The identifying features that mark this figure as a velvet-shirt katsina are a partially pink case mask; three flowers on the forehead; the prominent dark velvet shirt; white body paint; red boots and ears; and the characteristic inverted V over the mouth. (The diagnostic fur ruff is missing.) The slight stoop and spindly legs lend this katsina a wizened, elderly air. It came to light at the Four Winds Trading Post, in Flagstaff, in 1987, and seemed to be begging for attention.

1. B. Wright 1973, p. 191.

Jimmy Keywaywentewa
Hopi, active 1930s–40s

| 162. Hemis katsina |

Late 1930s–early 1940s
Hopi Pueblo, Arizona
Painted cottonwood, feathers, wool yarn
16 ¾ x 5 ½ in. (42.5 x 14 cm)
RTCNA 657

The sculptured character of the case mask that the Hemis katsina wears makes it one of the most classically beautiful, and deservedly best known, of all the several hundred Hopi types. The stepped crown of the mask always displays ears of corn that can be interpreted as phallic symbols. Thus, the iconography of the crown combines the concepts of nature's fecundity and human fertility in a universal synthesis. The name Hemis would seem to indicate that this katsina was originally from Jemez, a distant pueblo west of the Rio Grande, in New Mexico. At Jemez, however, the dance in which the Hemis katsina appears is referred to as a Hopi dance.[1] This would explain why the present example, while appropriated by the Hemis, is Hopi in execution.

The Hopi Hemis katsina is often called a Niman katsina because it generally participates in the Niman, or Home Dance. This ceremony concludes the Hopi cycle of katsina dances held in mid- to late summer and marks the return of katsinas to the San Francisco Peaks in Arizona.

This Hemis katsina was carved by Jimmy Keywaywentewa, one of the finest twentieth-century Hopi artists and the chief at Old Oraibi (First Mesa). Politically innovative and sympathetic to social reform, he was nonetheless a conservative carver. Carefully delineated white crescent warrior motifs mark the front of the shirt; the case mask is classically structured; and the tablita (see cat. no. 150) is integral to the overall composition. The four vertically arranged white circles are a signature feature of Keywaywentewa's work. This katsina dates to the late 1930s or early 1940s, when the carver was at the height of his artistic powers, though at first glance one might suppose that, with its tight-fitting kilt, it was earlier than it actually is.

1. B. Wright 1973, p. 214.

163. Navajo Tasap katsina

ca. 1940s
Hopi Pueblo, Arizona
Painted cottonwood, feathers, wool yarn, ribbon, hair
9 ½ x 4 ⅞ in. (24.1 x 12.4 cm)
RTCNA 646

In the early 1990s, I used to visit Kachina House Gallery on Delgado Street in Santa Fe. It was owned by two women who were avid collectors of katsinas, and from time to time they would sell work from their large, ever-changing display. To purchase something, one simply had to be there when this occurred. One day, the proprietors were willing to part with this small katsina from the 1940s, and I was told then that it was Navajo. While this is not one of the specialized Navajo gods or long-haired katsinas adopted by the Hopi, in its identifying characteristics it relates sufficiently to Harold S. Colton's no. 137[1] and to the image of Tasap katsina in Barton Wright's monograph[2] to be considered Navajo Tasap. It has the prominent pink and yellow upper body paint, although a slash of turquoise has been added at the left, and it wears a case mask of the same color. It has, additionally, tufts of red hair for ears, a foxlike tail, and wears a wedding sash and the requisite red Navajo-style moccasins. The katsina once held a rattle in the right hand and carries, as a special touch, a small Hopi wicker plaque. The latter is an idiosyncratic element in work by this artist. Although it lacks the upturned, pothook eyes often seen on Hopi/Navajo katsinas, it does have the characteristic narrow black-and-white band carried across the bottom edge of the case. The Tasap example in Wright's book is a later, less rigid representation, lacking the wood angularity of the katsina pictured here.

1. Colton 1959, p. 60, no. 171.
2. B. Wright 1973, p. 180.

164. Katsina

ca. 1940
Laguna Pueblo, New Mexico
Painted cottonwood, feathers, wool yarn,
cotton and velvet cloth, beads
11 ¼ x 5 ½ in. (28.6 x 14 cm)
RTCNA 644

This chubby Laguna katsina from western New Mexico, which I purchased in Santa Fe in 1962 from William S. Dutton, was carved in any one of the five villages that constitute the most populous pueblo group. Shaking a pair of flower-shaped rattles in its hands, it seems almost to pout and stomp its feet. The face is concealed behind a yellow case mask, the eyes are shaded with ash, and a green wool ruff encircles the neck. The apparel reflects at least two instances of repair and/or replacement, considered a process of renewal and change rather than simply restoration. The coral-colored necklaces are not of the same date, and the "pajamas" may also be a later replacement. The detached wool hair is loosely worn and may have been replaced or added to several times over. Laguna katsina dances are held in private and are not witnessed by the public.

XIII

SOUTHWESTERN POTTERY

From Earth to Ethos

165. Water jar (olla)

ca. 1875
Acoma Pueblo, New Mexico
Ceramic
Height 12 in. (30.5 cm); diameter 13 ¼ in. (33.7 cm)
RTCNA 638

Pottery from Acoma Pueblo was initially geometric in design. It was also highly symbolic in its representation of cloud terraces, rainbirds, and life-giving waters. The jar, or olla, was made to hold water, and is thus in itself a prayer for sustenance.

By the middle of the nineteenth century, the designs on Acoma water jars had evolved into heavy bars joined together in a rainbow band and discernible parrot motifs appeared that are more representational than the earlier rainbird abstractions.[1] The next phase, which began about 1875, when this jar was made, brings split-leaf designs with a suggestion of berries and other vegetation, while the bar designs take on the shape of an hourglass.[2] These developments set the stage for the introduction of motifs that are more fine-lined and calligraphic and which impart a greater sense of repetition around the pot.

Stylistically, this jar is on the cusp between Acoma pottery traditions of the early nineteenth century and those that appeared in the late nineteenth and early twentieth century. It is an early precursor of the archetypal Acoma design vocabulary still in use today.

A nearly identical jar is in the collection of the Museum of Primitive Art and Culture, in Peace Dale, Rhode Island, with the notable exception that the black and white colors are reversed; the ellipses are black and the leafy elements are white.[3]

1. Dillingham and Elliot 1992, p. 32, fig. 2.8.
2. Ibid., p. 33, fig. 2.9.
3. Turnbaugh and Turnbaugh 1991, p. 42, fig. 24.

Nampeyo, Hopi/Tewa, ca. 1860–1942

| *166. Jar* |

ca. 1900
Hopi Pueblo, Arizona
Ceramic
Height 8 ¼ in. (21 cm); diameter 14 ¼ in. (36.2 cm)
RTCNA 666

Born into a Hopi/Tewa family about 1860, the legendary potter Nampeyo was given the name Nung-beh-yong, the Tewa word for "sand snake."[1] Nampeyo is the corrupted version of that name. Nampeyo's Tewa (Rio Grande) Pueblo ancestors settled among the Hopi about 1702, and Nampeyo was raised at the Hopi Third Mesa, in a culture still untouched by outside influences. It is this deep grounding in traditional life that accounts for the strength of the artist's accomplishments as a potter. In the 1890s, Nampeyo's husband, Lesou, worked with the amateur archaeologist Thomas Keam, excavating ruins near the Hopi mesas. Many of the designs found on the ancient shards and vessels that they unearthed Lesou copied on paper for Nampeyo, and these she sometimes used as inspiration, adapting and transforming them to her own vision while maintaining an integral relationship to the past.[2]

This wide-shouldered jar was formerly in the collection of Tony Abeyta, former governor of Taos Pueblo, and Victor Higgins (1884–1949), one of the prominent figures in the circle of modernist painters working in Taos in the early twentieth century. All of Nampeyo's works have been left unsigned, and most examples of her pottery are qualified by the term "attributed to." There would seem to be no question about the authenticity of this example, however, which was sold on the art market by a descendant of Higgins's. It is ivory to pale yellow in color, with two geometric and two curvilinear motifs, swabbed in black and red and placed in opposed pairs. The fawn-colored clay is characteristic of Hopi pottery and is seen also in the contemporary jar by Nathan Begaye (cat. no. 169). The eminent dealer in Southwestern pottery Martha H. Struever has described this finely constructed pot as follows: "Certain elements of this large, elaborate layout are diagnostic of Nampeyo's work: the graceful swooping areas ending in a pair of feathers, and the use of sets of feathers within the large triangular element. The entire layout may be a highly stylized bird with widespread wings, dissected body and tail feathers. Separating these large design units is a pair of cross-like motifs consisting of a diamond with appendages pointing in four directions. Appearing on other vessels made by Nampeyo, according to her granddaughter, Dextra [Quotskuyva], these motifs represent both whirlwinds and 'four directions,' popular Hopi symbols."[3]

1. See Kramer 1996.
2. Blair and Blair 1999, p. 96.
3. Letter to Ralph T. Coe, ca. 2000.

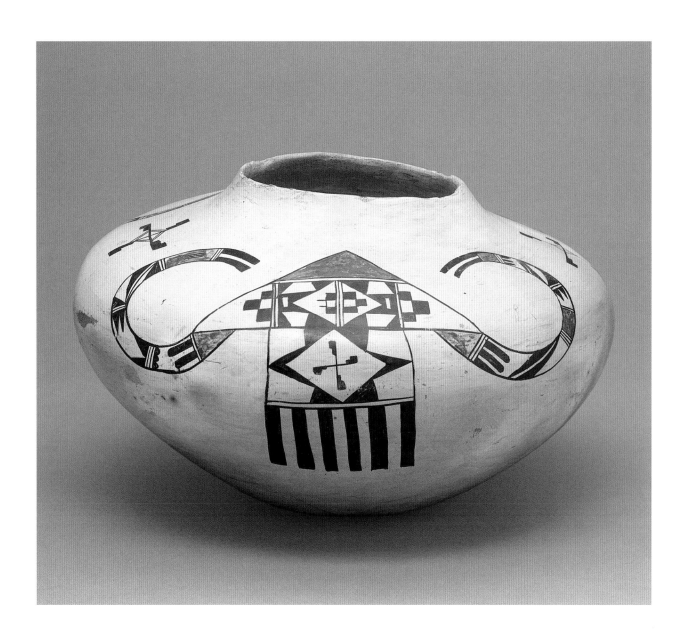

Martina Vigil, San Ildefonso, 1856–1916
Florentino Montoya, San Ildefonso, 1858–1917

| 167. Storage jar |

1904–5
San Ildefonso Pueblo, New Mexico
Ceramic
Height 11 in. (27.9 cm); diameter 11 ¼ in. (28.6 cm)
RTCNA 641

Because Maria Martinez and her husband, Julian, have become such household names in Southwestern pottery (see cat. no. 168), the importance of an equally gifted couple also active at San Ildefonso Pueblo has sometimes been overlooked. Martina Vigil and Florentino Montoya were older than Maria and Julian, and their work therefore reflects an earlier stage in the later history of San Ildefonso pottery. In his study of these two potters, the Southwestern ceramics expert Jonathan Batkin sets the record straight: "The pottery of this husband and wife team is that of artists and innovators who introduced new materials and techniques to other potters. Martina's experimentation with shapes and slip and Florentino's distinctive painting style facilitate the identification of many of their pots. If imitation is the greatest form of flattery, then Maria and Julian Martinez admired Martina and Florentino greatly: Julian often copied designs from their pottery and Maria said of them, 'they were very good potters, nobody can touch them.'"[1]

Between 1902 and 1905, Martina and Florentino moved from San Ildefonso to Cochiti Pueblo, west of Santa Fe, where Martina's father had been born. At Cochiti, they were introduced to a new ceramic technology that employed a white slip composed of bentonite. This slip required the use of a rag or leather for polishing rather than a stone. While the finish of San Ildefonso pottery is smooth and satiny, the surface of Cochiti pottery "appears soapy: the marks of the rag or leather applicator and polisher are preserved as numerous parallel lines, as if the slip were painted on with a brush."[2] A pot made with bentonite slip can also be finished more quickly. Batkin suggests that the pottery which Martina and Florentino made during their stay in Cochiti should nevertheless be considered, stylistically, San Ildefonso. And indeed, the ceramic forms they continued to use—such as a jar with a concave neck and shoulder joined to a rounded or slightly tapered body—are in the classic San Ildefonso tradition. The storage jar seen here exemplifies this type, and it preserves the streaks of the Cochiti slip. The strongly articulated step and feather designs together with the triangular motifs edging the inner rim demonstrate the succinctness of Florentino Montoya's draftsmanship at its best.[3]

1. Batkin 1987, p. 29.
2. Ibid., p. 33.
3. For a pair of ollas (water jars), one made with Cochiti slip but polished with a stone (San Ildefonso method) and the other also showing Cochiti slip but polished with a rag, see ibid., p. 35, figs. 12 and 13.

Attributed to Maria Martinez, San Ildefonso, 1887–1980

Julian Martinez, San Ildefonso, 1885–1943

| 168. Bowl |

ca. 1914–15

San Ildefonso Pueblo, New Mexico

Ceramic

Height 5 ⅞ in. (14.9 cm); diameter 9 ¾ in. (24.8 cm)

RTCNA 637

This bowl is attributed to the renowned San Ildefonso Pueblo potters Maria and Julian Martinez. Over their long partnership, Maria coiled the pots and her husband, Julian, painted them. I bought this bowl, which is unsigned, in 1988. Three specialists in Southwestern pottery had earlier held an informal conclave to discuss its attribution—the late potter Rick Dillingham, the ceramics expert Jonathan Batkin, and Bruce Bernstein, now curator of collections at the National Museum of the American Indian, Washington, D.C. By a process of elimination, they came to the conclusion that the pot was most probably by these two artists. They dated it to about 1914–15, several years before their famous "first firing"

that marked the debut of black-on-black matte ceramic, today considered a landmark in the history of pueblo pottery. The present example is a clear antecedent of what was to come. While it lacks the sophisticated refinement of form of the first firing pots, it is interesting not only historically but artistically as well. It is coated with a red slip, is vigorously formed, and *Avanyu,* or Water Serpent—an invention of Julian's—here makes an early appearance.[1]

1. For a typical black-on-black Maria and Julian Martinez bowl with a more developed *Avanyu* design, see Wardwell 1998, p. 86, no. 97.

Nathan Begaye, Hopi/Navajo, b. 1958

| *169. Jar* |

ca. 1990
Arizona
Ceramic
Height 15 ½ in. (39.4 cm); diameter 13 ¼ in. (33.7 cm)
RTCNA 639

I purchased this jar by the widely exhibited potter Nathan Begaye from Letta Wofford, Indian trader, collector, and patron of Native American art. Along with such legendary denizens of the Southwest in the 1920s and 1930s as Mabel Dodge Luhan, Letta was one of the early cultural pioneers to make her home in New Mexico. She lived quite near me in Santa Fe, and to her I am indebted for deepening my appreciation of the Native American ethos. Nathan Begaye is one of the gifted young ceramists she sponsored.

This jar is one of the largest works the artist has produced. It makes reference to both his Hopi and his Navajo heritage.

The clay is an exquisitely redefined Hopi buff, and the figure on one side (above left), painted in a personal but traditional idiom, represents the Hopi sun katsina. On the opposite side (above right), the same katsina is portrayed in a startlingly radical and graphic manner, as a nakedly sexual, ambiguous male. The figure has a graphic energy that is characteristic of contemporary Navajo pottery. As Nathan, turning the pot, explained to me: "Here's the old katsina . . . and here is the new."

Diego Romero, Cochiti, b. 1964

170. "Chungo Brothers" dough bowl

1994
Cochiti Pueblo, New Mexico
Ceramic
Height 5 ⅝ in. (14.3 cm); diameter 12 in. (30.5 cm)
RTCNA 649

Diego Romero, a member of the prominent Cochiti Pueblo family that includes the artist's equally well known brother, the painter Mateo Romero (b. 1966), has achieved fame as a master satirist in clay. He takes calculated liberties with the long history of pueblo pottery that convey a Native American's view of how contemporary Western values have influenced the mores of his people. In this pot, he gently ridicules the non-Native approach to academic archaeology, enclosing, within a satiric adaptation of ancient Mimbres pottery designs, a cameo cartoon of two Mimbres-style figures, the Chungo Brothers, so named for their traditional knotted hairstyle, known as a chungo. The two characters have obviously been infected with the Anglo bug of materialistic ambition, which has inflated their already substantial egos.

On the left, Dan-Yei Bachata, presented as a self-important young painter, is shown in plaid Bermuda shorts lounging against a mantel above a kiva-style fireplace—in itself, a sign that you have "made it" in Santa Fe. The rendering of his

eye is pure Mimbres, and he sports just the right T-shirt, with an image, on the front, of Kokopelli, the prehistoric hunchback flute player. In this context, Dan-Yei Bachata can be understood as a sort of Pied Piper of success. His lifelong ambition is "to be the next Indian Market poster boy!" At the right is the mad sculptor Jorge Lujan, who hacks away at a self-portrait bust. Lujan's T-shirt bears a fish motif, a standard emblem of ancient Mimbres pottery design, and his ambition is "to be the next Don Trump of Indian gaming!!"—a reference to the casino culture so prevalent in Native American life today.

The spirit line through which the spirit of the pot escapes, at the very edge of the rim just above Dan-Yei Bachata, is a sacred reference deeply embedded in Indian culture. By contrast, the kiln firing of the pot is a defiant rejection of tradition and the deeply held belief in man's connection to the earth. The artist's signature, like a manufacturer's logo, is impersonally rendered in garish gilt paint. Surely this pot is dressed for success.

XIV

CREST DISPLAYS

Heraldic Art of the Northwest Coast

171. Button blanket

ca. 1850–60
Tsimshian peoples, British Columbia
Wool trade cloth, shell buttons
60 ½ x 77 ½ in. (153.7 x 196.9 cm)
RTCNA 663

This large appliqué wearing blanket, also known as a button blanket, is generally recognized as one of the finest early examples extant.[1] It was probably made between 1850 and 1860, not long after northern-style button blankets were first produced. Still made even today, such blankets are a testament to the resilience of Northwest Coast Indian culture.

Known as the Wellington blanket, this monumental textile was bought from Midas Wesley at Kitsegukla (Skeena Crossing), a Gitk'san town sufficiently inland from the coast to have remained relatively undisturbed long after European contact. Totem poles were still raised there by eminent local families as late as the 1940s. When I first visited Kitsegukla in the late 1960s, I was astonished to find that many of these poles had survived, standing like sentinels around the village. At one time, this crest blanket may have been stored in one of these houses. I sat on the steps of the general store with Coke in hand and felt I was in paradise!

The central figure on the blanket is a bear. The consistent outline of the head and body is classically Tsimshian in profile and would immediately proclaim the family crest affiliation for one and all to admire. Two pairs of childlike figural designs in red appliqué seem to sprout organically from each side of the great head, indicating that the bear is a female. Joint designs, anthropologically called "hockers," are clearly indicated on the palms of the bear's upraised front paws and at the shoulder and pelvic joints. Below the ribs is a uterine ovoid probably encasing a bear fetus, denoted by its face. These unusual features would suggest that the design represents an underlying mythical narrative, that of the Bear Mother.[2] The pulsating button borders of the Bear Mother help proclaim her power as the founder of the tribe. Here myth mediates between the animal and human worlds, linked by the magic of design.

The story of the Bear Mother is an important origin myth of the Northwest Coast. One version recounts the story as follows: "The heroine, a haughty young woman, is abducted by a grizzly or brown bear and becomes the mother of his children. With his knowledge, she betrays him, sending a signal to her brothers, who become his killers."[3] Another version goes: "Kats, a member of the Tékwedi clan, married a grizzly bear woman and had children by her. Later, when he returned to his human wife, the bear wife warned him to bring food only to his bear children. Because he broke this rule, the bears killed him."[4]

Another important button blanket depicting this same myth by the same maker is in the collection of the Museum of Archaeology and Anthropology, University of Pennsylvania, in Philadelphia.[5] It was collected, probably in the 1920s, on the Nass River by Louis Shotridge. On this blanket, the bear children appear as faces terminating the dramatically outsize Bear Mother's ears.[6]

1. It has been reproduced several times. See, e.g., Coe 1976a, p. 124, fig. 352 (and as a color poster for the same exhibition); Maxwell 1978, p. 327, colorpl.; Ewing 1982, p. 213, no. 208, colorpl. 4; Mathews 1984, p. 5; Bancroft-Hunt 1992, p. 68, colorpl. p. 69.
2. A Tlingit killer-whale crest blanket in the Portland Art Museum would also appear to have narrative content. It displays a beaded-head motif below the image of a whale that "represents a rock on which [the whale] was stranded while chasing a seal"; Gunther and Rasmussen 1966, p. 203, no. 121. The recent revival of button blankets has encouraged the personalized content of this art. See Jensen and Sargent 1986.
3. Bierhorst 1985, p. 50.
4. Ibid.
5. Museum of Archaeology and Anthroplogy, University of Pennsylvania, Philadelphia, acc. no. NA 8516
6. Feder 1971a, p. 282, no. 162.

172. Button blanket

ca. 1880

Kaigani Haida peoples, Prince of Wales Island, Alaska

Wool trade cloth, shell buttons

56 x 70 in. (142.2 x 177.8 cm)

RTCNA 212

While this button blanket represents a bear crest similar to that of the Wellington blanket (cat. no. 171), the treatment and concept are quite different. While the X-ray-like exposed ribs and skeletal pose are shared motifs, the particular style of this blanket is specific to Kaigani Haida tunics and blankets. It is more folkish than the Wellington blanket, as exemplified in the bear's outlines, which are animated by a less subtle, more quirky sense of sudden, quick movement. Nonetheless, while less artistically pleasing, the impact is powerfully direct.

I visited the Kaigani people at Hydaburg, Alaska, about 1980. Several of the elders told me they had obtained the buttons for their blankets by ordering them from the B. K. Button Company in Muscatine, Iowa. Back in the Midwest, I went to Muscatine and found that the company still existed (it is now defunct) but had long since turned to making only plastic buttons. Clamshell buttons purchased on the Muscatine trip were later used to replace a number of the missing buttons on this blanket. The B. K. Button Company had records dating back more than seventy years, citing people and names known to me from Hydaburg, including my mentor in the culture of the Kaigani Haida, the late Jessie Natkon, who made for me one of the X-ray bear tunics now in the Nelson-Atkins Museum of Art, Kansas City.

This Kaigani Haida button blanket once belonged to Charlie Swan, a Makah traditionalist and dance leader—one of the few Native Americans of the Northwest Coast who collected tribal art professionally in order to preserve it.[1]

1. Charlie Swan is depicted wearing this blanket in Inverarity 1950, pl. 103.

173. Frontlet

ca. 1820–40

Tsimshian peoples, Metlakatla village area, British Columbia

Painted wood, abalone-shell inlay

8 ¾ x 6 ¼ in. (22.2 x 15.9 cm)

RTCNA 179

This Northwest Coast frontlet, worn on the forehead at chiefly occasions, is attributed to the Tsimshian peoples, who occupied a pivotal position in the geography of the northern Northwest Coast. They lived on the central British Columbian mainland directly across from the Queen Charlotte Islands, where the Haida dwelled, and encompassing as well the Skeena and Nass River valleys that led inland between the Tlingit to the north and the Haisla to the south. Thus, they served as an intersection through which coronation headdress frontlets traveled both north and south to become widespread in Northwest Coast art.[1]

This early frontlet exemplifies the generic Tsimshian type. It has a humanoid animal face below which is a truncated body with joined hands, arms, legs, and feet in two symmetrical units framed by a halolike rim.

In these early examples, abalone shell is customarily used for inlays; in this case, it is restricted to six vertically aligned panels that help to define the figure's limbs. It is also employed, with great restraint, to emphasize eyes and teeth. At this stage, the encircling border has no abalone inlay, and the body of the humanoid animal is carved in a very summary style. Only a faint articulation of the ribs separates the shoulder and chest area from the rest of the highly compressed body. Though small, this frontlet projects an aura of majesty and nobility. Its forceful simplicity would indicate a date between 1820 and 1840.

The frontlet has a highly distinguished provenance, having belonged to the famous (or infamous) missionary William Duncan in 1863, who sold it to Edmund Hope Verney about 1864. Taken back to England, it was part of the collection of the Cranmore Ethnographical Museum, a now defunct private museum in Chislehurst, Kent, owned by the celebrated early-twentieth-century collector Harry Beasley. About 1962, it came into the possession of John Wise, of New York City, and was subsequently purchased by Adelaide de Menil, in 1976. The frontlet was put up for auction in New York in 1998, after which I was fortunate enough to acquire it.[2] There is a similarly composed Tsimshian frontlet in the U'mista Kwakwaka'wakw Cultural Society at Alert Bay, British Columbia, which has been "updated" for a later audience: at some point, several abalone-shell plaques were affixed to the rim, which had been previously unadorned.

1. While there is no surviving documentation on the beginnings of Northwest Coast frontlet carving, two frontlets collected during the late eighteenth century are known, one by the Italian navigator Alessandro Malaspina and the other by Captain James Cook. The former was collected at Yakutat village in southeastern Alaska, in 1791, far to the north of Tlingit territory, and Captain Cook's was collected in 1778, with unknown attribution. It is to be assumed that the core style of Tsimshian frontlet carving was developed over a period of time before it spread north, west, and south.
2. Sotheby's, New York, May 19, 1998, sale no. 7137, lot 556.

174. Frontlet

ca. 1885
Tlingit peoples, Chilkat area, southeastern Alaska
Painted wood, abalone-shell inlay
6 ⅜ x 5 in. (16.2 x 12.7 cm)
RTCNA 153

This frontlet has an interesting collection history. Shortly after I acquired it, in 1986, its authenticity was questioned. An obviously old accession number on the back, beginning with the letter *E* and covered with faded varnish, was regarded as evidence of forgery, as was the tiny relief panel representing the body of a bear set between the legs of the larger, primary bear. Stylistically, however, the relief suggested an origin in the Alaska Panhandle. Such flat reliefs in full size, often monumental, were typical of the northern Tlingit. In this uppermost area of the Panhandle, the Tlingit made low-relief screens and houseposts rather than totem poles, as did their Tlingit neighbors to the south, because the small diameter of the trees in their district made carving full-size poles impossible.

In the catalogue for the American Indian exhibition at the Seattle World's Fair of 1962, organized by the anthropologist Erna Gunther, I noticed that objects from the Peabody Essex Museum in Salem, Massachusetts, bore accession numbers preceded by the letter *E*. The number on the present frontlet was then identified as belonging uniquely to the museum's cataloguing system. The original card reference, still in the museum files, described the piece as "[a] very fine, very old frontlet, probably from the far north, Chilkat." Not only did the numbers correspond but the frontlet was attributed to the far northern part of Tlingit territory, and thus bore out the style of the object as Chilkat. The registrar of the museum explained that the frontlet, though not part of the museum's collection, was probably given an accession number because it was assumed that it would be given to the museum or, at the very least, placed there on exhibition. However, it was returned to the owners, a family in Maine, perhaps around 1930. It was subsequently bought from them by the New York dealer Eleanor Tulman Hancock, who sold it to me.

The somewhat crowded composition, together with the elaborate, closely spaced shell ornamentation, indicates a late stage of Northwest Coast frontlet carving—about 1885—when decoration with abalone-shell was lavish compared with its more restrained use during the early and classic period, between 1790 and the 1840s, as seen in catalogue number 173.

| 175. Crest helmet |

ca. 1860
Haida peoples, Haida Gwaii (Queen Charlotte Islands),
British Columbia
Painted wood
14 x 14 ½ x 17 ½ in. (35.6 x 36.8 x 44.5 cm)
RTCNA 205

The Haida are divided into two principal divisions, or moieties, based on descent through the line of the maternal uncles. The moieties are subdivided into clans, or kinship groups that claim an animal crest, a symbol of lineage affiliation. The owner of this crest helmet belonged to the bear clan and was entitled to wear its crest over his head. The helmet represents the mythological sea bear, indicated by the finlike projection that extends from the back of the head, cutting the air like a blade. Most likely, it was worn during many potlatches and processions, as the base has suffered what is evidently water damage, a result of the rains and fogs so prevalent on the Northwest Coast in the winter season, traditionally the ceremonial time of year.

The solid forms of the helmet are typically Haida in their volumetric self-containment. A sense of balance and a concentration more on massive curves than on detail lend it a gravitas that in conception places it firmly in the mid-nineteenth century, within the classic period of Haida art. Weighing almost ten pounds, it is heavy enough to discourage wearing by any but the most hardy. With its aggressive, martial bearing, this crest helmet perfectly combines the protective function of military armor with the civil honors and political glory associated with animal heraldry, thus creating a visual record of acts of leadership attributed to the wearer's family. A variant of this helmet is in the John H. Hauberg collection at the Seattle Art Museum.[1]

1. Seattle Art Museum 1995, pp. 108–9, no. 39.

XV

MASKS

Healing and Catharsis: Myth and Mystery

176. Mosquito mask

Before 1843
Tlingit peoples, southeastern Alaska
Painted wood, copper, abalone-shell inlay, Native-tanned skin ties
4 ½ x 6 ¾ in. (11.4 x 17.1 cm)
RTCNA 141
The Metropolitan Museum of Art, Gift of Ralph T. Coe, 2002 (2002.602.1)

Among the Tlingit of southeastern Alaska, the mosquito, because of its craving for human blood, was believed to have associations with the supernatural world, and mosquito masks were danced during shamanistic rituals as supernatural aids. This mosquito mask came to light several years ago at a small auction sale in New York. It was considered to be a "modern" mask, modeled after a shaman's mask of the Northwest Coast. It brought a very low price and ended up with a New York dealer. I spied the mask tucked away in a cabinet and asked to see it, although I was warned that it could be of recent date. Nevertheless, it has every characteristic of great age and is undoubtedly quite early.

The mask is virtually identical to a mosquito mask in the Peter the Great Museum of Anthropology and Ethnography, St. Petersburg, which was collected at Sitka, Alaska, by the Russian naturalist Ilia G. Voznesenskii in 1843.[1] There are, however, slight differences between the two. The St. Petersburg version, which is somewhat larger, has more original features

preserved. The exuberant outcropping of feathers and sea-lion whiskers, for example, are still attached, as are the painted hide flaps glued onto the cheeks. On the present mask, only one sea-lion bristle remains (it has been removed for preservation). Here, also, the connection between the eyebrows and the nose is more distinct, creating separate ocular areas. And the eyebrows are copper, whereas those of the St. Petersburg version are painted. The extraordinary, extended proboscis is given a more curvilinear twist on the present example, which makes it seem almost to buzz or whine. Additionally, the mask has sustained harsh treatment, which accounts for its condition. Nevertheless, the comparable form and design of these two masks, as well as the very old paint and signs of wear, indicate that they were possibly once paired. One wonders where this mask has been since it was made and why it was not, evidently, also collected by Voznesenskii.

1. Wardwell 1996, p. 154, no. 176.

177. Transformation mask

1820–30
Tlingit peoples, southeastern Alaska
Painted wood, metal coins, Native-tanned skin ties
8 x 7 ½ in. (20.3 x 19.1 cm)
RTCNA 145
The Metropolitan Museum of Art,
Gift of Ralph T. Coe, 2002 (2002.602.2)

Magical transformations from the supernatural to the natural and from the animal to the human were dramatized by transformation masks. This example takes the form of an owl, a common symbol of death on the Northwest Coast. Quite possibly, it was never buried, as indicated by its generally fine condition. Shamans' paraphernalia was often buried with the owner, but if this mask once had such apparatus it is now missing.

The combination of the sharply overhanging beak and the semicircular arched eyebrows convey an owlish, predatory alertness that is only slightly tempered by humanoid lateral mouth extensions. Faded celestial symbols, both round and lunate, are painted in silhouette across the forehead and above the eyes. The ears are prominently indicated in Chinese vermilion, and the eyes appear to glance backward, as though the mask is reacting to something it has heard. The Chinese coin eyes are not stationary but attached with old square nails that can be joggled and the coins removed to reveal the staring blackness within. One can picture the wearer of the mask in performance, turning away from the audience and then quickly reappearing, the Chinese coins having been transformed into haunted spaces.

As is often the case with such Tlingit transformation masks, the features are compressed toward the center, with less vertical elongation than in masks made by the Tsimshian in the central part of the Northwest Coast. While there was exchange—even exchange of carvers—between the Tsimshian and the southern Tlingit, Tlingit masks generally have a more pinched expression, as does this one, which lends an aspect of morbid concentration. While the features of this type of Tlingit mask—cheekbones, forehead, chin, and projecting beak—are sharply rendered, the smoothness of the carving suggests an otherworldly inner harmony. It is this tension between the inner and the outer worlds that fills these masks with their powerful primordial mystery.

178. Mask

ca. 1840–60
Tlingit peoples, southeastern Alaska
Wood, copper, fur
10 ½ x 6 ¼ in. (26.7 x 15.9 cm)
RTCNA 149

This Tlingit mask once belonged to the Surrealist painter and collector Wolfgang Paalen. Following a collecting trip he made along the Northwest Coast in 1939, Paalen published a seminal essay on the art of the Northwest Coast in *Dyn,* the Surrealist magazine he edited in Mexico City.

The mask first caught my eye in graduate school, when I saw it illustrated in Robert Bruce Inverarity's pioneering volume on Northwest Coast Indian Art.[1] One can imagine my delight at finding the actual mask for sale in California in 1960. Seven years later, walking along the Rainch, the old Tlingit quarter of Sitka, I saw an old Indian gentleman with a long face and prominent moustache. He seemed the very personification of the mask, signifying the living continuity of the Tlingit peoples.

The mask has an iconlike gravity that makes one wonder if the carver was familiar with the Russian icons that were at St. Michael's Cathedral in Sitka, among other places, during the nineteenth-century Russian occupation of Alaska.

An old label on the back reads: "Thlinget [*sic*] Indian Shaman's mask, used at dancing Totem of Frog and Bear, from Hoonah. $3.50." The double row of figures staring out across the crown represents mythical land-otter men, which as shamans' aides can be associated with mental disturbance. Here, the frog being expelled from the mouth, and thus effecting a cure, may represent the affliction of the supplicant.

A very similar mask is in the collection of the National Museum of the American Indian, Washington, D.C.[2] That mask is also from the town of Hoonah. It is more volumetric than the mask seen here, and it retains significant traces of old paint. One has to imagine the present example with copper eyes and eyebrows (probably from old ship plating), polished and gleaming, and with the moustache bristling with seal fur, of which only the skin remains.

1. Inverarity 1950, no. 97.
2. Illustrated in Wardwell 1996, frontis. Wardwell notes that George Emmons, the collector of the Washington mask, who acquired it directly from the shaman and later attended the shaman's funeral, identifies it as a depiction of an old woman. There are no remnants of a moustache, as in the present mask, which represents an old man. Whether these two masks, documented as from the same village, were ever used together remains unknown.

179. Komokwa mask

1880s
Kwakwaka'wakw peoples, Rivers Inlet, British Columbia
Painted wood
15 x 12 in. (38.1 x 30.5 cm)
RTCNA 203

Masks from the Rivers Inlet subdivision of the northern Kwakwaka'wakw (Kwakiutl) peoples from coastal British Columbia are of fairly rare occurrence. Stylistically, they fall into the broad category of Kwakwaka'wakw carvings, but they also feature the protruding eye sockets, seen here, that are a characteristic of Nuxalk (Bella Coola) masks from about fifty miles farther north.

The basic form of this Kwakwaka'wakw mask is a half cylinder, as opposed to the usual hemispheric form of many Nuxalk masks. Alan Hoover, the cultural and art historian of the Northwest Coast, noted on the export permit application for this piece from Canada to the United States that while the structure of the lips, forehead, and chin are more like Heiltsuk (Bella Bella) than Nuxalk examples,

the nose is typically Kwakwaka'wakw. The painting style is characteristically Nuxalk in the repeated starfish-like motifs and in the connected U forms on the forehead. Indeed, the blue paint used on this mask is informally referred to as Bella Coola blue. Known to have been made in the village of Oweekeno, the mask, in its combining of styles and influences, may be seen as an example of cross-cultural exchange, which could have resulted from reciprocal visits for feasts or marriages.

The face painting offers a clue to the meaning of the mask, as does its blocky configuration. The features may refer to the marine world inhabited by Komokwa, Lord of the Undersea World. The triangular elements may be the fins of killer whales, and the asterisks may represent starfish, riches of Komokwa's underwater domain. The bulky shape of the mask derives in part from Komokwa masks of the nearby Kwakwaka'wakw peoples.

The mask was collected by a local store owner, a Mr. Hunt, in the 1920s, apparently from a neighboring Oweekeno family. It was bought, together with a Nuxalk mask from the previous store owner, a Dr. Green, by the dealer Howard Roloff, in 1986.

180. Crooked Beak of Heaven mask

Late 19th century
Kwakwaka'wakw peoples, Vancouver Island, British Columbia
Painted wood, plant fiber, commercial cord
18 ¼ x 40 ⅛ in. (46.4 x 101.9 cm)
RTCNA 215

Perhaps the best-known cycle of all Northwest Coast Indian dance performances—except for the potlatch—is the Hamatsa (cannibal) initiation ceremonial, an elaborate winter ritual of four nights' duration held by the Hamatsa Society. The philosophy behind this complex ritual rests on the belief that humanity becomes civilized by ascending a timeless path that leads from an uneducated, primitive state to a state of enlightened awareness. On this journey, qualities of leadership and social responsibility are developed that produce a cultured civilization. For the Kwakwaka'wakw, this pathway is a paradigm for human progression.

Each of the four performances in the ceremonial marks a stage on the way to achieving a state of knowledge and self-discipline. During his training for initiation, the candidate is taught the songs of the cannibal spirit by a woman. In the dances, he travels to the end of the earth and is given masks and other ritual paraphernalia, including bark, a symbol of spirituality. After his journey, he returns home. On the last night of the performance cycle, he is regaled wearing a long-beaked mask, the Cannibal Raven, which is so heavy that attendants have to hold him up. The Cannibal Raven is escorted by masked attendants, including a cannibal spirit called Crooked Beak of Heaven. This is the mask exhibited here. Wearers of the Crooked Beak of Heaven mask are completely concealed in shredded cedar bark, and the beaks are elevated to a forty-five-degree angle while circling the dance floor. The dancers make high-pitched sounds and move with a springy, angular step, turning their heads from side to side while they pull a hidden string apparatus that causes the beak to open and close with a resounding, cracking noise. Little by little, the Cannibal Raven, becomes less frenetic and enters a state of serenity. The initiate, having

thus traveled the path from cannibalism to mature cultural awareness, is now a civilized and full-fledged member of the Hamatsa Society.

The Crooked Beak of Heaven mask is not as long as that of the Cannibal Raven. But it is crowned by a dramatic cockscomblike superstructure, a signifying device of Kwakwaka'wakw dramatic art. This version was carved in the late nineteenth century and is therefore more boxy in its proportions and the comb more elemental in design than the highly baroque Crooked Beak masks of the twentieth century. These are complex masks composed of two or even three conjoined images, such as those made in the 1930s by such master carvers as Mungo Martin and Willie Sewid. A notable feature in the present example are the pink eye sockets. This coloration also appears in a Hok'kwa mask from Smith Inlet that was collected by George Hunt in 1905.[1]

1. Jonaitis 1991, p. 99, fig. 2.28.

George Walkus, Kwakwaka'wakw, active 1920s–1930s

| 181. Yagim mask |

1920–25
Vancouver Island, British Columbia
Painted wood
33 x 18 in. (83.8 x 45.7 cm)
RTCNA 155

Here, indeed, is a sea monster for all seasons. He recalls another mythological undersea denizen, Komokwa (cat. no. 179), but while Komokwa dwells in a submerged domain, Yagim (or Yagis) prowls, furtively aggressive. His fixated eyes seek out a victim. His suckers quiver at either side of his pinched nose. Around the edge of his face six barnacles protrude. And crowning his head is a grotesque fish-bird with sickle-shape fins. Like Crooked Beak of Heaven (cat. no. 180), Yagim exudes great authority and evokes overwhelming awe.

A spirit ancestor, Yagim figures in the Tseyka cycle of the southern Kwakwaka'wakw complex of winter dances. Bill Holm has described Yagim's participation at these events: "The dancer appears in the firelight hung with fringes of shredded bark or draped with a dark blanket. His movements are slow and flowing, befitting a monstrous undersea being. He turns his head from side to side staring into the shadows of the house . . . fanciful and unlike any credible living creature, Yagim comes alive for the hushed audience in the spirit-charged atmosphere of the Tseyka."[1] More than providing entertainment, Yagim offers his audience catharsis, an emotional physic akin to the purging effect of classical theater.

In 1958, this powerful mask turned up at the Carlebach Gallery in New York. I had to wait several months before it arrived. Julius Carlebach had agreed to rent it to Columbia Pictures as a prop in the feature film *Bell, Book, and Candle*, starring Kim Novak as a young art dealer, Jack Lemmon as a happy-go-lucky warlock, Hermione Gingold as the coven's den mother, and James Stewart as a befuddled suitor. Yagim turned up having survived the sentimental, romantic notions of "primitive" art that characterized his use by Hollywood.

At that time I had no idea of the real history of the mask. Fortunately, its first collector, the ethnologist and art historian Edward Malin, kindly wrote to me in 1965 that he had acquired the mask from the family of the carver, George Walkus, at Smith Inlet, British Columbia. Walkus had carved the mask during the 1920s, at a time when Kwakwaka'wakw traditional culture was being severely undermined by the Canadian government. Yagim has thus managed to brave not only Hollywood but also social persecution—finally to be understood and respected.

1. Holm and Calderón 1987, p. 102, no. 36. Another, quite different, a Yagim mask is illustrated in this publication.

Joe David, Nuu-chah-nulth/Tla-o-qui-aht, b. 1946

| *182. Pair of maskettes* |

1981–88
Vancouver Island, British Columbia
Painted wood
a. 4 ¼ x 2 ¾ in. (10.8 x 7 cm)
b. 2 x 3 ¼ in. (5.1 x 8.3 cm)
RTCNA 163a, b

This charming, sprightly pair of miniature sculptures are a very personal expression of the artist's aesthetic. Joe David, from the Tla-o-qui-aht band, is among the most prominent contemporary Nuu-chah-nulth (Nootka) carvers, including Tim Paul, Ron Hamilton, and the late Art Thompson, all of whom are known for ritual masks that adhere to traditional imagery, albeit with a freshness of style. David, however, has not shied away from investigating new fields of endeavor, such as painting the image of a gigantic whale on the tail of a British Airways Boeing 757.[1]

Here, we see him in a lighthearted mode. Considered together, this intimately conceived pair of maskettes, one with a playful human face, the other with a winsome animal face, have about them a beguiling Punch-and-Judy aspect. According to Leona Lattimer, the Vancouver art dealer who sold them to me, the human face mask alludes to Joe David himself, while the forehead maskette portrays a muskrat, a reference to the zoological vocation of one of his girlfriends.

1. See Hoover 2000, p. 71, and King 2000.

Robert Davidson, Haida, b. 1946

| 183. Woman's portrait mask |

ca. 1977–78
Old Masset, Haida Gwaii (Queen Charlotte Islands)
or White Rock, British Columbia
Painted wood
9 ½ x 6 ½ in. (24.1 x 16.5 cm)
RTCNA 169

Three masks have contributed to Robert Davidson's development of the "woman mask" theme. The first one, Woman with Labret (private collection),[1] was executed in 1975 and was conceived by the artist as "an imitation of a [traditional] portrait mask and was not intended for a 'doings' [potlatch] per se, but was part of my own personal program of study."[2]

Part of Davidson's acknowledged genius is his extraordinary ability to revisit, in each work, every facet, trait, and nuance of Haida carving art—almost as if he were reconstructing its history. This process is exemplified by Woman with Labret. Of this mask, Davidson has written: "When I finished it, I didn't care for it, and disliked the heavy blueness of it. I was surprised to see how well it was received. I placed

it with Bud Mintz [a much respected dealer and advocate of Northwest Coast Indian art, now deceased], whose widow, Jean, sold it for $CDN 67,500, which simply amazed me. . . . I carved your mask later, about 1977–1978, as another step in my study of the Haida woman, also not intending it for use."[3]

On a tip from a local ethnology dealer, the Australian woman to whom Davidson gave this second mask, called me and, at my request, sold it to me literally on my doorstep,

in April 2000. She had been gifted with this mask, as I learned later from Davidson, when living in Vancouver, B.C., and had subsequently brought it with her to Santa Fe. No one knew she owned it, and its appearance was a revelation.

1. For a reproduction of Woman with Labret, see Macnair, Joseph, and Grenville 1998, p. 182, no. 155. See also Thom 1993, pp. 48–49.
2. Personal communication from Robert Davidson, June 18, 2002.
3. Ibid.

Robert Davidson, Haida, b. 1946

| 184. Noble Woman mask |

2001
Old Masset, Haida Gwaii (Queen Charlotte Islands), or White Rock, British Columbia
Painted alder, copper, abalone-shell inlay, human hair
13 x 12 in. (33 x 30.5 cm)
RTCNA 495

A year after I purchased Robert Davidson's portrait mask (cat. no. 183), I spied a small colorplate of another woman's mask by Davidson, known as the Noble Woman, in an advertisement for the Spirit Wrestler Gallery in Vancouver, and I filed it in the back of my mind.[1] Luckily, I was able to visit the gallery in the late summer of 2001, and I purchased the mask on the spot.

More than a quarter century of steadily expanding artistic development separates the portrait mask from the Noble Woman mask. The earlier one is realistic in its program. The later one is a redefinition of the same theme. Not only is it more monumental in conception, but the facial features are carved with a stylistic fluidity that gives it a mystical profundity. The gaze of the Noble Woman is conceptually related to the masks of the ancient Roman and Japanese Noh theatre. The mask is loosely based on a corpus of Haida painted portrait masks dating to the period between 1824 and 1830 that were probably made for sale to early-nineteenth-century visitors to the Queen Charlotte Islands. These were associated in the literature with a female portrait mask with an old label on the reverse that had

been misread as "Jenna Cass."[2] Today, the label has been transliterated as Dija Kons, a mythical ancestress of the Haida eagle phratry, who gave birth to the eagles living on Haida Gwaii. Although portrait masks constitute a specific stylistic type, differences in the carving indicate that they were made by more than one hand.[3] Davidson's contemporary interpretation of the woman's portrait mask is based on a far more personal aesthetic. No longer the embodiment of a mythical being, she has been given a more human aspect and an evanescent smile, with features rendered to express feminine nobility. The painted forehead refers to the affiliation of the Davidson family with the Raven clan, while the abalone-shell labret is a traditional symbol of nobility itself. Endowed with a conceptualized beauty, the mask breaks through the reserve of earlier Haida traditions.

1. American Indian Arts Magazine, autumn 2001, p. 39.
2. Vaughan and Holm 1982, p. 97, no. 61.
3. The best group of illustrations of the type are to be found in King 1979, pls. 46, 47, 50, 51, 52, 53, 56, 57, 58. Two similar masks are in the Donald D. Jones collection at the Nelson-Atkins Museum of Art, Kansas City.

| 185. Seal mask |

Late 19th century
Yup'ik peoples, Kuskokwim/Yukon River delta, western Alaska
Painted wood
19 x 8 ¾ in. (48.3 x 22.2 cm)
RTCNA 609

| 186. Face mask |

Late 19th century
Yup'ik peoples, Kuskokwim/Yukon River delta, western Alaska
Painted wood
7 ⅞ x 5 ⅜ in. (20 x 13.7 cm)
RTCNA 610

| 187. Face mask |

Late 19th century
Yup'ik peoples, Kuskokwim/Yukon River delta, western Alaska
Painted wood
7 x 5 ¾ in. (17.8 x 14.6 cm)
RTCNA 611

These three masks represent, in different ways, the subtle and imaginative carving style of the Yup'ik peoples of the Kuskokwim/Yukon River delta of western Alaska. They do not display the whimsical appendages and feather embellishments often found on masks from this region, although the twisted face mask (above right) has five holes along the upper rim for the addition of goose or gull plumes. Rather, the emphasis is on delicacy of portrayal and the capturing of expressions of serenity and gentle humor, which invest western Alaskan Eskimo wood carvings with their unique charm. During my field experience in the far north, my discovery of the sociable and poetic character of the Yup'ik peoples made my Alaskan and Canadian Arctic travels among the most rewarding of my life.

All three masks were collected at the end of the nineteenth century by Bishop Farhout, a French-born cleric in charge of the Mackenzie River diocese, which was a short distance

from the Alaskan border. After the Second World War, the bishop's Parisian family sold the masks to John J. Klejman. I purchased them from Klejman at his New York gallery in the late fifties and early sixties. The mask shown at the upper right on the preceding page, with twisted features, crooked nose, leering mouth, and eyes askew, represents a *tugendaht,* or evil spirit, who hovers threateningly and unseen. While the *tugendaht* mask, with its dark message, has features that are roughcast, the smiling face of the mask below is softly carved. Held in the hand, it seems as fragile as parchment. These two masks were accompanied by a third, from the same source and now in the collection of Ramona Morris.

The largest mask (see p. 294), with its Harlequin-like face, presents a female seal seen from above, basking in the water, with two baby seal effigies appended at the bottom. The seal's flippers gently frame a large round humanoid mask set in the center of her body. The mask represents the *inua,* or soul element, of the animal, a symbol of cyclical regeneration. The pair of holes at the bottom edge would have allowed access into the spirit world. This mask was possibly displayed and danced at celebratory festivals of continuance and renewal. However, the fresh condition of the paint surface may indicate that it was never used and was collected directly from the carver.

1. For an example of another *tugendaht* mask, see Fitzhugh and Kaplan 1982, p. 196.

XVI

BOXES, BOWLS, AND

IMPLEMENTS

Making the Mundane Magical

188. Kerfed storage chest panels

1780–1820

Tlingit peoples, southeastern Alaska

Painted wood

Assembled: 12 ¾ x 25 x 15 ¾ in. (32.4 x 63.5 x 40 cm)

RTCNA 561

This celebrated set of four panels was originally a three-dimensional kerfed (steam-bent) chest used to store clothing, valuables, and house effects. At some unknown time, the panels were separated. An attempt was made to reassemble them into box form, but the edges were flattened and could not be rejoined. For this reason, they are exhibited here as a frieze. Other separate panels have survived either singly or in pairs, and some are of excellent quality.[1] The panels were exhibited in "The Native American Heritage: A Survey of North American Indian Art," a seminal exhibition held at the Art Institute of Chicago in 1977, and in "Spirits of the Water: Native Art Collected on Expeditions to Alaska and British Columbia, 1774–1910," an exhibition held at Fundación "la Caixa," Barcelona, in 1999, which traveled to Houston, Texas, the following year.[2] Allen Wardwell, in his

masterly tome on Northwest Coast shamanic art, writes that Bill Holm "dates such carvings to the late eighteenth century through their 'massive formlines, minimal background, simple details and ovoid reliefs in eyes and joints.' Although there is no documentation to associate this chest with shamanic use, the central face with the protruding tongue suggests the depiction of a shaman in a trance."[3] The face relief carvings certainly support such an association, as does the owl, with its rounded eyes, immediately below, since the owl is acknowledged as a shaman's helper and a symbol of death (see also cat. no. 177).

An image in relief of a shaman either in a trance or dying occupies the top center of each of the two longitudinal panels, indicating that the chest, when assembled, may have been used to hold a shaman's remains or that it once contained

paraphernalia belonging to a specific shaman. The entire image appears to represent a bear-monster, perhaps the shaman himself, tansformed into an owl. The bear's mouth, with elongated teeth and a shallow tongue, seems to double as the wings of the owl.

This composition is also seen on a chest panel from about 1850, preserved in the National Museum of the American Indian, Washington, D.C.[4] By this time, the design has lost its fluidity and is rigidly patternlike. The image of the owl, however, is clearly recognizable and its wings more visible

within the mouth cavity. The design of repeating circles can be interpreted as the wings of the owl or as rows of suckers from another shamanic animal, the octopus.

1. Brown 1998, p. 110; Inverarity 1950, no. 16, in which the separate panels are shown digitally reassembled; and Sturtevant 1974, no. 74, for an example in similar archaic style.
2. Maurer 1977 and Brown 2000 are the catalogues to these exhibitions.
3. Wardwell 1996, pp. 300–301, no. 455, colorpl.
4. Ibid., p. 301, no. 456.

189. Kerfed storage chest

Mid- to late 19th century
Heiltsuk peoples, Bella Bella, British Columbia
Painted wood
18 ½ x 33 x 18 in. (47 x 83.8 x 45.7 cm)
RTCNA 170

Until recently, what used to be known generically as northern Kwakwaka'wakw (Kwakiutl) art was neglected, and there was considerable confusion about the distinction between the art styles of several tribes in this central region of British Columbia. Every Northwest Coast art tradition that was not of Nuxalk (Bella Coola) origin tended to be lumped together under that catchall. Recent scholarship, however, has now distinguished the artistic contributions of the Heiltsuk, dwelling principally in the town of Bella Bella, from those of the neighboring Haisla and Oweekeno. Among the first to have received artistic reappraisal are the Heiltsuk, the subject of a recent monographic exhibition at the Royal Ontario Museum, Toronto, organized by the art historian Martha Black.[1]

Bella Bella art is a fascinating convergence of various influences from neighboring tribes and yet invested with vernacular and unconventional features that proclaim it a unique orthodoxy easily recognized. Among the most striking products of this style, which is transitional between the tradition of the central and northern Northwest Coast, is a series of painted kerfed oblong chests by, or attributed to, the Heiltsuk artist Captain Carpenter (1841–1931), who lived in Bella Bella and whose name reflects his profession of canoe and boat maker. Certainly the front and back panels of this storage chest are more sophisticated in style than the two end panels, which are more rudimentary in craft and design, suggesting that they are by a less gifted painter. The most identifiable characteristics of Captain Carpenter's style are the slim, elongated formlines that arc from one side of the box to the other, providing compositional balance and continuity. This approach to design is a hallmark of many storage boxes from Bella Bella, and it would be interesting to know more fully how the style developed and how it migrated to tribes both to the north and to the south of the Heiltsuk. The standing figure, with hands raised in the orans position, is a particularly refined example of Heiltsuk style.[2] The figural type migrated northward as far as the Tsimshian tribe of northern British Columbia and on to Alaska. It is seen on Alaskan Tlingit basketry, as well as on large wood screens such as the famous Shakes screen originally from the house of Chief Shakes, Wrangell, Alaska, and now in the Denver Art Museum.[3]

Bill McLennan and Karen Duffek, in their recent survey of Northwest Coast painted designs, include a reconstructed Heiltsuk house front with an orans figure originally from Kimsquit and dating to 1881, in Nuu-chah-nulth territory on Vancouver Island, south of Bella Bella. A Tsimshian painted fabric screen from north of Bella Bella shows eighteen squatting figures around a standing figure, all of whom display the orans gesture.[4] And a Tsimshian button blanket in this volume (cat. no. 171) displays a bear in the orans position. The orans figure also appears in the iconography of the Tlingit at the northern limit of the Northwest Coast, as cited above. Thus, the present storage box in its imagery, occupies geographically a midpoint between the northern and southern extremes.

1. Black 1997, pp. 110–14.
2. The orans position, of prayer with open hands extended, has been interpreted as a charismatic gesture of blessing. It is common to almost all ancient religions as an outward sign of glorification. The Northwest Coast version has a squatting, rather than standing, position.
3. Inverarity 1950, no. 12.
4. McLennan and Duffek 2000, p. 119, fig. B.

190. Kerfed grease bowl

Early 19th century
Haida or Tlingit peoples, Alaska or British Columbia
Wood
3 ¾ x 5 ¼ x 4 ¾ in. (9.5 x 13.3 x 12.1 cm)
RTCNA 191

In 1990, I spied this simple grease dish on a desk in a gallery in Santa Fe, where it was being used to hold pens and pencils. Its total lack of ornamentation probably led to its being overlooked as a work of art. But, in fact, in its great formal purity it offers a basic lesson in Northwest Coast carving fundamentals. Dating to the early nineteenth century, it is either Haida or Tlingit in origin. Such carved bowls are used to store and to offer guests eulachon (candlefish) grease, which is reserved for important visitors at events such as potlatches or feasts and has something of the same prestige value in the Northwest Coast that the finest caviar has in the West. Portions of fish or meat are dipped in the grease in such bowls or related, carved dishes (see cat. no. 191) and used as a condiment. Today, a gallon of rendered eulachon grease from the fisheries at the mouth of the Nass River can cost several hundred dollars. In this particular case, at the center of each side the wood has worn through the oil patination, which is exceedingly rich and dense, confirming its great age and usage and thus increasing its appeal.

191. High-end bowl

Mid-19th century
Haida or Tlingit peoples, Alaska or British Columbia
Wood
3 ⅜ x 6 ½ in. (8.6 x 16.5 cm)
RTCNA 159

This type of eating container, called a high-end bowl because of its crownlike terminals, is found by the hundreds by ethnologists collecting along the northern part of the Northwest Coast. The form has a generic relationship to canoes (the inner edge of such bowls are finished in the manner of tribal canoe gunwales), but the striations at the midpoint of the longitudinal sides recall the grain of the birchbark used for containers made by inland Athabaskan tribes east of the Haida/Tlingit cultural area. Some elaborately delineated feast dishes of this general size are carved in the form of animals such as bear, beaver, or seal effigies and do not have this profile.[1] Here, too, the face at either terminal depicts a schematized animal, probably a bear, in shallow relief.

Other animals—otters, seals, beavers, even hawks—can also appear on high-end bowls, although the carving may be too generalized for specific animal attribution. It is a tribute to the makers of this widespread type that, despite similarities in imagery, almost each bowl has subtle variations that make it unique. This bowl shows, by its greasy patination, that it has been well used.[2]

1. These features are detailed in the catalogue of a 1973–75 exhibition organized at the Renwick Gallery of the Smithsonian American Art Museum; see Sturtevant 1974. For a particularly close example, see ibid., no. 41, attributed to the Tlingit.
2. For additional, similar examples, see Holm 1983, p. 76, and Varjola 1990, p. 81, fig. 71.

| 192. Halibut hook |

Early 19th century
Tlingit peoples, southeastern Alaska
Wood, plant fiber, Native-tanned skin ties, string
6 x 10 ¼ in. (15.2 x 26 cm)
RTCNA 151
The Metropolitan Museum of Art,
Gift of Ralph T. Coe, 2002 (2002.602.3)

Halibut was a staple of the Tlingit diet, and halibut fishing was a perennial activity all up and down the Northwest Coast. Hooks of wood were fashioned for this purpose, customarily by the fishermen who actually used them. Bill Holm has noted that the quality of the carving depended very much on the abilities of the fisherman who made the hook, but an expert fisherman did not necessarily guarantee an artistically successful product.

This typical halibut hook takes the form of a V, which requires the joining of two pieces at the inner angle. The barb points inward from the opening at the front. Sometimes the upper part of the hook is extensively carved with traditional imagery. In this case, a sculpin forms the upper prow of the hook, its bony openwork mouth and receding gills exquisitely rendered with a clarity of style typical of early-nineteenth-century design. The detached bird in the hollowed-out top section of the sculpin can move freely within its cavity and thus acts as a sort of rudder to steady the hook as it moves through the water, all designed with the hope of attracting a bountiful catch. The Northwest Coast art specialist Steven C. Brown has suggested that this particular hook might well be by the famous carver of the Wrangell houseposts of about 1816, preserved today in the Wrangell Museum in Wrangell, Alaska.[2]

1. Holm 1983, p. 89.
2. Personal communication from Steven C. Brown, ca. 1995.

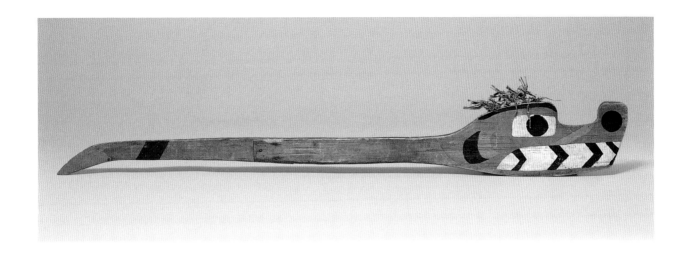

193. Dance wand

1890–1900
Nuu-chah-nulth peoples, west coast of Vancouver Island,
British Columbia
Painted wood, plant fiber
6 ⅞ x 55 in. (17.5 x 139.7 cm)
RTCNA 562

This sparse, but impressive, Nuu-chah-nulth (Nootka) dance wand was used long ago during the Klukwana, an elaborate wolf ritual that is at the heart of Nuu-chah-nulth spirituality. The ritual apparently took place over an eight-day season, with "wind up" ceremonies on the ninth through the eleventh day, although the masked dancing continued in private houses, so that the season in fact continued indefinitely.[1] At what point the dramatic wand entered into the ceremonial remains uncertain, but its vital association with the wolf ritual is certain because the flattened wolf image follows exactly the profile of the better-known headdress masks worn by the dancers.

The wolf ritual centers on the dramatization of a legend that tells of the abduction of several young initiates to the secret wolf society; their eventual rescue by members of the society; and their receiving the power and wisdom of the wolves, accomplished by the exorcism of the wolf spirit by

which they had been possessed. This coming-of-age ritual is related to the Hamatsa (cannibal) ceremonial among the Kwakwaka'wakw peoples, who occupied lands to the north. But while the carving style of the Kwakwaka'wakw became more complex (see cat. no. 180), that of the Nuu-chah-nulth, as exemplified by this wand, remained more elemental.

In addition to being danced in the now rarely performed full Klukwana, dance wands and wolf masks, worn by men or boys, are danced today at many events. In 1988, I was fortunate to be invited to a party (the Nuu-chah-nulth name for a potlatch) near Port Alberni, British Columbia. Given by the David family (see cat. no. 182), it was held as a memorial for the deceased and as a child's naming, honoring past and present in one extended ceremony. It is an occasion I will never forget.

1. Ernst 1952, p. 63.

194. Steering paddle

Late 19th century
Tlingit or Haida peoples, Alaska or British Columbia
Painted wood
63 x 5 ½ in. (160 x 14 cm)
RTCNA 168

This paddle, used for steering as indicated by its size,[1] unmistakably displays an octopus, a motif that was used on Tlingit paddles over a long period of time. The octopus was noted for its liquidlike speed through the water and ability to hide from enemies, characteristics valued by Northwest Coast canoeists and seamen. The pattern on an older Haida steering paddle in the National Museum of American History, Washington, D.C., is very similar to this one and also depicts an octopus with suckers hanging downward.[2] The carver of the present paddle may have known of the earlier one, or both may have descended from the same tradition. Indeed, the largest Tlingit canoes were often carved by and acquired from the Haida, who lived not far away across the Hecate Strait and with whom the Tlingit traded. This steering paddle may or may not have been part of that trade.

1. Emmons 1991, p. 84.
2. Fitzhugh and Crowell 1988, p. 157, fig. 190.

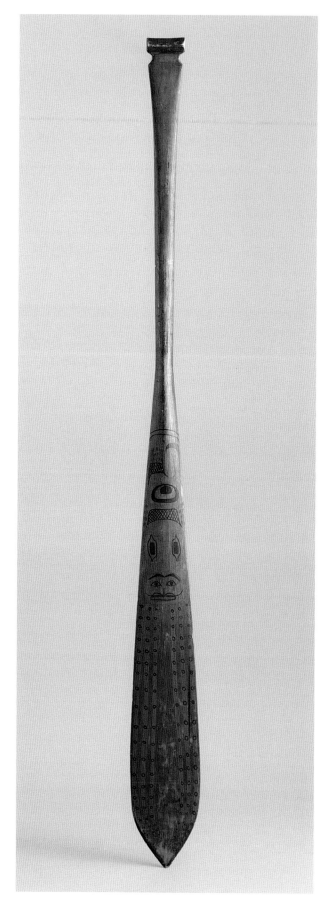

195. Spindle whorl with otter

ca. 1860
Salish (Comox or Cowichan) peoples, east coast of
Vancouver Island, British Columbia
Wood
Diameter 7 ¼ in. (18.4 cm)
RTCNA 177

Spindle whorls were used to spin the fibers for southern Salish blankets, once made from dog's hair. Although utilitarian objects, spindle whorls were often embellished with animal imagery that is, at its best, among the most stunning from the southern part of the coast. Here, the spinning motion of the whorl is signified by the circular movement of a sea otter carved in relief. The depiction of the otter is somewhat more vernacular than the elegant designs on eighteenth-century examples, but it has a dynamic of its own, with a staccato rhythm created by the otter's spiky back and the aggressive mouth with bared teeth. The whorl once belonged to the distinguished Native American art historian Norman Feder, who field-collected it on Vancouver Island over forty years ago.

| 196. Bird effigy dish |

Late 19th century
Yup'ik peoples, Kuskokwim/Yukon River delta, western Alaska
Painted wood, copper inlays
16 ¾ x 5 ¾ in. (42.5 x 14.6 cm)
RTCNA 658

| 197. Oval dish |

Late 19th century
Yup'ik peoples, Kuskokwim/Yukon River delta, western Alaska
Painted wood
10 ¾ x 20 in. (27.3 x 50.8 cm)
RTCNA 659

This pair of dishes, one depicting a bird and the other with a seemingly abstract design, were sold together and are probably by the same artist. Dishes such as these were used at Yup'ik feasts and also, by the 1930s, were made for sale, first for ethnologists and then for visitors and servicemen. They demonstrate the simplicity of form and sensitivity to nuance that mark the western Alaskan and the pan-Eskimo–Inuit approach to decorative art. More elaborately painted dishes often were embellished with designs of monstrous imaginary creatures, but even these pieces have about them something of the disarming quality that applies as well to Eskimo mask and even to the very smallest objects—buttons, seal plugs, spear guard amulets, and toggles. The designs may not be as simple as they appear. The painted interior of the oval dish may be a sky chart or map of the heavens, a prototype of the diagram of the Big Dipper in gold against a deep blue background on the Alaska state flag—which was designed by an Alaskan Eskimo.

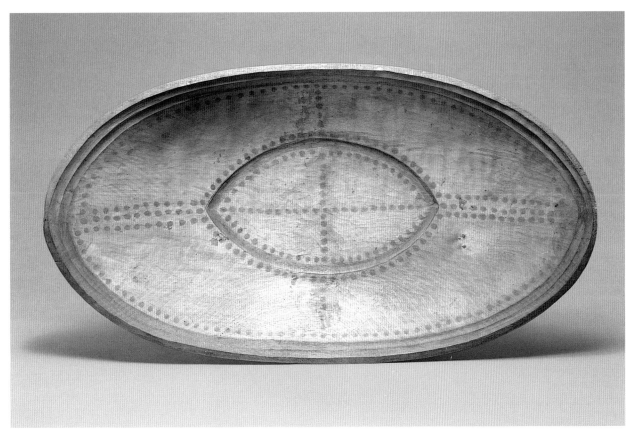

198. Utility box

1825–30
Supiak peoples, Kodiak Island, southern Alaska
Wood, metal
6 ½ x 10 ½ in. (16.5 x 26.7 cm)
RTCNA 623

This utility, or, more properly, tea box is one of the rarest surviving examples of Pacific Eskimo art. Only three other examples have been published. It was probably made between 1825 and 1830. The four side drawers and two top compartments, accessible only from above, indicate that it could have been commissioned by a Russian patron as a tea caddy, as a container for spices, or even as a writing box. Russian influence figured prominently during the occupation of Alaska, from 1784 to 1867, and this box reflects cross-cultural exchange. The construction is Euro-inspired, down to the non-Eskimo drawer pulls and the iron nails on the base used for repairs, and the framing of the compartments is modeled on European toolboxes and sea chests. Except for the tiny metal ring handles, the drawers are concealed. The incised designs are fascinating in their ambiguity and clearly in imitation of Tlingit motifs, although they are not well understood and lack the formline system basic to Tlingit art.

These quasi motifs were perhaps transmitted through the Eyak, a small Athabaskan tribe that lived northeast of the Tlingit, with whom they shared certain artistic traditions. The Supiak of Kodiak Island, who made this utility box, may also have been influenced by the Northwest Coast manner, either from their own trade or from Russian impressments, quite common during this period. The charm of Supiak boxes derives from their reference to Tlingit motifs. These were better understood on another Supiak painted chest of similar date in the Peter the Great Museum of Anthropology and Ethnography, St. Petersburg, which lacks the obscuring coats of varnish on the present example.[1] These Tlingit characteristics may also have been transmitted by the other Pacific Eskimo group, the Chugash, who lived on Prince William Sound, east of Kenai Peninsula. Two other similar utility boxes are preserved in the Etholén collection at the National Museum of Finland, Helsinki, and were probably donated in 1834.[2]

1. Fitzhugh and Crowell 1988, p. 284, fig. 391.
2. Varjola 1990, p. 79, figs. 65–67.

Bibliography

COMPILED BY JEAN WAGNER

Abbott, Donald N., ed.
1981   *The World Is as Sharp as a Knife: An Anthology in
Honour of Wilson Duff.* Victoria: British Columbia
Provincial Museum in association with Donors Fund,
Friends of the Museum.

Abel-Vidor, Suzanne, Dot Brovarney, and Susan Billy
1996   *Remember Your Relations: The Elsie Allen Baskets,
Family and Friends.* Introduction by Malcolm Margolin.
Exh. cat. Ukiah, Calif.: Grace Hudson Museum, 1993;
Oakland Museum of California, 1996; Berkeley, Calif.:
Heyday Books.

ACPAC Newsletter
1994   "General Electric's Hopewell Site." *ACPAC Newsletter,*
October.

Alsop, Joseph
1982   *The Rare Art Traditions: The History of Art Collecting and
Its Linked Phenomena Wherever These Have Appeared.*
Bollingen Series, xxxv, 27. New York: Harper and Row.

Antes, Horst, and Wolfgang Haberland
1981   *Kachina-Figuren der Pueblo-Indianer Nordamerikas aus
der Studiensammlung Horst Antes.* Exh. cat. Karlsruhe:
Badisches Landesmuseum Karlsruhe.

Archambault, JoAllyn, and William C. Sturtevant
1996   "Museums and Collectors." In *Encyclopedia of North
American Indians,* edited by Frederick E. Hoxie,
pp. 407–10. Boston and New York: Houghton Mifflin.

Archuleta, Margaret, and Rennard Strickland
1991   *Shared Visions: Native American Painters and Sculptors
in the Twentieth Century.* Essays by Joy L. Gritton and
W. Jackson Rushing. Exh. cat. Phoenix, Ariz.: Heard
Museum; New York: New Press.

Bancroft-Hunt, Norman
1979   *People of the Totem: The Indians of the Pacific Northwest.*
London: Orbis Publishing.
1992   *North American Indians.* Philadelphia: Courage Books.

Batkin, Jonathan
1987   "Martina Vigil and Florentino Montoya: Master Potters
of San Ildefonso and Cochiti Pueblos." *American
Indian Art* 12 (autumn 1987), pp. [28]–37.
1999   as editor. *Clay People: Pueblo Indian Figurative
Traditions.* Exh. cat. Santa Fe: Wheelwright Museum
of the American Indian.

Bedford, Clay P.
1980   *An Exhibition of Western North American Indian
Baskets from the Collection of Clay P. Bedford.*
Exh. cat. San Francisco: California Academy of
Sciences.

Benndorf, Helga, and Arthur Speyer
1968   *Indianer Nordamerikas, 1760–1860: Aus der Sammlung
Speyer.* Exh. cat. Offenbach: Deutsches Ledermuseum,
Deutsches Schuhmuseum.

Bercht, Fatima, ed.
1997   *Taíno: Pre-columbian Art and Culture from the
Caribbean.* Exh. cat. New York: El Museo del Barrio;
Monacelli Press.

Bierhorst, John
1985   *The Mythology of North America.* New York:
Morrow.

Black, Lydia T.
1982   *Aleut Art: Unangam Aguqaadangin / Unangan of the
Aleutian Archipelago.* Anchorage: Aang Angagin,
Aleutian / Pribilof Islands Association.

Black, Martha
1997   *Bella Bella: A Season of Heiltsuk Art.* Toronto: Royal
Ontario Museum; Vancouver and Seattle: University
of Washington Press.

Blackard, David M.
1990   *Patchwork and Palmettos: Seminole/Miccosukee Folk Art
Since 1820.* Exh. cat. Fort Lauderdale, Fla.: Fort
Lauderdale Historical Society.

Blair, Mary Ellen, and Laurence Blair
1999 *The Legacy of a Master Potter: Nampeyo and Her Descendants.* Tucson, Ariz.: Treasure Chest Books.

Blomberg, Nancy J.
1988 *Navajo Textiles: The William Randolph Hearst Collection.* Tucson: University of Arizona Press.

Boas, Franz
1907 "Notes on the Blanket Designs." Following "The Chilkat Blanket," by George T. Emmons, with notes by Franz Boas, in *Memoirs of the American Museum of Natural History, Whole Series,* vol. 3, pp. 351–401.
1908 "Decorative Designs of Alaskan Needlecases: A Study in the History of Conventional Designs, Based on Materials in the U. S. National Museum." *Proceedings of the U. S. National Museum* 34, pp. 321–44.
1927 *Primitive Art.* Instituttet for Sammenlignende Kultur- forskning, [Publikationer], ser. B, Skrifter, 8. Oslo: H. Aschehoug; Cambridge, Mass.: Harvard University Press.
1955 *Primitive Art.* Reprint of 1927 ed. New York: Dover.

Boas, Franz, and George Hunt
1902–5 *Kwakiutl Texts.* 3 parts. Memoirs of the American Museum of Natural History, vol. 5; Jesup North Pacific Expedition, Publications, vol. 3. New York.
1906 *Kwakiutl Texts—Second Series.* Memoirs of the American Museum of Natural History, vol. 14, part 1; Jesup North Pacific Expedition, Publications, vol. 10, part 1. Leiden and New York.

Bolz, Peter, and Hans-Ulrich Sanner
1999 *Native American Art: The Collections of the Ethnological Museum Berlin.* Seattle: University of Washington Press.

Brain, Jeffrey P., and Philip Phillips
1996 with Susan P. Sheldon. *Shell Gorgets: Styles of the Late Prehistoric and Protohistoric Southeast.* Cambridge, Mass.: Peabody Museum Press.

Brasser, Ted J.
1976 *"Bo'jou, Neejee!": Profiles of Canadian Indian Art, a Travelling Exhibition of the National Museum of Man, Ottawa.* Catalogue of artifacts by Judy Thompson and Ted J. Brasser. Exh. cat. Ottawa: National Museum of Man, National Museums of Canada.

Brody, J. J.
1997 *Pueblo Indian Painting: Tradition and Modernism in New Mexico, 1900–1930.* Santa Fe: School of American Research.

Brose, David S., James Allison Brown, and David W. Penney
1985 *Ancient Art of the American Woodland Indians.* Exh. cat. Washington, D.C.: National Gallery of Art; Detroit: Detroit Institute of Arts; Houston: Museum of Fine Arts; New York: Harry N. Abrams, in association with Detroit Institute of Arts.

Browman, David L.
2002 "The Peabody Museum, Frederic W. Putnam, and the Rise of U. S. Anthropology, 1866–1903." *American Anthropologist* 104, pp. 508–20.

Brown, Steven C.
1998 *Native Visions: Evolution in Northwest Coast Art from the Eighteenth through the Twentieth Century.* Exh. cat. Seattle: Seattle Art Museum; University of Washington Press.
2000 as editor. *Spirits of the Water: Native Art Collected on Expeditions to Alaska and British Columbia, 1774–1910.* Essays by Paz Cabello et al. Exh. cat. Barcelona: Fundación "la Caixa"; Seattle: University of Washington Press; Vancouver: Douglas and McIntyre.

Brumwell, Stephen
2002 *Redcoats: The British Soldier and War in the Americas, 1755–1763.* Cambridge: Cambridge University Press.

Bunzel, Ruth Leah
1972 *The Pueblo Potter: A Study of Creative Imagination in Primitive Art.* Reprint. New York: Dover. Originally published Columbia University Press, New York, 1929.

Burch, Wanda
1990 "Sir William Johnson's Cabinet of Curiosities." *New York History* 71, no. 3, pp. 261–82.

Burland, Cottie A.
1959 *Man and Art.* London and New York: Studio Publications.
1965 *North American Indian Mythology.* London: Hamlyn.
1973 *Eskimo Art.* London and New York: Hamlyn.

Burnett, Edwin K.
1944 *Inlaid Stone and Bone Artifacts from Southern California.* Contributions from the Museum of the American Indian, Heye Foundation, vol. 13. New York.

Butterfield and Butterfield sale
1991 *American Indian and Ethnographic Art.* Sale cat., Butterfield and Butterfield, San Francisco and Santa Fe, April 25, 1991.

Canadian Museum of Civilization
1993 *In the Shadow of the Sun: Perspectives on Contemporary Native Art.* Mercury Series; Canadian Ethnology Service, no. 124. Hull, Quebec: Canadian Museum of Civilization.

Chatwin, Bruce
1988 *Utz.* London: J. Cape.

Clifford, James

1987 "Of Other Peoples: Beyond the 'Salvage' Paradigm." In *Discussions in Contemporary Culture,* edited by Hal Foster, vol. 1, pp. 121–30. Seattle: Bay Press.

1988 *The Predicament of Culture: Twentieth-Century Ethnography, Literature, and Art.* Cambridge, Mass.: Harvard University Press.

Coe, Ralph T.

1954 "Camille Pissarro in Paris: A Study of His Later Development." *Gazette des Beaux-Arts,* ser. 6, 43 (February), pp. 93–118.

1962 *The Imagination of Primitive Man: A Survey of the Arts of the Non-Literate Peoples of the World.* Exh. cat. Kansas City: William Rockhill Nelson Gallery of Art and Mary Atkins Museum of Fine Arts.

1972 "Asiatic Sources of Northwest Coast Art." In *American Indian Art: Form and Tradition,* pp. 85–91. Minneapolis: Walker Art Center.

1976a *Sacred Circles: Two Thousand Years of North American Indian Art.* Exh. cat. London: Hayward Gallery; Kansas City: William Rockhill Nelson Gallery of Art and Mary Atkins Museum of Fine Arts; [London]: Arts Council of Great Britain. Also published Kansas City, 1977.

1976b "Animal Style in Indian North America." *Apollo,* n.s., 104 (September), pp. 169–75.

1986 *Lost and Found Traditions: Native American Art, 1965–1985.* Edited by Irene Gordon. Exh. cat. Seattle: University of Washington Press; New York: American Federation of Arts. Circulated 1986–93.

Cohodas, Marvin

1992 "Louisa Keyser and the Cohns: Mythmaking and Basket Making in the American West." In *The Early Years of Native American Art History: The Politics of Scholarship and Collecting,* edited by Janet C. Berlo, pp. 88–133. Seattle: University of Washington Press.

Cole, Douglas

1985 *Captured Heritage: The Scramble for Northwest Coast Artifacts.* Seattle: University of Washington Press.

Collins, Henry Bascom

1973 *The Far North: 2000 Years of American Eskimo and Indian Art.* Exh. cat. Washington, D.C.: National Gallery of Art.

Colton, Harold Sellers

1959 *Hopi Kachina Dolls, with a Key to Their Identification.* Rev. ed. Albuquerque: University of New Mexico Press.

Cope, Gilbert, comp.

1871 *Genealogy of the Dutton Family of Pennsylvania, Preceded by a History of the Family in England from the Time of William the Conqueror to the Year 1669; with an Appendix Containing a Short Account of the Duttons of Conn.* West Chester, Pa.: F. S. Hickman, for the author.

Covarrubias, Miguel

1954 *The Eagle, the Jaguar, and the Serpent: Indian Art of the Americas. North America: Alaska, Canada, the United States.* New York: Knopf.

Crowell, Aron L., Amy F. Steffian, and Gordon L. Pullar, eds.

2001 *Looking Both Ways: Heritage and Identity of the Alutiiq People.* Fairbanks: University of Alaska Press.

Dalzell, Kathleen E.

1968 *The Queen Charlotte Islands, 1774–1966.* Terrace, B. C.: C. M. Adam.

Dam-Mikkelsen, Bente, and Torben Lundbæk, eds.

1980 *Etnografiske genstande i det Kongelige Danske Kunstkammer, 1650–1800 / Ethnographic Objects in the Royal Danish Kunstkammer, 1650–1800.* National-museets skrifter; Etnografisk række, vol. 17. Copenhagen: Nationalmuseet.

Dillingham, Rick, and Melinda Elliot

1992 *Acoma and Laguna Pottery.* Edited by Joan Kathryn O'Donnell. Santa Fe: School of American Research Press.

Douglas, Frederic H., and René d'Harnoncourt

1941 *Indian Art of the United States.* Exh. cat. New York: Museum of Modern Art.

1969 *Indian Art of the United States.* Reprint of 1941 ed. New York: Arno Press for the Museum of Modern Art.

Drew, Leslie, and Douglas Wilson

1980 *Argillite: Art of the Haida.* North Vancouver: Hancock House.

Duff, Wilson

1967 *Arts of the Raven: Masterworks by the Northwest Coast Indian. An Exhibition in Honour of the One Hundredth Anniversary of Canadian Confederation.* Contributions by Bill Holm and Bill Reid. Exh. cat. Vancouver: Vancouver Art Gallery.

1981 "Thoughts on the Nootka Canoe." In Abbott 1981, pp. 201–6.

Duncan, Kate C.

1989 *Northern Athapaskan Art: A Beadwork Tradition.* Seattle: University of Washington Press.

Dunn, Dorothy

1968 *American Indian Painting of the Southwest and Plains Areas.* Albuquerque: University of New Mexico Press.

Emmons, George Thornton

1911 *The Tahltan Indians.* University of Pennsylvania, The Museum, Anthropological Publications, vol. 4, no. 1. Philadelphia: University Museum.

1991 *The Tlingit Indians.* Edited and with additions by Frederica de Laguna; a biography by Jean Low.

Anthropological Papers of the American Museum of
Natural History, vol. 70. Seattle: University of
Washington Press; New York: American Museum
of Natural History.

Ernst, Alice Henson
1952   *The Wolf Ritual of the Northwest Coast.* Eugene:
University of Oregon Press.

Ewers, John C.
1967   "William Clark's Indian Museum in St. Louis, 1816–
1838." In *A Cabinet of Curiosities: Five Episodes in the
Evolution of American Museums,* by Whitfield J. Bell Jr.
et al., pp. 49–72. Charlottesville: University Press of
Virginia.

Ewing, Douglas C., ed.
1982   *Pleasing the Spirits: A Catalogue of a Collection of
American Indian Art.* With essays by Craig Bates and
Ted J. Brasser. New York: Ghylen Press.

Feder, Norman
1964   *Art of the Eastern Plains Indians: The Nathan Sturges
Jarvis Collection.* Guides to the Collection, 2.
Brooklyn: Brooklyn Museum.
1965   "American Indian Art Before 1850." *Denver Art Museum
Quarterly,* summer. Exh. cat. Denver: Denver Art
Museum.
1971a *American Indian Art.* New York: Harry N. Abrams.
1971b *Two Hundred Years of North American Indian Art.* Exh.
cat. New York: Whitney Museum of American Art;
Praeger Publishers.

Feest, Christian F., ed.
2001   *Studies in American Indian Art: A Memorial Tribute
to Norman Feder.* ERNAS Monographs, 2. Altenstadt,
Germany: European Review of Native American Studies.

Fields, Virginia M.
1985   *The Hover Collection of Karuk Baskets.* Eureka, Calif.:
Clarke Memorial Museum.

Fitzhugh, William W., and Aron Crowell, eds.
1988   *Crossroads of Continents: Cultures of Siberia and
Alaska.* Exh. cat. Washington, D.C.: National
Museum of Natural History; Smithsonian
Institution Press.

Fitzhugh, William W., and Susan A. Kaplan
1982   *Inua: Spirit World of the Bering Sea Eskimo.* Contributions
by Henry Bascom Collins et al. Exh. cat. Washington,
D.C.: Smithsonian Institution Press for the National
Museum of Natural History.

Flint Institute of Arts
1973   *The Art of the Great Lakes Indians.* Exh. cat. Flint,
Mich.: Flint Institute of Arts.

Force, Roland W.
1999   *Politics and the Museum of the American Indian: The
Heye and the Mighty.* Honolulu: Mechas Press.

Frank, Larry, and Francis H. Harlow
1974   *Historic Pottery of the Pueblo Indians, 1600–1880.*
Boston: New York Graphic Society.

Gibbon, Guy E., ed.
1998   *Archaeology of Prehistoric Native America: An
Encyclopedia.* New York: Garland Publishing.

Greenberg, Clement
1961   *Art and Culture: Critical Essays,* pp. 139–45. Boston:
Beacon Press.

Greenfeld, Howard
1987   *The Devil and Dr. Barnes: Portrait of an American Art
Collector.* New York: Viking Press.

Grimes, John R., Christian F. Feest, and Mary Lou Curran
2002   *Uncommon Legacies: Native American Art from the
Peabody Essex Museum.* Exh. cat. New York:
American Federation of Arts; Seattle: University of
Washington Press.

Grinnell, George Bird
1923   *The Cheyenne Indians: Their History and Ways of Life.*
2 vols. New Haven: Yale University Press.
1972   *The Cheyenne Indians: Their History and Ways of Life.*
2 vols. Reprint of 1923 ed. Lincoln: University of
Nebraska Press.

Gunther, Erna
1962   *Northwest Coast Indian Art: An Exhibit at the Seattle
World's Fair Fine Arts Pavilion.* Exh. cat. Seattle:
[Century 21 Exposition], 1962.

Gunther, Erna, and Axel Rasmussen
1966   *Art in the Life of the Northwest Coast Indians. With a
Catalog of the Rasmussen Collection of Northwest Indian
Art at the Portland Art Museum.* Portland, Oreg.:
Portland Art Museum.

Haddon, Alfred C.
1895   *Evolution in Art; as Illustrated by the Life-Histories of
Designs.* London: W. Scott.

Haeberlin, Herman K.
1918   "Principles of Esthetic Form in the Art of the
North Pacific Coast." *American Anthropologist* 20
(July–September), pp. 258–64.

Hail, Barbara A.
1980   *Hau, Kóla!: The Plains Indian Collection of the
Haffenreffer Museum of Anthropology.* Bristol, R.I.:
The Museum.

Halle, David

1993   *Inside Culture: Art and Class in the American Home.* Chicago: University of Chicago Press.

Harris, Marvin

1968   *The Rise of Anthropological Theory: A History of Theories of Culture.* New York: Crowell.

Harrison, Julia D., et al.

1987   *The Spirit Sings: Artistic Traditions of Canada's First Peoples.* With essays by Ruth Holmes Whitehead, Ruth B. Phillips, Ted J. Brasser, Judy Thompson, Bernadette Driscoll, and Martine J. Reid. Exh. cat. Calgary, Alberta: Glenbow Museum; Toronto: McClelland and Stewart.

Herold, Joyce

2001   "Norman Feder's Double Standard." In Feest 2001, pp. 4–15.

Holm, Bill

1965   *Northwest Coast Indian Art: An Analysis of Form.* Thomas Burke Memorial Washington State Museum, Monograph, no. 1. Seattle: University of Washington Press.

1983   as editor. *The Box of Daylight: Northwest Coast Indian Art.* Contributions by Peter L. Corey et al. Exh. cat. Seattle: Seattle Art Museum; University of Washington Press.

Holm, Bill, and Eduardo Calderón

1987   *Spirit and Ancestor: A Century of Northwest Coast Indian Art at the Burke Museum.* Thomas Burke Memorial Washington State Museum, Monograph, no. 4. Seattle: University of Washington Press.

Holm, Bill, and William Reid

1975   *Form and Freedom: A Dialogue on Northwest Coast Indian Art.* Exh. cat. Houston: Institute for the Arts, Rice University.

1978   *Indian Art of the Northwest Coast: A Dialogue on Craftsmanship and Aesthetics.* Reissue of Holm and Reid 1975.

Hoover, Alan L., ed.

2000   *Nuu-chah-nulth Voices, Histories, Objects, and Journeys.* Victoria: Royal British Columbia Museum.

Horse Capture, Joseph D., and George P. Horse Capture

2001   *Beauty, Honor, and Tradition: The Legacy of Plains Indian Shirts.* Exh. cat. Washington, D.C.: National Museum of the American Indian, Smithsonian Institution; Minneapolis: Minneapolis Institute of Arts.

Howard, Kathleen H., and Diana F. Pardue

1996   *Inventing the Southwest: The Fred Harvey Company and Native American Art.* Flagstaff, Ariz.: Northland Publishing.

Illinois Archaeological Survey

1968   *Hopewell and Woodland Site: Archaeology in Illinois.* Illinois Archaeological Survey, Bulletin 6. Urbana: University of Illinois.

Inverarity, Robert Bruce

1950   *Art of the Northwest Coast Indians.* Berkeley: University of California Press.

Jacknis, Ira

1992   "'The Artist Himself': The Salish Basketry Monograph and the Beginnings of a Boasian Paradigm." In *The Early Years of Native American Art History: The Politics of Scholarship and Collecting,* edited by Janet C. Berlo, pp. 134–61. Seattle: University of Washington Press; Vancouver: UBC Press.

James, Henry

1987   *The Spoils of Poynton.* Reprint of 1963 ed. with a new introduction by David Lodge and notes by Patricia Crick. London: Penguin. Originally appeared in *Atlantic Monthly* from April to October 1896; published in book form in Boston and New York, 1897.

Jennings, John, Bruce W. Hodgins, and Doreen Small, eds.

1999   *The Canoe in Canadian Cultures.* [Toronto]: Natural Heritage Books. Proceedings of a conference held at Queen's University in 1996.

Jensen, Doreen, and Polly Sargent

1986   *Robes of Power: Totem Poles on Cloth.* University of British Columbia Museum of Anthropology, Museum Note, no. 17. Vancouver: University of British Columbia Press in association with the UBC Museum of Anthropology.

Jonaitis, Aldona, ed.

1991   *Chiefly Feasts: The Enduring Kwakiutl Potlatch.* Exh. cat. with essays by Douglas Cole, Ira Jacknis, Gloria Cranmer Webster, Judith Ostrowitz, and Aldona Jonaitis. Seattle: University of Washington Press; New York: American Museum of Natural History.

1995   *A Wealth of Thought: Franz Boas on Native American Art.* Seattle: University of Washington Press; Vancouver: Douglas and McIntyre.

Kahlenberg, Mary Hunt

1998   *The Extraordinary in the Ordinary: Textiles and Objects from the Collections of Lloyd Cotsen and the Neutrogena Corporation: Works in Cloth, Ceramic, Wood, Metal, Straw, and Paper from Cultures throughout the World.* Exh. cat. Santa Fe: Museum of International Folk Art; New York: Harry Abrams.

Kapoun, Robert W., and Charles J. Lohrmann

1997   *Language of the Robe: American Indian Trade Blankets.* Salt Lake City: Gibbs Smith.

Kent, Timothy J.

1997   *Birchbark Canoes of the Fur Trade.* 2 vols. Ossineke, Mich.: Silver Fox Enterprises.

Kersey, Harry A., Jr.

1975   *Pelts, Plumes, and Hides: White Traders among the Seminole Indians, 1870–1930.* Gainesville: University Presses of Florida.

King, J. C. H.

1979   *Portrait Masks from the Northwest Coast of America.* London: Thames and Hudson Press.

2000   "Nuu-chah-nulth Art at The British Museum." In Hoover 2000, pp. 257–72.

Knoblock, Byron W.

1939   *Banner-stones of the North American Indian: A Specialized Illustrated Volume Prepared for the Primary Purpose of Putting Forth Conclusions Regarding Distribution, Possible Uses, Methods of Manufacture, Evolution of Types, Adoption of Special Materials for Particular Types, and to Establish a System for Classifying the Diversity of Shapes of Banner-stones by Their Lines and Planes.* Contributions by Charles E. Brown, Fay-Cooper Cole, et al. LaGrange, Ill.: The Author.

Kramer, Barbara

1996   *Nampeyo and Her Pottery.* Albuquerque: University of New Mexico Press.

Krause, Aurel

1956   *The Tlingit Indians: Results of a Trip to the Northwest Coast of America and the Bering Straits.* Translated by Erna Gunther. Seattle: University of Washington Press for the American Ethnological Society.

Krauss, Rosalind E.

1996   *The Optical Unconscious.* 2nd printing. Cambridge, Mass.: MIT Press.

Krech, Shepard, III, ed.

1994   *Passionate Hobby: Rudolf Frederick Haffenreffer and the King Philip Museum.* Exh. cat. Studies in Anthropology and Material Culture, vol. 6. Bristol, R.I.: Haffenreffer Museum of Anthropology, Brown University.

Krech, Shepard, III, and Barbara A. Hail, eds.

1999   *Collecting Native America, 1870–1960.* Washington, D.C.: Smithsonian Institution Press.

Krinsky, Carol Herselle

1996   *Contemporary Native American Architecture: Cultural Regeneration and Creativity.* New York: Oxford University Press.

Kroeber, A[lfred] L[ouis]

1901   "Decorative Symbolism of the Arapaho." *American Anthropologist,* n.s., 3, pp. 308–36.

[Lee, Sherman]

1960   "In Memoriam: Ralph M. Coe." *Bulletin of the Cleveland Museum of Art* 47, no. 1 (January), p. 2.

Leland, Charles Godfrey

1992   *Algonquin Legends.* Reprint. New York: Dover. Originally published as *The Algonquin Legends of New England; or, Myths and Folk Lore of the Micmac, Passamaquoddy, and Penobscot Tribes.* Boston: Houghton, Mifflin, 1884.

Lester, Joan A.

1993   *History on Birchbark: The Art of Tomah Joseph, Passamaquoddy.* Exh. cat. Bristol, R.I.: Haffenreffer Museum of Anthropology, Brown University; Bar Harbor, Maine: Robert Abbe Museum.

MacCauley, Clay

1887   "The Seminole Indians of Florida." *Fifth Annual Report of the Bureau of Ethnology, 1883–84,* pp. 469–531. Washington, D.C.: Government Printing Office.

2000   *The Seminole Indians of Florida.* Reprint with a new introduction by William C. Sturtevant. Gainesville: University Press of Florida.

MacDonald, George F.

1996   *Haida Art.* Vancouver: Douglas and McIntyre; Hull, Quebec: Canadian Museum of Civilization.

MacGregor, Arthur, ed.

1983   *Tradescant's Rarities: Essays on the Foundation of the Ashmolean Museum, 1683, with a Catalogue of the Surviving Early Collections.* Oxford: Clarendon Press; New York: Oxford University Press.

Macnair, Peter L., Alan L. Hoover, and Kevin Neary

1980   *The Legacy: Continuing Traditions of Canadian Northwest Coast Indian Art.* Exh. cat. Edinburgh International Festival. Victoria: British Columbia Provincial Museum.

1984   *The Legacy: Tradition and Innovation in Northwest Coast Indian Art.* 2nd ed. Vancouver: Douglas and McIntyre; Seattle: University of Washington Press.

Macnair, Peter L., Robert Joseph, and Bruce Grenville

1998   *Down from the Shimmering Sky: Masks of the Northwest Coast.* Vancouver: Vancouver Art Gallery and Douglas and McIntyre; Seattle: University of Washington Press.

Mallett, Donald

1979   *The Greatest Collector: Lord Hertford and the Founding of the Wallace Collection.* London: Macmillan.

Malloy, Mary

2000   *Souvenirs of the Fur Trade: Northwest Coast Indian Art and Artifacts Collected by American Mariners, 1788–1844.* Cambridge, Mass.: Peabody Museum of Archaeology and Ethnology, Harvard University.

Marriott, Alice

1956 "The Trade Guild of Southern Cheyenne Women." *Bulletin of the Oklahoma Anthropological Society* 4, pp. 19–27. Reprinted in *Native North American Art History: Selected Readings,* compiled by Zena Pearlstone Mathews and Aldona Jonaitis. Palo Alto, Calif.: Peek Publications, 1982.

Mathews, Zena Pearlstone

1984 *Symbol and Substance in American Indian Art.* Exh. cat. New York: The Metropolitan Museum of Art.

Maurer, Evan M.

1977 *The Native American Heritage: A Survey of North American Indian Art.* Exh. cat. Chicago: Art Institute of Chicago.

Maxwell, James A., ed.

1978 *America's Fascinating Indian Heritage.* Pleasantville, N.Y.: Reader's Digest Association.

McLennan, Bill, and Karen Duffek

2000 *The Transforming Image: Painted Arts of Northwest Coast First Nations.* Vancouver: UBC Press; Seattle: University of Washington Press.

McMaster, Gerald, and Lee-Ann Martin, eds.

1992 *Indigena: Contemporary Native Perspectives.* Exh. cat. Hull, Quebec: Canadian Museum of Civilization; Vancouver: Douglas and McIntyre.

McMullen, Ann, and Russell G. Handsman, eds.

1987 *A Key into the Language of Woodsplint Baskets.* With essays by Joan A. Lester et al. Washington, Conn.: American Indian Archaeological Institute.

Meiss, Millard

1974 *French Painting in the Time of Jean de Berry: The Limbourgs and Their Contemporaries.* With the assistance of Sharon Off Dunlap Smith and Elizabeth Home Beatson. 2 vols. New York: Braziller.

Meldgaard, Jørgen

1960 *Eskimo Sculpture.* Translated by Jytte Lynner and Peter Wait. New York: Clarkson N. Potter.

Meyer, Karl

1977 *The Plundered Past.* New York: Atheneum.

Monroe, Dan L., ed.

1996 *Gifts of the Spirit: Works by Nineteenth-Century and Contemporary Native American Artists.* Contributions by Dan L. Monroe, Richard Conn, Richard W. Hill, and Suzan Shown Harjo. Exh. cat. Salem, Mass.: Peabody Essex Museum.

Montiel, Anya

2002 "Remarkable Story Uncovered." *National Museum of the American Indian* 3, 2 (spring 2002), pp. 24–25.

Mowat, Farley

1952 *People of the Deer.* Toronto: McClelland and Stewart.

Moxey, Keith P. F.

1994 *The Practice of Theory: Poststructuralism, Cultural Politics, and Art History.* Ithaca: Cornell University Press.

Muir, John

1978 *Travels in Alaska.* Reprint. New York: AMS Press. Originally published Boston: Houghton Mifflin, 1915.

Munroe, Mrs. Kirk

1909 "Seminole Indian Women." *Florida Times-Union,* June 6.

Muther, Richard

1895–96 *The History of Modern Painting.* 3 vols. New York: Macmillan.

Nemiroff, Diana, Robert Houle, and Charlotte Townsend-Gault

1992 *Land, Spirit, Power: First Nations at the National Gallery of Canada.* Exh. cat. Ottawa: National Gallery of Canada.

Newman, Peter C.

1985 *The Company of Adventurers.* Vol. 1, *The Story of the Hudson's Bay Company.* Harmondsworth and New York: Penguin Books.

Nunley, John W., and Cara McCarty

1999 *Masks: Faces of Culture.* With contributions by John Emigh and Lesley Ferris. Exh. cat. New York: Abrams, in association with the Saint Louis Art Museum.

Ostrowitz, Judith

1999 *Privileging the Past: Reconstructing History in Northwest Coast Art.* Seattle: University of Washington Press.

Paalen, Wolfgang

1943 "Totem Art." *Dyn,* no. 4–5 (December), pp. 7–37.

Painter, John W.

1991 *American Indian Artifacts: The John Painter Collection.* Cincinnati: George Tassian Organization.

Panhandle-Plains Historical Museum

1986 *Masterpieces of Native American Basketry.* Exh. cat. Canyon, Tex.: Panhandle-Plains Historical Museum.

Parker, Arthur C.

1935   *A Manual for History Museums.* New York State Historical Association Series, no. 3. New York: Columbia University Press.

Parks, Cameron

1972   *Who's Who in Indian Relics, No. 3.* Saint Louis: Parks and Thompson.

Penney, David W., ed.

1989   *Great Lakes Indian Art.* Detroit: Wayne State University Press and Detroit Institute of Arts.

1992   *Art of the American Indian Frontier: The Chandler-Pohrt Collection.* Exh. cat. Detroit: Detroit Institute of Arts; Seattle: University of Washington Press.

Phillips, Ruth B.

1984   *Patterns of Power: The Jasper Grant Collection and Great Lakes Indian Art of the Early Nineteenth Century.* Kleinburg, Ontario: McMichael Canadian Collection.

1998   *Trading Identities: The Souvenir in Native North American Art from the Northeast, 1700–1900.* Seattle: University of Washington Press; Montreal: McGill-Queen's University Press.

Pissarro, Camille

1943   *Camille Pissarro: Letters to His Son Lucien.* Edited by John Rewald, with the assistance of Lucien Pissarro; translated by Lionel Abel. New York: Pantheon Books.

Pohrt, Richard A., Sr.

1989   "Pipe Tomahawks from Michigan and the Great Lakes Area." In Penney 1989, pp. 95–103.

1992   "A Collector's Life: A Memoir of the Chandler-Pohrt Collection." In Penney 1992, pp. 299–323.

Pohrt, Richard A., Jr., ed.

1996   *Bags of Friendship: Bandolier Bags of the Great Lakes Indians.* Exh. cat. Santa Fe: Morning Star Gallery and Martha Hopkins Struever.

Pope-Hennessy, John

1991   *Learning to Look. My Life in Art: An Autobiography.* New York: Doubleday.

Price, Sally

1989   *Primitive Art in Civilized Places.* Chicago: University of Chicago Press.

Purdy, Barbara A.

1996   *Indian Art of Ancient Florida.* Gainesville: University Press of Florida.

Rewald, John

1989   *Cézanne and America: Dealers, Collectors, Artists,* *and Critics, 1891–1921.* Bollingen Series, XXXV, 28. Princeton: Princeton University Press.

Reynolds, Christopher

2002   "Southwest Museum Loses Deal." *Los Angeles Times,* November 19, calendar section / art, pp. E1, E7.

Ring, Grete

1949   *A Century of French Painting, 1400–1500.* London: Phaidon Press.

Rubin, William, ed.

1984   *"Primitivism" in 20th Century Art: Affinity of the Tribal and the Modern.* 2 vols. Exh. cat. New York: Museum of Modern Art.

Ruby, Robert H., and John A. Brown

1976   *Myron Eells and the Puget Sound Indians.* Seattle: Superior Publishing Co.

Rudenko, Sergei I.

1970   *Frozen Tombs of Siberia: The Pazyryk Burials of Iron Age Horsemen.* Translated by M. W. Thompson, with author's revisions. Berkeley: University of California Press.

Rushing, W. Jackson

1992   "Marketing the Affinity of the Primitive and the Modern: René d'Harnoncourt and 'Indian Art of the United States.'" In *The Early Years of Native American Art History,* edited by Janet C. Berlo, pp. 191–236. Seattle: University of Washington Press.

1995   *Native American Art and the New York Avant-garde.* Austin: University of Texas Press.

Schoolcraft, Henry Rowe

1857   *History of the Indian Tribes of the United States: Their Present Condition and Prospects, and a Sketch of Their Ancient Status.* Vol. 6. Philadelphia: J. B. Lippincott.

Seattle Art Museum

1995   *The Spirit Within: Northwest Coast Native Art from the John H. Hauberg Collection.* New York: Rizzoli; Seattle: Seattle Art Museum.

Sellers, Charles Coleman

1996   *Mr. Peale's Museum: Charles Willson Peale and the First Popular Museum of Natural Science and Art.* New York: W. W. Norton.

Shadbolt, Doris

1967   Foreword. In Duff 1967.

Sheehan, Carol

1981   *Pipes That Won't Smoke; Coal That Won't Burn: Haida Sculpture in Argillite.* Exh. cat. Calgary, Alberta: Glenbow Museum.

Simard, Cyril, and Jean-Louis Bouchard
1977   *Indiens et Esquimaux.* Vol. 3 of *Artisanat québécois.* Montreal: Éditions de l'Homme.

Southwest Museum
1983   *Akicita: Early Plains and Woodlands Indian Art from the Collection of Alexander Acevedo.* Exh. cat. Los Angeles: Southwest Museum.

Speck, Frank G.
1940   *Penobscot Man: The Life History of a Forest Tribe in Maine.* Philadelphia: University of Pennsylvania Press. Reprinted New York: Octagon Books, 1970.

Stevenson, James
1883   "Illustrated Catalogue of the Collections Obtained from the Indians of New Mexico and Arizona in 1880." *Second Annual Report of the Bureau of American Ethnology,* pp. 423–65. Washington, D.C.: Government Printing Office.

Stocking, George W., ed.
1985   *Objects and Others: Essays on Museums and Material Culture.* History of Anthropology 3. Madison: University of Wisconsin Press.

Struever, Martha H.
2001   *Painted Perfection: The Pottery of Dextra Quotskuyva.* Exh. cat. Santa Fe: Wheelwright Museum of the American Indian.

Sturtevant, William C.
1969   "Does Anthropology Need Museums?" *Proceedings of the Biological Society of Washington* 82 (November 17), pp. 619–50.
1974   *Boxes and Bowls: Decorated Containers by Nineteenth-Century Haida, Tlingit, Bella Bella, and Tsimshian Indian Artists.* Exh. cat. Washington, D.C.: Renwick Gallery of the National Collection of Fine Arts, Smithsonian Institution; Smithsonian Institution Press.

Sturtevant, William C., and David Damas
1984   *Handbook of North American Indians.* Vol. 5, *Arctic.* Washington, D.C.: Smithsonian Institution.

Sturtevant, William C., and Wayne P. Suttles
1990   *Handbook of North American Indians.* Vol. 7, *Northwest Coast.* Washington, D.C.: Smithsonian Institution.

Swanberg, W. A.
1962   *Citizen Hearst: A Biography of William Randolph Hearst.* London: Longmans.

Swanton, John Reed
1905   *Haida Texts and Myths: Skidegate Dialect.* Bureau of American Ethnology, Bulletin, vol. 29. Washington, D.C.: Government Printing Office.

Takashina, Shūji, et al.
1988   *Japonisumu ten: 19-seiki seiyo bijutsu e no Nihon no eikyo / Le japonisme.* Exh. cat. Paris: Galeries Nationales du Grand Palais; Éditions de la Réunion des Musées Nationaux. Tokyo: National Museum of Western Art.

Thom, Ian M., ed.
1993   *Robert Davidson: Eagle of the Dawn.* With essays by Aldona Jonaitis, Marianne Jones, and Ian M. Thom. Exh. cat. Vancouver: Vancouver Art Gallery; Seattle: University of Washington Press.

Torrence, Gaylord
1994   *The American Indian Parfleche: A Tradition of Abstract Painting.* Exh. cat. Des Moines: Des Moines Art Center; Seattle: University of Washington Press.

Treue, Wilhelm
1960   *Art Plunder: The Fate of Works of Art in War, Revolution, and Peace.* Translated by Basil Creighton. London: Methuen.

Turnbaugh, Sarah Peabody, and William A. Turnbaugh
1986   *Indian Baskets.* West Chester, Pa.: Schiffer Publishing, in collaboration with the Peabody Museum of Archaeology and Ethnology, Harvard University.
1991   *The Nineteenth-Century American Collector: A Rhode Island Perspective. Selections from the Museum of Primitive Art and Culture, Peace Dale, Rhode Island.* Peace Dale: Museum of Primitive Art and Culture.

Varjola, Pirjo
1990   *The Etholén Collection: The Ethnographic Alaskan Collection of Adolf Etholén and His Contemporaries in the National Museum of Finland.* Contributions by Julia P. Averkieva and Roza G. Liapunova. Helsinki: National Board of Antiquities.

Vaughan, Thomas, and Bill Holm
1982   *Soft Gold: The Fur Trade and Cultural Exchange on the Northwest Coast of America.* Exh. cat. Portland: Oregon Historical Society; Cambridge, Mass.: Peabody Museum of Archaeology and Ethnology, Harvard University. 2nd ed., rev., Portland: Oregon Historical Society Press, 1990.

Veblen, Thorstein
1965   *The Theory of the Leisure Class. 1899.* Reprint. New York: A. M. Kelley.

Venturi, Lionello
1939   *Les archives de l'Impressionnisme: Lettres de Renoir, Monet, Pissaro, Sisley et autres. Mémoires de Paul Durand-Ruel. Documents.* 2 vols. Paris and New York: Durand-Ruel.

Vincent, Gilbert Tapley, Sherry Brydon, and Ralph T. Coe, eds.

2000   *Art of the North American Indians: The Thaw Collection.* Cooperstown, N.Y.: Fenimore Art Museum; New York State Historical Association; Seattle: University of Washington Press.

Viola, Herman J., and Carolyn Margolis, eds.

1985   *Magnificent Voyagers: The U.S. Exploring Expedition, 1838–1842.* With the assistance of Jan S. Danis and Sharon D. Galperin. Washington, D.C.: Smithsonian Institution Press.

Wade, Edwin L., ed.

1986   *The Arts of the North American Indian: Native Traditions in Evolution.* New York: Hudson Hills Press, in association with Philbrook Art Center, Tulsa.

Walker Art Center

1972   *American Indian Art: Form and Tradition.* Exh. cat. Minneapolis: Walker Art Center, Indian Art Association, Minneapolis Institute of Arts; New York: E. P. Dutton.

Walton, Ann T., John C. Ewers, and Royal B. Hassrick

1985   *After the Buffalo Were Gone: The Louis Warren Hill, Sr., Collection of Indian Art.* Saint Paul, Minn.: Northwest Area Foundation in cooperation with the Indian Arts and Crafts Board of the United States Department of the Interior, Washington, D. C., and the Science Museum of Minnesota.

Wardwell, Allen

1996   *Tangible Visions: Northwest Coast Indian Shamanism and Its Art.* New York: Monacelli Press, with Corvus Press.

1998   as editor. *Native Paths: American Indian Art from the Collection of Charles and Valerie Diker.* Contributions by Janet Catherine Berlo et al. Exh. cat. New York: The Metropolitan Museum of Art.

Whitehead, Ruth Holmes

1982   *Micmac Quillwork: Micmac Indian Techniques of Porcupine Quill Decoration, 1600–1950.* Appendix by Deborah Jewett. Halifax: Nova Scotia Museum.

Willoughby, Charles

1935   *Antiquities of the New England Indians, with Notes on the Ancient Cultures of the Adjacent Territory.* Cambridge, Mass.: Peabody Museum of Archaeology and Ethnology, Harvard University.

Wilson, Chris

1997   *The Myth of Sante Fe: Creating a Modern Regional Tradition.* Albuquerque: University of New Mexico Press.

Wissler, Clark

1904   "Decorative Art of the Sioux Indians." *Bulletin of the American Museum of Natural History* 18, pp. 231–77.

Wooley, David, and William T. Waters

1988   "Waw-no-she's Dance." *American Indian Art* 14 (winter 1988), pp. 36–45.

Wright, Barton

1973   *Kachinas: A Hopi Artist's Documentary.* Original oil paintings by Cliff Bahnimptewa. Flagstaff, Ariz.: Northland Press, in cooperation with the Heard Museum, Phoenix.

Wright, Robin K.

2001   *Northern Haida Master Carvers.* Seattle: University of Washington Press; Vancouver: Douglas and McIntyre.

Yale Art Gallery

1956   *Pictures Collected by Yale Alumni.* Exh. cat. New Haven: Yale University, Art Gallery.

Zevi, Bruno, and Edgar Kaufmann Jr.

1965   *La casa sulla cascata di F. Ll. Wright / F. Lloyd Wright's Fallingwater.* 2nd ed. Milan: ETAS Kompass.

Index

Page numbers in *italics* refer to illustrations.